Scholarship and Engagement

T0355504

Scholarship and Engagement in Mainland Southeast Asia
A festschrift in honor of Achan Chayan Vaddhanaphuti

Edited by

Oscar Salemink

in collaboration with

Patcharin Lapanun
Benjaporn Deekhuntod
Malee Sitthikriengkrai

The publication of this book is made possible in part by grants from the Interchurch Organization for Development Cooperation and the Ford Foundation.

ISBN: 978-616-215-118-7

First published in 2016 by
Silkworm Books
104/5 Chiang Mai-Hot Road, M. 7, T. Suthep
Chiang Mai 50200 Thailand
info@silkwormbooks.com
www.silkwormbooks.com

Cover artwork by Timothy Joseph Erb

Typeset in Arno Pro 11 pt. by Silk Type

Printed in Thailand by O.S. Printing House, Bangkok

5 4 3 2 1

Contents

Acknowledgments

Although this book was conceived as a tribute to Achan Chayan Vaddhanaphuti, the authors wish to also dedicate this book to the memory of Dr. Ronald D. Renard, who sadly and prematurely passed away on December 27, 2014, having just finished a first draft of his contribution to this volume. I would like to thank his wife, Dr. Anchalee Singhanetra, and Khun Chanida Puranapun of RCSD, for their efforts to make Achan Ron's paper—with handwritten editorial comments on it—available for publication.

This volume would not have been possible without the unflinching support of Dr. Patcharin Lapanun of Khon Kaen University and Dr. Malee Sitthikriengkrai and Dr. Benjaporn Deekhuntod, both of the Regional Center for Social Science and Sustainable Development at Chiang Mai University. They conceived of the idea for this volume and contacted contributors and potential funders. In addition, they are involved in editing Thai language volumes that serve as companion volumes to this one.

I would also like to mention the generous financial support from the Interchurch Organization for Development Cooperation in the Netherlands and from the Ford Foundation, which made the publication of this book logistically possible.

Finally, I would like to thank the contributors who went out of their way to make this volume in honor of our friend and esteemed colleague, Achan Chayan Vaddhanaphuti, happen.

Oscar Salemink

Chayan Vaddhanaphuti, riding in a horse cart used to transport luggage at Ratanakiri Airport in Cambodia, before attending a workshop with local NGOs organized by UNDP Highland's People Project (see chapter 8). (Photo: Ron Renard)

Chayan Vaddhanaphuti and Ms. Tran Thi Lanh meet villagers of Ban Long Lan, Laos, in March 1999 during a research project for the Social Policy Ecology Research Institute, for which Chayan serves on the scientific board.

Introduction

UPSTREAM AND DOWNSTREAM POLITICS IN THAILAND

In 1996 an art exhibition opened on the premises of Chulalongkorn University in Bangkok, celebrating the natural diversity of Thailand's forests. Bangkok-based artists had been invited to spend time in forests in northern Thailand in the company of "forest-dwellers" in order to enjoy and appreciate the forest environment and, more importantly, express their impressions and enhanced understanding through visual art—mostly paintings. The opening took place with a symbolic act involving a piece of performance-cum-installation art consisting of a series of bamboo and wooden pipes that would lead water to a place where fruits of the land were the symbolic result of the nourishing water. The performance part consisted of the main Chiang Mai protagonist, Dr. Chayan Vaddhanaphuti, pouring water into the top end of the installation, making it run downstream in order to symbolically fertilize the delta and produce rice, vegetables, and fruits.

The symbolism was clear: the downstream environment depended on the upstream environment; the hydrology and ecology downstream depended on the rainfall and water retention upstream; the people and their economy downstream—read "Bangkok"—depended on the way that northern rural people treated the forests in what was a shared watershed area. Not surprisingly, the exhibition had been organized by northerners, in particular by scholar-activists from Chiang Mai University who wanted to impress on a metropolitan public the importance of environmental issues and the mutual interdependence between urban and rural, southern and northern populations. They

1

also wanted to increase their funding base in big-city middle classes, with reference to the technical concept of "watershed," which had become the rallying cry of environmentalist NGO activism in Thai society in the 1980s and 1990s (Buergin and Kessler 2000; Chantana 2004; Hirsch 1996; Hirsch and Lohmann 1989; Iorns and Hollick 1998; Lohmann 1993, 2000; Pinkaew 2000, 2002; Quinn 1996; Roth 2004; Taylor 1996, 1998; Vandergeest 2007).

This notion of watershed had become a political concept during the 1980s and 1990s in the course of a series of high-profile conflicts in Thai society that saw the rise of NGOs as part of a democratization movement against military rule, notably over the protection of national parks and the construction of dams like the Nam Choan dam. The movement against the dams was predicated on a newfound environmentalism that bound disparate groups of activist students, activist Buddhist monks, urban middle classes, lowland farmers, and upland ethnic minorities together in an alliance of various civil society organizations. These NGOs rallied against a course of industrial development that was perceived as detrimental to Thai nature and culture alike and, more broadly, against authoritarian rule. Representing diverse constituencies, these NGOs had diverse linkages with various state agencies and international NGOs and donors. For instance, some NGOs embraced King Bhumibol's theory of "sufficiency economy" which promoted a moderate, self-dependent life without greed or over-exploitation of labor or natural resources, and which was promoted in the king's Royal Projects, which targeted the "hill tribes." The civil-society movement in Thailand, pairing notions of environmentalism with calls for democratization, culminated in the Thai constitution of 1997, based on broad consultation with various groups in society, and a draft Community Forestry Act that was supposed to legislate the way that people could live with forests.[1]

This coalition of civil-society organizations fell apart violently in what has become known as the Chom Thong incident in northern Thailand, well-documented in scholarly publications. This conflict

1. After the 2006 coup a new constitution was adopted in 2007, which also mentioned the king's sufficiency theory as an inspiration.

pitted various civil-society organizations against one another, all claiming to protect the watershed. To summarize the conflict, a national park had been established around Doi Inthanon, encompassing places inhabited by ethnic minorities (Karen, Hmong) living in upstream villages and managing the land and natural resources as common property in shifting cultivation.[2] These villagers were accused by the Royal Forestry Department, by park officials, by lowland ethnic Thai farmers, and by environmentalist NGOs like the Dhammanaat Foundation and WWF Thailand of destroying the forest and the watershed. These NGOs found support among urban middle-class environmental groups that conceived of "nature" as "pristine" and devoid of human population that would be antagonistic towards "nature" (Kritsada 2002; Rajah 2005; Tomforde 2003).

Against these "dark green" NGOs, the upstream ethnic minority villagers had support from "light green" NGOs like the Northern Farmers Alliance and the Inter-Mountain Peoples Education and Culture in Thailand Association (IMPECT) which argued that these farmers had lived with and managed the forest successfully and sustainably over the years, and should not be blamed for the abuse by logging companies and others. These groups, which held that the "dark green" environmentalist NGOs simply blamed the victims, were also supported by high-profile scholars from Chiang Mai University, most notably Achan Chayan Vaddhanaphuti. After an incident when a protest demonstration by ethnic minority farmers and their supporters was violently broken up by personnel of the Royal Forestry Department (RFD) and a group of "downstream" farmers, effigies of Achan Chayan and some of his colleagues were burned in street protests in Chiang Mai by RFD personnel and downstream farmers mobilized by the RFD. The ethnic minority groups also sought international support, in particular from indigenous-rights groups and academics. When the Chiang Mai governor heard a recording of Dr. Chayan's presentation on the issue to a Thai Studies Conference in 1999, he branded him a

2. In fact, since the 1980s many "hill tribe" communities—in particular Hmong—successfully adopted cash crop farming, aided by good roads and hence market access.

traitor. When he and his family started to receive death threats, Achan Chayan used his international contacts—including myself, as Ford Foundation program officer at the time—to spend time as a visiting fellow at the University of Washington at the invitation of Professor Charles Keyes.[3]

CIVIL AND POLITICAL SOCIETY, SCHOLAR AND ACTIVIST

The vignette above shows that civil society in Thailand is an arena of struggle. At first, the struggle was in unison against authoritarian forms of government; later it was internal, over various definitions of watershed and how best to protect watersheds. After the 2006 military coup against the controversial prime minister and business tycoon Thaksin Shinawatra, the main issue was the high-profile conflict over access to and ownership of the state between so-called red shirts and yellow shirts—a conflict that was and remains suppressed by another military coup in 2014 led by General Prayuth Chan-ocha. Inevitably, civil-society activism revolves around the intersection with two other sectors—namely, the state and the market—which is one of the reasons that Andrew Walker (2012) prefers the term "political society" to "civil society." Walker thus invokes Partha Chatterjee's distinction between civil society (voluntary associations based on individual freedoms, rights, and—largely urban—cultural competencies) on one hand, and political society on the other hand, which deals with (collective) populations that are not organized in formal associations but where mobilization occurs through the flow of life (Chatterjee 2004). In his village study in northern Thailand, Walker shows that villagers don't seek autonomy from the state—in contrast to James Scott's (2009) thesis on the Southeast Asian highlands as a zone of state avoidance—but that instead they seek direct benefits from the state through tangible exchanges.

But what should also be clear from the vignette above is the important role of sympathetic or activist scholars in activism. Much—but certainly not all—scholarly activism in Thailand and beyond seeks to connect rural political society up with urbanite civil society from a

---

3. For more information on this, please see the next chapter, by Keyes.

privileged, liberal position. This was not the case with Achan Chayan Vaddhanaphuti, who consistently sided with the poor and destitute in society, whether they be farmers or ethnic or sexual minorities, while at times risking his own safety. Taking a political-society stance he forfeited class, ethnic, and gender privilege, cultivating himself as a scholarly activist on behalf of underprivileged groups in Thai society and beyond. He combined his scholarly activism with the choice to become an activist scholar in the sense that he traveled the mainland Southeast Asia region, converting younger scholars to at once high-quality *and* activist research; this is also the hallmark of Chiang Mai University's Regional Center for Social Science and Sustainable Development (RCSD), of which he is the founding director.

This book is dedicated to Achan Chayan, who on June 5, 2015, reached the auspicious age of seventy-two. A number of his friends and colleagues have taken the initiative to honor him with the publication of a book inspired by Chayan's remarkable career as an "activist intellectual"[4]—alternatively, he has been called a "scholar-activist." As transpires from the 2004 interview with Celia Lowe in *Positions* but also from his entire career, the terms "scholar-activist" and "activist intellectual" can be understood in two senses. The first sense is the sense that Celia Lowe gives, namely that of a scholar—in Achan Chayan's case an academic working at a university—who engages in social and political activism on behalf of underprivileged communities or oppressed categories of people in Thailand, usually against powerful elites. Examples of such marginalized people in Thailand are upland ethnic groups in northern Thailand and Isan, Muslim Malays in the deep south, and refugees and stateless people. After a period as director of Chiang Mai University's Social Research Institute, Achan Chayan brought his scholarly activism to the university's Center for Ethnic Studies and Development, for which he acts as director. His advocacy for marginal groups brought Achan Chayan sometimes into conflict with authorities, both within the university system and in society at large. As is clear from the interview, that scholarly activism also permeates his approach to

---

4. Celia Lowe calls him such in a 2004 interview with Chayan Vaddhanaphuti published in *Positions: Asia Critique*.

scientific research and influences the theoretical, methodological, and epistemological paradigms that he adopts.

The second sense of the term "scholar-activist" can also be gleaned from the interview with Celia Lowe, as Achan Chayan spoke a lot about the region of mainland Southeast Asia beyond Thailand—China, Vietnam, Laos, Cambodia, and Myanmar in particular. Over the last two decades Achan Chayan has worked tirelessly to promote critical social-science scholarship in the region, predicated on independent thinking, as an activist promoting scholarship or perhaps as a secular missionary of critical social science. From its inception in 1998, the institutional springboard for Achan Chayan's scholarly activism in this sense was the Regional Center for Social Science and Sustainable Development (RCSD) of Chiang Mai University. The RCSD's main mission is to train graduate students and scholars from the Greater Mekong Subregion, but Achan Chayan and his colleagues also reach out and work directly with and in universities and research institutes in the region—over the last five years focusing especially on Burma through RCSD's Burma Concern project. Working with colleagues in universities in marginalized areas of Thailand (Isan, the deep south) as well as in other countries, Achan Chayan tirelessly held master classes and workshops, trained junior and senior staff, supervised research, offered study opportunities, and so on, all with the aim of promoting critical social science that aims to be close to the communities in those places and that would speak and act on their behalf.

SCHOLARLY ACTIVISM IN THAILAND AND MAINLAND SOUTHEAST ASIA

Taking its cue from this perspective on Achan Chayan's career, this *liber amicorum* will offer a number of papers at the intersection of politics, (scholarly) activism, and cross-border connections in the Greater Mekong Subregion. One axis concerns the politics of research in marginal regions in and beyond Thailand. The second axis addressed in a number of papers concerns the relationship between scholarship and politics by tackling questions of how scholarship—embodied in scholars, researchers, lecturers, and professors—engages with the powers that be or seeks to change existing power relations. To a major extent the contributions mirror the activist politics of Achan Chayan himself, but in most cases the empirical basis for the book is the research by the contributors in the places where they worked.

The book consists of three parts. Part 1, "The Scholarly Activism of Chayan Vaddhanaphuti," consists of a single chapter by Charles Keyes about Achan Chayan as an exemplary scholar and activist within the Thai and mainland Southeast Asian contexts. Besides a brief biographical sketch, Keyes discusses the various political fields in which Achan Chayan has worked most visibly on behalf of underprivileged groups and issues—namely, ethnic minorities, the environment, and refugees. Keyes does not neglect to mention Achan Chayan's tireless efforts toward the training of a new generation of scholar-activists in Thailand and in the mainland Southeast Asia region, or Greater Mekong Subregion. One could argue that Achan Chayan's remit effectively spreads beyond the region, as the RCSD has increasingly emerged as a host for foreign researchers and lecturers from around the world, who in various ways contribute to RCSD programs and, in turn, become infected by the scholarly activism permeating the RCSD under Achan Chayan. These researchers include many of the contributors to this volume.

Part 2 addresses the theme "Politics, Activism, and Cross-Border Connections in the Greater Mekong Subregion," and opens with the chapter "Highlanders' Mobility and Colonial Anxieties: A Political History of the Khmu Laborers in Siam," by Olivier Evrard. Evrard focuses on colonial-era transborder migration by ethnic minorities between Laos and northern Siam/Thailand, looking at the various interpretations and policies on both the Siamese/Thai side and the Lao/French side with reference to labor migration by ethnic Khmu from colonial Laos to Chiang Mai, and documenting the volte-face of the French and Thai authorities regarding migration. At first, the French authorities attempted to restrict migration of their "protégés" before seeing migration as beneficial for the Lao colony. The Siamese initially saw the Khmu as indispensable workers, before adopting a strong anti-immigration stance in the 1930s. This article is noteworthy historical background reading for understanding current migration policies in the Greater Mekong Subregion.

In her chapter "A Mat-Weaving Cooperative and a Military Coup: The Challenges of Fieldwork in the 1970s in Thailand," Katherine Bowie documents her involvement in a mat-weaving cooperative in a village in northern Thailand after the military coup of 1976. Bowie follows the attempts to organize poor villagers into cooperatives as part of an effort to wean them away from any potential communist influence, and interweaves her own story of overcoming distrust, gaining access, and relating to various categories of villagers to paint a lively, personal picture of fieldwork at a time of multiple political tensions that seemed to have militated against overt scholarly activism.

In chapter 4 Christopher Joll assumes an activist approach by revisiting and critiquing stereotypical clichés about ethnicity and religion that are often invoked to understand the tensions and conflicts in the South. In "Revisiting Ethnic and Religious Factors in Thailand's Southern Discomfort," Joll contests the salience of ethnicity and religion as explanatory concepts for the emergence of the conflicts in the deep south of Thailand, and instead urges us to pay more attention to detailed local histories against the backdrop of national and transnational processes.

In chapter 5, Shigeharu Tanabe offers a very different take on activism by interpreting the meditation practices of hermit monks in northern Thailand as resistance against what he calls "diverse material and spiritual hardships and distress, in short, against the power structures in existential, religious, economic, or political terms in contemporary society." In "Resistance through Meditation: Hermits of King's Mountain in Northern Thailand," Tanabe asserts that hermits employ specific meditative practices as "technologies of the self" geared toward self-transformation in the hope of becoming a Buddha and hence escaping the cycle of hardship and distress.

Part 3 of the book zooms in more directly on the theme "Scholarly Activism in the Greater Mekong Subregion." In Chapter 6, "'Learning Across Boundaries': Grantmaking Activism in the Greater Mekong Subregion," Rosalia Sciortino recounts how the program she managed when she worked for the Rockefeller Foundation supported scholarly and activist initiatives in the Greater Mekong Subregion and their emergent networks across borders and boundaries. Perhaps counterintuitively, Sciortino depicts grantmaking as an activist and potentially subversive strategy. Less counterintuitively, the Rockefeller Foundation terminated this program when it reoriented not just its investments but its funding programs along neoliberal lines by adopting a "technocratic approach to philanthropy," which devastated "humanistic" and "social justice" approaches. Unfortunately, as somebody who worked with the Ford Foundation before, I have seen similar tendencies at work there.

My own chapter, "Scholarship, Expertise, and the Regional Politics of Heritage," looks at scholarship invoked as "expert knowledge" dealing with heritage policies in the region, in particular the UNESCO-inscribed "Space of Gong Culture" in Vietnam's Central Highlands. In my chapter I explore the role of experts and scholars as applied or engaged researchers, with reference to what I call spectacularization, dispossession, and disenfranchisement in the framework of intangible cultural heritage in Vietnam. Asking what modalities there are for scholars who choose to engage with the state—as initiator and guarantor of heritage—and with local heritage communities, I argue that the room for maneuver for Vietnamese scholars is limited but that also in other countries anthropologists supporting local communities articulate their opposition not in terms of opposing heritagization but of alternative heritage management and conservation, thus keeping scholarly activism within certain discursive bounds—not unlike the discourses of environmentalism and watershed protection with which I began this introduction.

Chapter 8, titled "The Rise and Fall of UNODC's Alternative Development Program," was written by the late Ronald D. Renard, who sadly passed away before he could finalize the paper. As mentioned in the acknowledgments, this book is also dedicated to the memory of Ron Renard. Like the authors of the two preceding chapters, Renard wrote about projects that he had been deeply involved in, in particular the Alternative Development Program under the auspices of the United Nations Office on Drugs and Crime (UNODC). Rather than simply a repressive program, the Alternative Development Program did not just wield a stick but held out a carrot to people who would stop cultivating or trading poppy or producing its hallucinogenic derivatives by promoting alternative sources of income for highland farmers, especially in the Wa Region of Burma. Sadly, these programs were discontinued—in spite of demonstrable and demonstrated successes—when UNODC reverted to its default mode of repressing crime. Again, this story serves as a reminder that there are limits to what scholarly activism may achieve, especially when it faces entrenched institutional interests and discursive dogmas.

The last chapter was contributed by historian Mandy Sadan, who wrote the authoritative book *Being and Becoming Kachin: Histories Beyond the State in the Borderworlds of Burma* (2013). In her chapter, "Meeting Educational Needs in Marginal Areas of the State: Reflections on Research in Myanmar," Sadan documents not only her own "research-activist collaboration" in the 1990s with specific groups in Burma but more importantly the scholarly activism of older and younger Kachin people in and out of Kachin State. Young Kachin intellectuals create religious, educational, cultural, and research institutions against all odds but with the full support of their local constituencies, who realize the importance of these networks for the viability of an autonomous Kachin State within Myanmar. In that context, almost any scholarly endeavor becomes a demonstration of activism.

The volume is capped by an afterword by Michael Herzfeld, who is known himself as an activist scholar and whose next book will concern the struggle against eviction of the Pom Mahakan community around a heritage site in Bangkok. Herzfeld offers a number of reflections on Achan Chayan and his approach to engaged scholarship.

This brings us back to the theme of the volume: scholarly activism and transborder engagement in mainland Southeast Asia, as eminently embodied by Achan Chayan Vaddhanaphuti and also by other activists and researchers from the region and beyond, including some of the contributors to this volume. Together, the various contributions explore the possibilities and limits of scholarly activism and activist scholarship in the Greater Mekong Subregion, documenting successes in working with and for underprivileged communities while also pointing to discursive, institutional, and political constraints to change. By bringing together a wide variety of experiences from different situations and positions, I would hope that this collection of essays will contribute to more effective scholarly activism and activist scholarship in the region.

REFERENCES

Buergin, R., and Chr. Kessler. 2000. "Intrusions and Exclusions: Democratization in Thailand in the Context of Environmental Discourses and Resource Conflicts." *GeoJournal* 52:71–80.

Chantana Banpasirichote. 2004. "Civil Society Discourse and the Future of Radical Environmental Movements in Thailand." In *Civil Society in Southeast Asia*, edited by Lee Hock Guan, 234–64. Singapore: ISEAS.

Chatterjee, Partha. 2004. *Politics of the Governed: Reflections on Popular Politics in Most of the World*. New York: Columbia University Press.

Hirsch, Philip. 1996. "Environment and Environmentalism in Thailand: Material and Ideological Bases." In *Seeing Forests for Trees: Environment and Environmentalism in Thailand*, edited by Philip Hirsch, 15–36. Chiang Mai: Silkworm Books.

Hirsch, Philip, and Larry Lohmann. 1989. "Contemporary Politics of Environment in Thailand." *Asian Survey* 29 (4): 439–51.

Iorns Magallanes, Catherine J., and Malcolm Hollick, eds. 1998. *Land Conflicts in Southeast Asia: Indigenous Peoples, Environment and International Law*. Bangkok: White Lotus Press.

Kritsada Boonchai. 2002. "Social Movement and the Making of Cultural Identity Rights of Karen Communities in Thungyai Naresuan." Foundation for Ecological Recovery.

Lohmann, Larry. 1993. "Green Orientalism." *The Ecologist* 23 (6): 202–4.

———. 2000. *For Reasons of Nature: Ethnic Discrimination and Conservation in Thailand*. Unpublished paper for "Reassessing Resources: Teaching, Writing and Civic Action," a working conference of the Cornell University Southeast Asia Program, Ithaca, New York, April 7–9.

Lowe, Celia. 2004. "The Potential of People: An Interview with Chayan Vaddhanaphuti." *Positions: Asia Critique* 12 (1): 71–91.

Pinkaew Laungaramsri. 2000. "The Ambiguity of 'Watershed': The Politics of People and Conservation in Northern Thailand." *Sojourn* 15 (1): 52–75.

———. 2002. "Competing Discourses and Practices of 'Civil Society': A Reflection on the Environmental Movement in Thailand and Some Implications for the Mekong Region." Paper presented at the Mekong Dialogue Workshop "International Transfer of River Basin Development Experience: Australia and the Mekong Region," September.

Quinn, Rapin. 1996. "Competition over Resources and Local Environment: The Role of Thai NGOs." In *Seeing Forests for Trees: Environment and Environmentalism in Thailand*, edited by Philip Hirsch, 89–115. Chiang Mai: Silkworm Books.

Rajah, Ananda. 2005. "Political Assassination by Other Means: Public Protest, Sorcery and Morality in Thailand." *Journal of Southeast Asian Studies* 36 (1): 111–29.

Roth, Robin. 2004. "Spatial Organization of Environmental Knowledge: Conservation Conflicts in the Inhabited Forest of Northern Thailand." *Ecology and Society* 9 (3). http://www.ecologyandsociety.org/vol9/iss3/art5/.

Sadan, Mandy. 2013. *Being and Becoming Kachin: Histories Beyond the State in the Borderworlds of Burma*. Oxford: Oxford University Press.

Scott, James C. 2009. *The Art of Not Being Governed: An Anarchist History of Southeast Asia*. New Haven: Yale University Press.

Taylor, Jim. 1996. "Thamma-Chaat: Activist Monks and Competing Discourses of Nature in Northeastern Thailand." In *Seeing Forests for Trees: Environment and Environmentalism in Thailand*, edited by Philip Hirsch, 37–53. Chiang Mai: Silkworm Books.

———. 1998. "Community Forests, Local Perspectives and the Environmental Politics of Land Use in Northeastern Thailand." In *Land Conflicts in Southeast Asia: Indigenous Peoples, Environment and International Law*, edited by Catherine J. Iorns Magallanes and Malcolm Hollick, 21–56. Bangkok: White Lotus Press.

Tomforde, Maren. 2003. "The Global in the Local: Contested Resource-Use Systems of the Karen and Hmong in Northern Thailand." *Journal of Southeast Asian Studies* 34 (2): 347–60.

Vandergeest, Peter. 2007. "Displacements in Neoliberal Land Reforms: Producing Tenure (In)securities in Laos and Thailand." In *Development's Displacements: Ecologies, Economies, and Cultures at Risk*, edited by Peter Vandergeest, Pablo Idahosa, and Pablo S. Bose, 136–54. Vancouver: University of British Columbia Press.

Walker, Andrew. 2012. *Thailand's Political Peasants: Power in the Modern Rural Economy*. Madison, WI: University of Wisconsin Press.

Part 1

The Scholarly Activism of Chayan

Chayan Vaddhanaphuti: Exemplary Scholar-Activist

Charles Keyes

INTRODUCTION

In July 1999, Dr. Chayan Vaddhanaphuti, the founding director of the Regional Center for Social Science and Sustainable Development at Chiang Mai University, was publicly accused by the then governor of Chiang Mai Province of *khai chat*, literally "selling the nation," or defaming the nation. The accusation stemmed from Achan Chayan's organizing a panel at the International Thai Studies Conference held earlier in the month in Amsterdam at which panelists discussed the confrontation between some northern Thai villagers and Hmong (an upland minority) villagers on Doi Inthanon in Chiang Mai Province regarding the Hmong use of forestlands in the watershed. The governor's rage was impelled by the fact that Achan Chayan had joined with foreigners (Westerners, including myself, and Japanese—notably, Shigeharu Tanabe) not only in making what the governor considered should have been an internal Thai matter a focus of international attention in the conference, but also by giving an interview to BBC about the conflict. The governor had learned of this from then prime minister Chuan Leekpai, who had personally given him a copy of the taped BBC interview.

The governor's accusation followed protests organized the previous year by the Chom Thong Watershed Conservation Group, at one of which Chayan and Nidhi Eoseewong, another prominent faculty member from Chiang Mai University, had been burned in effigy. The Chom Thong Watershed Conservation Group represented the interests of northern Thai villagers living below the Hmong on Doi

Inthanon in Chiang Mai Province. These protests also prompted someone to send Achan Chayan a threat to kill him or his family.

Fortunately, not only for Achan Chayan but also for those seeking a better understanding of the upland peoples in Thailand and neighboring countries whose rights have not been recognized and respected by the dominant peoples of these countries, the threat against his life was never acted upon. Achan Chayan continued as the director of the Regional Center for Social Science and Sustainable Development and the Social Science (RCSD) and went on to found the Center for Ethnic Studies and Development (CESD) at Chiang Mai University.[1] He has now reached the end of his sixth cycle. In the many other roles he has played in Thai public as well as academic life, Achan Chayan has become widely recognized as an exemplary activist scholar. The Doi Inthanon/Chom Thong controversy added to his prominence as a public intellectual, a role he has continued to play until today. It was a role, however, that had significant antecedents.

Although I had taught in the Faculty of Social Science at Chiang Mai University in 1972–74, a faculty of which Achan Chayan was a member, he was at the time studying for his PhD at Stanford University. I really came to know him after I returned to the US and was invited to be an external member of his dissertation committee.

In the 1970s, American social science was undergoing a significant transformation. In no small part this was a consequence of the growth of anti–Vietnam War protests on American university campuses. Like other Thais who studied in the US during this period, Achan Chayan was impressed by those American academics who recognized that although they were committed to adhering to academic standards of scholarship or science in carrying out their research, the choice of what to inquire into was always constrained by politics.[2] It has followed for many scholars and scientists that when one's research leads to knowledge that is counter to premises on which policies are based, it

1. See http://rcsd.soc.cmu.ac.th/v2012/index.php and http://www.cesd.soc.cmu.ac.th (accessed January 19, 2015).
2. This understanding is for many social scientists rooted in the work of Max Weber (see Weber 1958a and 1958b and Roth and Schluchter 1979).

is morally imperative that one challenge those premises. It was apparent to me that Achan Chayan saw his own role as a student in the US as providing him the opportunity not only to become a scholar but also to follow many of his mentors and fellow students in using his knowledge to speak truth to power.

Chayan has done so with regard to social justice, especially concerning ethnic group relations, environmental conflicts, and refugee issues. He has, moreover, done so not only through drawing on findings from his own research but also through the recruitment and mentoring of a new generation of scholar-activists both in Thailand and, significantly, in neighboring countries as well.

ETHNIC GROUP RELATIONS

A major focus of Achan Chayan's research since he was a graduate student has been on ethnic group relations in Thailand. Northern Thailand, where Chayan was born and raised and where he became a researcher and then a teacher at Chiang Mai University, is known for its upland minorities. Minorities in northern Thailand who speak Austroasiatic or Karen languages have long lived in the region—indeed, such Austroasiatic-speaking people as the Lua (Lawa) and Htin are descendants of the most ancient peoples of the region, peoples whose presence in the area antedates the settlement of Tai-speaking people in the region. Although more Karen-speaking people are found in Myanmar than in Thailand, Karen-speaking Sgaw and P'wo have also lived in what is now northern Thailand for several hundred years.[3] Beginning a little over a century and a half ago other upland peoples—Hmong, Mien, Akha, Lahu, and Lisu—began to migrate from neighboring countries into northern Thailand. These newcomers, like most Karen in Thailand, practiced swidden, or "slash-and-burn," agriculture. Khon Muang—the dominant Tai-speaking people of northern Thailand, as well as many Austroasiatic-speaking peoples and some Karen, were primarily wet-rice cultivators who lived in the lowlands or upland valleys.

3. See Keyes (1979) and Renard (1980).

Prior to World War II, the Khon Muang maintained a symbiotic relationship with the upland peoples, exchanging such lowland products as metal tools for upland products such as medicinal plants. Some upland peoples—most notably the Hmong—like their kinsmen in neighboring French Indochina and southern China, also cultivated opium that they sold in lowland markets. The Thai governments of the period ignored the upland peoples, being more concerned with integrating the Khon Muang, who had once lived in an autonomous polity, into the Thai state (then called Siam).[4]

The situation changed radically in the 1950s when the Thai government acquiesced to international pressure to eradicate opium production. Since opium was produced by upland minorities, mainly by Hmong—although those who benefited from the trade in opium were primarily Chinese or Sino-Thai middlemen and Thai officials— the efforts to eradicate opium production targeted upland peoples. In the 1960s when Thailand allied itself with the United States in seeking to stop the spread of the influence of communism, especially that associated with the newly founded Peoples Republic of China, upland peoples who had kinsmen living in China, Laos, or Vietnam were also deemed to be problematic citizens. The Thai government also grew concerned as conflicts in Myanmar (then Burma) and Laos as well as in southern China stimulated increased migration of upland peoples into northern Thailand. The "hill tribe problem" (*panha chao khao*)— construed to mean the combination of producing an illegal crop, being illegal migrants who had presumably moved to Thailand from Laos, and being likely supporters of communist insurrection—thus began.[5] And with it came both a growing demand for more research about the characteristics of upland peoples as well as an impetus for the Thai government to adopt new policies to address the problem.

Until the 1970s, most research among and about hill tribes in northern Thailand was carried out by foreign scholars, although the

4. See Keyes (1971); Tej Bunnag (1977); Ramsay (1976, 1979); Thongchai Winichakul (1994).

5. For an excellent review of Thai government policies toward hill peoples see Pinkaew Laungaramsri (1995). Also see Cooper (1979), Kammerer (1986, 1988), Keyes (1986), and Anthony Walker (1983).

Tribal Research Institute (later the Tribal Research Center) employed several Thai anthropologists.[6] Beginning in 1970 the role of American and Australian researchers among upland peoples in Thailand came under sharp attack from anti–Vietnam War activists in the United States.[7] Although I have had only passing discussions with Chayan about what became known as the "Thailand Controversy," I am sure that when he was a student at Stanford in the 1970s he was aware of the criticisms of research linked to policies designed to bring about radical changes in the lives of upland peoples.

As a student in international comparative education at Stanford, Chayan chose to do his own dissertation research on how Khon Muang village culture was shaped by a national education curriculum while still maintaining a distinctive local character (Chayan 1984; also see Chayan 1991). Because the Khon Muang village he carried out his research in bordered on a village with Akha who had been resettled, he also became aware of the cultural as well as economic poverty consequent on resettlement. As a faculty member in sociology and anthropology at Chiang Mai University, Chayan began to encourage students and colleagues to undertake politically engaged research among upland minorities as well as among Khon Muang.

THE POLITICS OF THE ENVIRONMENT

Beginning in the late 1960s some researchers working with upland minorities in Thailand began to concern themselves with questions of how upland minorities adapted to highland environments and, more particularly, how their activities in forested areas led them into conflict with expanding state interests in these areas. In Thailand, a government policy adopted soon after the end of World War II sought to end swidden, or slash-and-burn, agriculture, the long-standing method

---

6. On the role of the Tribal Research Institute/Center, see Kwanchewan Buadaeng (2006). The foreign researchers who were the main students of hill tribe cultures and societies from the early 1960s through the early 1990s were primarily Americans and Australians, although there were also Austrians, Swedes, Danes, British, and Japanese.

7. On what became known as the "Thailand Controversy" see Wakin (1992) and Jonsson (2014).

used not only by minorities but also by some Khon Muang who cultivated crops on highland fields.

Although researchers have shown that traditional slash-and-burn cultivation was a mode of adaptation that was not destructive of forests, as these reemerged after fields were allowed to lie fallow for many years, and that swidden cultivators did not destroy watersheds, as the amount of area under cultivation was limited to what could be watered by rainfall, modern governments throughout not only Asia but also most parts of the world have deemed slash-and-burn cultivation to be unacceptable. Initially this policy was adopted primarily because these governments sought to gain income from commercial exploitation of forests and because the people who supported themselves with this mode of agriculture were constantly moving and thus were not easily kept under the supervision of the state.[8]

In the 1980s following devastating floods that were determined to have been particularly intense because of deforestation, the Thai government shifted its policy regarding forested lands from one based on commercial interests to one predicated on environmental conservation. This shift did not, however, allow for people to pursue cultivation in areas deemed by the government to be in forests managed by the Royal Forestry Department in the Ministry of Natural Resources and the Environment. In response to this policy, Chayan, along with other activists (including his Chiang Mai University colleague Anan Ganjanapan [1998]), began to use social-scientific research to demonstrate that environmental concerns should not be used to undermine ongoing patterns of community forestry, especially among non-Thai minorities.[9] For its part, the Royal Forestry Department

8. For good analysis of the practice of swiddening in northern Thailand and the politics that emerged around this practice, see Kunstadter, Chapman, and Sanga (1978). On this mode of agriculture as a means whereby upland people escaped the supervision of the state, see Scott (2009).

9. For a history of the community forestry movement in Thailand, see United Nations Food and Agricultural Organization, Regional Office for Asia and the Pacific (2009). The community forestry movement has been criticized not only by Thai officials, but also by some scholars. Andrew Walker (2004), for example, argues that NGOs should seek to promote upland *commercial* agriculture as a means to

maintained that only the government had the right to determine how forests in designated national parks and national forests should be maintained and managed regardless of whatever the customary rights of local peoples who had long lived in these forests might be. Plodprasop Suraswadee, the director-general of the Royal Forestry Department at the time of the Doi Inthanon controversy, asserted that "we have to put people in the right place. We have to accept that there are some places that we should not live. I am not supposed to sleep on Ratchadamnoen Avenue [in Bangkok]. Likewise, some of you should not live in watershed forests."[10]

Successive governments in Thailand, whether led by a democratically elected parliament or put in place by a military junta, have continued to insist that the central government has ultimate authority over all land and land use in Thailand. In late July 2014, two months after a military junta had again assumed power in the country, the National Human Rights Commission "called on the Department of National Parks, Wildlife, and Plant Conservation to suspend legal action against forest dwellers under the National Council for Peace and Order's encroachment crackdown." In particular the commission observed that the government has failed to take into account "those whose ancestors had lived in forests for generations, or those who had occupied areas before territories were declared forest reserves" (*Bangkok Post*, July 30, 2014). The recent case of the disappearance the ethnic Karen grassroots activist Porlajee Rakchongchar, better known as Billy, who had led protests against the eviction of long-settled Karen villagers from the Kaeng Krachan National Park in Phetchaburi and

secure land rights rather than promote traditional practices, In fact, in practice many upland peoples have long been seeking secure land tenure rights both to produce for their own use and for markets.

10. Quoted in Pingkaew Laungaramsri's (2000) detailed analysis of the Doi Inthanon conflict. Also see Anan Ganjanapan (1996) and Delang (2002). Plodprasop, who holds a PhD from the University of Manitoba, has had a controversial history, most recently as deputy prime minister in the Pheu Thai government of Yingluck Shinawatra when he was given responsibility for leading the efforts in 2011–12 to devise means to prevent future disastrous flooding in Bangkok. Some basic biographical information on Plodprasop can be found in Thai at http://th.wikipedia.org/wiki/ปลอดประสพ_สุรัสวดี (accessed 18 January 2015).

who had filmed park officials engaged in illegal logging, demonstrates not only how the traditional rights of minorities living in forests have continued to be denied, but that many officials are complicit in the illegal cutting of timber in these same forests.[11]

Chayan has continued to encourage public attention to issues of ethnicity and the environment by organizing academic and activist conferences, sponsoring public speeches, and supervising graduate students working on one or another of these issues, as well as through his own lectures and writings (e.g., Chayan and Aquino 2000).[12] An underlining premise found in much of Chayan's work is that challenges to government policies that have ill consequences for local peoples are more effective if they are based on well-conceived research.

REFUGEES

Perhaps no social issue in Thailand is more fraught and long lasting than that which has emerged because of the large numbers of refugees who have made their way to Thailand since the 1970s. Although a small number of Vietnamese and Mon, Burmans, and Karen from Burma had arrived in Thailand because of earlier political conflicts in Vietnam and Burma, the numbers began to rapidly increase following the end in 1975 of the American war in the countries of Vietnam, Laos, and Cambodia. Tens of thousands from Laos and Cambodia sought refuge in Thailand in the late 1970s and early 1980s. Although a significant proportion of these refugees were either resettled in other countries

11. The case of Billy is but the latest example of how forestry officials of the Royal Thai Government have used their authority to deny rights of inhabitants of the forest—most of whom are minority people—to make their livelihoods by using forest resources and have usually done so to assist commercial interests. Billy disappeared after having been detained by Kaeng Krachan National Park's chief Chaiwat Limlikhit-aksorn for purportedly having illegally taken honey from the forest. Although Chaiwat was subsequently put on inactive duty, it is likely that unless more evidence—including Billy's corpse—can be produced, he will be returned to a position in the park service. The story of Billy's disappearance was well covered in the press, including in the English-language *Bangkok Post* and *The Nation*.

12. Chayan also contributed to the widespread protests by NGOs and other activists over the Pak Moon Dam project at the confluence of the Moon and Mekong Rivers in northeastern Thailand (see Chayan 2000).

or, for mainly Hmong refugees from Laos, repatriated, the escalation of civil conflict in Burma had by the mid-1980s led to an increasing number of mainly Karen seeking refuge in Thailand. Only a very small percentage of these refugees have found new homes in other (mainly Western) countries.

Earlier Thai governments saw Karen refugees as both a problem and a political asset when relations with Burma were tense.[13] They were considered a problem, in part, because they added significantly to an existing minority population—that of the Karen. But even more, their presence gave Burmese military forces cause for infringing on Thai territory. They were seen as an asset by some in the military as being justification for Thai hostility towards Burma.

The situation changed radically in the late 1990s when Burma, now renamed Myanmar, was admitted to the Association of Southeast Asian Nations (ASEAN). Now the refugees came to be seen by the Thai government as part of a larger problem that also involved hundreds of thousands of Burmese legal and illegal migrants who had come to Thailand in search of work. Because the Karen refugees have been overshadowed by the Burmese migrants, they have basically disappeared from Thai public consciousness.

The acceptance of Myanmar into ASEAN led to significant improvement in relations between Thailand and Myanmar. It now became possible for Thai people to travel easily to Myanmar and for some from Myanmar, mainly workers and students, to come legally to Thailand. Nonetheless, the legacy of a long history of confrontation between the two countries remains, as, for example, in popular Thai movies such as the *Naresuan* series, named after a sixteenth-century Siamese ruler who fought with the Burmese; the latest of these films has been used to promote Thai nationalism since the latest military government came to power.

13. The Thai view of these tense relationships that stemmed from Thailand's concern about adding to the Karen population in Thailand and the Thai view of Burmese as being brutal is apparent in the film *Salween*, directed by the famous Thai filmmaker Mom Chao Chatree Chalermyukhol—for details see http://en.wikipedia.org/wiki/Salween_(film).

RCSD under Chayan's direction established the Burma Concern Project, which

> aims to bridge the gap of understanding [between Thai and Burmese] that exists, and to facilitate information sharing and mutual learning, regarding Burmese issues among both Thai academic community and the public, by organizing regular seminars and public forums which will focus on historical, cultural, socio-economic, environmental and people issues associated with the situation in Burma, and in particular current issues arising along the Thai-Burmese border, those that give the area its "trans-border" nature.[14]

The Burma initiative of RCSD led to the recruitment to Chiang Mai University of a number of graduate students from Myanmar.

Chayan himself took particular interest in the Karen refugees from Myanmar living in refugee camps in Tak, Mae Hong Son, and Kanchanaburi Provinces. With some students from Chiang Mai University, including some enrolled in graduate programs under the RCSD and CESD, he has carried out research in these camps. The future of these camps, housing some 130,000 refugees, is now in question since General Prayuth Chan-ocha, the head of the military junta that took power in Thailand in May 2014, agreed in July 2014 with Myanmar's commander-in-chief, General Min Aung Hlaing, that the refugees should be repatriated.[15] Given this situation, the research findings of Chayan and his associates will certainly be of considerable relevance.[16]

14. See http://rcsd.soc.cmu.ac.th/v2012/index.php?sfile=burmaconcern (accessed January 18, 2015).

15. Even reassurances by General Prayuth that "an appropriate way to ensure a safe return of the refugees," and that "the significant matter is that human rights must not be violated" (*Bangkok Post*, July 27, 2014) have not assuaged concerns among the Karen refugees (see http://www.irrawaddy.org/burma/uncertainty-concern-surround-thai-govt-headcount-refugees.html, accessed January 18, 2015).

16. See Chayan Vaddhaphuti, Prasit Leeprecha, and Mali Sitthikriengkrai (2010).

TOWARD A NEW CADRE OF SOUTHEAST ASIAN RESEARCHER-ACTIVISTS

To promote research beyond what he himself could do, Chayan has since the 1980s been involved in facilitating and guiding the research of students, most of whom have come from Southeast Asia and many of whom are from ethnic minorities of the countries of which they are citizens. Initially he undertook this role as a member of the Faculty of Social Science at Chiang Mai University, a position he has continued to hold even after reaching the retirement age for Thai government officials. In the mid-1980s he was appointed the director of Chiang Mai University's Social Research Institute (SRI), an institute founded in 1981.[17] In this role, he was able to provide support for a number of students and colleagues to undertake research on ethnic group relations, environment and society, and social justice. While director of SRI, Chayan began to forge relations with a number of external funding agencies—the Ford Foundation, the Rockefeller Foundation, ORSTOM (Office de la recherche scientifique et technique d'outre-mer, now Institut de recherche pour le développement), and the Heinrich Böll Foundation, among others.

External funding—especially an endowment grant made in 1998 by the Ford Foundation—enabled Chayan to establish the Research Center for Social Science and Sustainable Development (RCSD) with the explicit purpose of assisting in the training of young researchers not only from Thailand but also from neighboring countries. RCSD quickly became and has remained the foremost interdisciplinary social science research and training institute in mainland Southeast Asia. In 1991–92, Chayan began to foster links between the Social Research Institute and what was then the Institute of Ethnology in the Lao National Center for Social Science. Links with institutions and scholars in Laos continue to the present primarily through a relationship between Chiang Mai University and the National University of Laos.

One of the most productive relationships in which Chayan was key was one funded by the Ford Foundation beginning in 1997 and

---

17. SRI under new directors would later become focused on socioeconomic rather than ethnographic research.

continued through 2005. With the assistance of the Ford Foundation and, especially, of Dr. Oscar Salemink, an anthropologist then serving as a program officer for the Ford regional office in Hanoi, a cooperative project was undertaken to train young researchers from Vietnam and Thailand to carry out research among upland minorities in the two countries. The project involved cooperation between RCSD at Chiang Mai University and the Institutes of Ethnology and Women's Studies in the Vietnamese National Center for Social Science and Humanities, with assistance from faculty in the Department of Anthropology at the University of Washington and the Department of Social Anthropology at the University of Gothenburg in Sweden.

The project was launched with a planning conference in Chiang Mai in early 1997 at which an intellectual agenda was shaped through presentations by senior scholars from all participating institutions as well as by a number of other scholars with specialist knowledge of indigenous peoples of either Thailand or Vietnam. The proceedings of this conference were published as *Ethnic Communities in Changing Environments* (Chayan 1997). In the next phase of the project, funding from the Ford Foundation and participating institutions was provided to enable twenty Vietnamese to formulate and carry out research projects of 4–6 months in duration. Several of these participants would go on to pursue master's or PhD programs abroad. A smaller Thai group, totaling twelve over the course of the project (of whom two pursued PhD degrees at the University of Washington and one a PhD degree at Sydney University), were also participants. In 2001 several of the grantees in the project presented findings at a special panel held at the International Convention of Asian Scholars in Berlin. In sum, the results of this project, being situated with reference to both international standards of research and academic and political contexts in Vietnam and Thailand, were impressive in laying the foundation for future research among ethnic minorities in Vietnam and Thailand.

Chayan's academic entrepreneurship continued in other guises as well. In 2004 Chayan was recruited by the dean of social science at Mahasarakham University in northeastern Thailand to administer an interuniversity PhD program in Tai studies at the university. Although based in Mahasarakham, this program involved faculty from all the major universities in Thailand as well as several foreigners, including myself from the US. Students were recruited not only from many universities in Thailand, but several came from Laos, and one Vietnamese who had been studying in Thailand also joined. The funding in this case came from the Thailand Research Fund as well as from participating Thai institutions. There were more than forty students affiliated with this program during the five years Chayan directed it.

Students were guided by Chayan to pursue projects that were of wide interest, many with implicit if not explicit political implications. Several projects related to problems of tension and conflict between local peoples and the Thai state over natural resources. Many projects concerned ethnic minorities, including not only upland groups like the Karen but others such as the Lao Phouan and Lao Song—both descendants of migrants from Laos—and the Sino-Thai in northeastern Thailand. One also concerned Tai-speaking people in northern Vietnam. Noteworthy were several projects relating to southern Thailand and the relations between Muslims and Buddhists in this strife-torn region. Several others concerned Laos, reflecting growing interest in relations between Thailand and Laos. Chayan not only was the director of this program but also took a personal interest in mentoring students. On the several occasions when I joined in workshops and joint supervision of several students, I was very impressed by how Chayan combined disciplined mentoring with remarkable empathy.

These same qualities have also been manifest in his guidance of the international MA program at Chiang Mai University under the jurisdiction of RCSD. From the beginning, this program was meant to attract, and has in fact attracted, students from a number of Asian countries—notably Vietnam, Laos, China, and, more recently, Myanmar. More recently he also took the lead in establishing the CESD at Chiang Mai University, under the Faculty of Social Science. This center offers an MA program, and many of the two-dozen students who have been in the program have been from ethnic or religious minority groups.

CONCLUSION

Taken together, Chayan's work in training students and researchers has led to a significant expansion of those in Thailand and neighboring countries who are engaged and will continue to be engaged in studies that will further understanding of issues connected to ethnic group relations, access to natural resources, and social justice. He has done more than any other Southeast Asian scholar of whom I am aware in fostering links between scholarly institutions in the region. In short, his scholarly activism is manifest not only in his own use of knowledge to speak to power but also in contributing to the training of a new cadre of scholar-activists who will also be socially and politically engaged.

In 2004 Chayan was awarded an honorary doctorate from Gothenburg University in Sweden. This honor, well deserved because of his long cooperation with Gothenburg faculty in training young researchers from Vietnam and Thailand, also underscored a message that was precisely the inverse of what the governor of Chiang Mai had asserted in 1999. Not only did Chayan's involvement with foreigners not result in "selling his nation," but Chayan's involvement had in fact resulted in international recognition of his prominent role in Thai academia. I can attest, having had the privilege of working with Chayan over nearly four decades, to his exceptional contribution to engaging in, promoting, and fostering scholarly activism not only in Thailand but also in many countries in Southeast Asia.

REFERENCES

Anan Ganjanapan. 1996. "The Politics of Environment in Northern Thailand: Ethnicity and Highland Development Programmes." In *Seeing Forests for Trees: Environment and Environmentalism in Thailand*, edited by Philip Hirsch, 202–22. Chiang Mai: Silkworm Books.

———. 1998. "The Politics of Conservation and the Complexity of Local Control of Forests in the Northern Thai Highlands." *Mountain Research and Development* 18 (1): 71–82.

Chayan Vaddhanaphuti. 1984. "Cultural and Ideological Reproduction in Northern Thai Society." PhD diss., Stanford University.

———. 1991. "Social and Ideological Reproduction in Rural Northern Thai Schools." In *Reshaping Local Worlds: Rural Education and Cultural Change in Southeast Asia*, edited by Charles F. Keyes, 153–73. New Haven: Yale University Southeast Asia Studies.

————, comp. 1997. *Ethnic Communities in Changing Environments.* Chiang Mai, Thailand: Center for Ethnic Studies and Development.

————. 2000. "Water, Livelihood and Dams: Experiences from Thailand." Paper presented at "Water and Indigenous Peoples" conference, sponsored by the World Water Forum, The Hague.

———— and K. Aquino. 2000. "Citizenship and Forest Policy: Community Forestry in Thailand," *Asia-Pacific Community Forestry Newsletter* 13 (1): 1, 14–15, 28.

————, Prasit Leeprecha, and Mali Sitthikriengkrai. 2010. *Citizens at the Western Border: The Quest for Thai Citizenship, Processes and Problems.* Chiang Mai: Chiang Mai University Center for Ethnic Studies.

Cooper, Robert G. 1979. "The Tribal Minorities of Northern Thailand: Problems and Prospects." In *Southeast Asian Affairs 1979*, 323–32. Singapore: Heinemann Educational Books.

Delang, Claudio O. 2002. "Deforestation in Northern Thailand: The Result of Hmong Farming Practices or Thai Development Strategies?" *Society and Natural Resources* 15:483–501.

Jonsson, Hjorleifur. 2014. "Phantom Scandal: On the National Uses of the 'Thailand Controversy.'" *Journal of Social Issues in Southeast Asia* 29 (2): 263–99.

Kammerer, Cornelia Ann. 1986. "Territorial Imperatives: Akha Ethnic Identity and Thailand's National Integration." In *Ethnicities and Nations: Processes of Interethnic Relations in Latin America, Southeast Asia, and the Pacific,* edited by R. Guidieri, F. Pellizzi, and S. J. Tambiah, 277–91. Houston: Rothko Chapel.

————. 1988. "Of Labels and Laws: Thailand's Resettlement and Repatriation Policies." *Cultural Survival* 12 (4): 7–12.

Keyes, Charles F. 1979. "The Karen in Thai History and the History of the Karen in Thailand." In *Ethnic Adaptation and Identity: The Karen on the Thai Frontier with Burma,* edited by Charles F. Keyes, 25–62. Philadelphia: ISHI.

————. 1986. "Tribal Peoples and the Nation-State in Mainland Southeast Asia." In *Southeast Asian Tribal Groups and Ethnic Minorities: Prospects of the Eighties and Beyond,* by Benedict O'G. Anderson, 19–26. Cambridge, Massachusetts: Cultural Survival.

Kunstadter, Peter, E. C. Chapman, and Sanga Sabhasri, eds. 1978. *Farmers in the Forest: Economic Development and Marginal Agriculture in Northern Thailand.* Honolulu: University of Hawai'i Press.

Kwanchewan Buadaeng. 2006. "The Rise and Fall of the Tribal Research Institute (TRI): 'Hill Tribe' Policy and Studies in Thailand." *Southeast Asian Studies* 44 (3): 359–84.

Pinkaew Laungaramsri. 1995. "On the Discourse of Hill Tribes." Unpublished MA paper, University of Washington.

————. 2000. "The Ambiguity of 'Watershed': The Politics of People and Conservation in Northern Thailand." *Sojourn* 15 (1): 52–75.

Ramsay, Ansil. 1976. "Modernization and Centralization in Northern Thailand, 1875–1911." *Journal of Southeast Asian Studies* 7 (1): 1–15.

————. 1979. "Modernization and Reactionary Rebellions in Northern Siam." *Journal of Asian Studies* 38 (2): 283–97.

Renard, Ronald D. 1980. "The Role of the Karens in Thai Society during the Early Bangkok Period, 1782–1873." *Contributions to Asian Studies* 15:16–28.

Roth, Guenther, and Wolfgang Schluchter. 1979. *Max Weber's Vision of History: Ethics and Methods.* Berkeley: University of California Press.

Scott, James C. 2009. *The Art of Not Being Governed: An Anarchist History of Upland Southeast Asia.* New Haven: Yale University Press.

Tej Bunnag. 1977. *The Provincial Administration of Siam, 1892–1915.* Kuala Lumpur: Oxford University Press.

Thongchai Winichakul. 1994. *Siam Mapped: A History of the Geo-Body of a Nation.* Honolulu: University of Hawai'i Press.

United Nations Food and Agricultural Organization, Regional Office for Asia and the Pacific. 2009. "Thailand Forestry Outlook Study." Bangkok. http://www.fao.org/docrep/014/am617e/am617e00.pdf

Wakin, Eric. 1992. *Anthropology Goes to War: Professional Ethics and Counterinsurgency in Thailand.* Center for Southeast Asian Studies, Monograph Number 7. Madison: University of Wisconsin,

Walker, Andrew. 2004. "Seeing Farmers for the Trees: Community Forestry and the Arborealisation of Agriculture in Northern Thailand." *Asia Pacific Viewpoint* 45(3): 311–24.

Walker, Anthony R. 1983. "In Mountain and Ulu: A Comparative History of Development Strategies for Ethnic Minority Peoples in Thailand and Malaysia." *Contemporary Southeast Asia* 4:451–85.

Weber, Max. (1946) 1958a. "Politics as a Vocation." In *From Max Weber,* edited and translated by H. H. Gerth and C. Wright Mills, 77–128. New York: Oxford University Press.

————. (1946) 1958b. "Science as a Vocation." In *From Max Weber,* edited and translated by H. H. Gerth and C. Wright Mills, 77–128. New York: Oxford University Press.

Part 2

Politics, Activism, and Cross-Border Politics in the Greater Mekong Subregion

Highlanders' Mobility and Colonial Anxieties: A Political History of the Khmu Laborers in Siam

Olivier Evrard

When he was a young boy, Achan Chayan used to live with his parents along the bank of the Mae Ping, in an area that was at that time the economic heart of the city of Chiang Mai, at the confluence of both riverine and overland trade networks. He remembers the horse caravans led by Haw traders that stopped near his father's house to sell their potatoes. He also recalls the large sawmill that collected and cut up the logs sent downriver from the northern regions by the teak companies. Most of the sawmill workers were of Khmu origin; they came from Laos and worked in Chiang Mai for months, sometimes years, before going back to their native areas. Achan Chayan got to know some of them personally because his father employed them as *samlo* drivers. One Khmu driver, who said he had been previously working as a mahout, married a Shan lady who ended up living with Chayan's family.

I chose this anecdote because it reflects both Achan Chayan's lifelong involvement with ethnic minorities and his inseparable interest in cross-border flows, networks, and politics. Coincidentally, labor migration of the Khmu between Laos and Thailand has been an important theme in my personal research itinerary and the subject of repeated discussions with Achan Chayan. When I first met him in Chiang Mai in 2007, I had been doing ethnographic fieldwork in remote Khmu upland villages of the Nam Tha area in northern Laos since the mid-1990s. I told him that in spite of the difficulties of access and the isolation of those settlements, their inhabitants had a much larger social space than I had initially assumed. Many elderly men had crossed the Mekong and traveled extensively in Thailand or in

Myanmar during their youth, and the same was true for the younger generations. Achan Chayan showed a keen interest in my findings and encouraged me to go on researching the lives of Khmu workers in Thailand. Thereafter, I interviewed many Khmu men and women working on building sites or in factories, markets, restaurants, shops, golf courses, hotels, sawmills, or rice mills in various cities of northern Thailand—not only Chiang Mai but also Chiang Khong, Chiang Rai, Phayao, Lamphun, and Lampang.

My fieldwork and archival research led me to two conclusions. First, and while they may appear negligible in volume (a few thousand per year), the labor migrations of the Khmu are remarkable in their historical durability: the accounts of the first colonial explorers show that it is an old phenomenon dating back to at least the nineteenth century, when Indian and Chinese labor migration was already booming but well before Lao lowlanders started also to cross the Mekong to engage in wage labor. These Khmu migrations went on throughout the twentieth century, interrupted only during the first decade of the communist regime in Laos, which came to power in 1975. A second contrasting feature relates to ethnic identity: these periodic migrations are only a well-established trend among the Khmu (and their close neighbors, the Rmet) of northern Laos. To my knowledge, no similar dynamics have been documented for other highlanders in mainland Southeast Asia over such a long period of time. If we consider in addition the fact that the Khmu and the Rmet are indigenous to northern Southeast Asia, or at least are considered as such, then their labor migrations bear a special significance for a social history of the Mekong basin. They offer the opportunity to unveil the old connections between upland hinterlands and lowland cities and to understand their transformation in the process of state formation and globalization. Unfortunately, available information is sketchy and refers mainly to the early colonial period. It is found scattered in the writings of various European explorers and administrators who traveled in northern Siam and Laos at the end of the nineteenth century and witnessed the presence of Khmu laborers in the teak plantations. For the postcolonial period, Franck Lebar is, to my knowledge, the only scholar who did research specifically on this topic (Lebar 1965 and 1967).

It is in this context that I discovered in 2007 an unpublished file in the archives of the French Ministry of Foreign Affairs entitled "Khmu migrations toward Siam."[1] It contains numerous letters and reports by French consuls in Chiang Mai, Chiang Rai, and Nan as well as correspondence with Siamese authorities regarding the legal status of those who were at that time considered as French "protégés." These documents cover the period between 1884 and 1939. They give precious indications of the fluctuations of the numbers and routes of migrants and of the changing attitudes of the French and Siamese officials toward them. They also allow us to catch a glimpse of the economic and social changes that affected development in northern Siam between the 1880s and the 1930s. Most importantly, they show how the figure of the migrant was constructed and became an object of political discourse during the colonial period. As modern conceptions of borders and citizenships were established, references to "legal" and "illegal" migrants as well as to "middlemen" and "smugglers" emerged and were the subject of minor but constant debates between Siamese and French officials as well as among personnel on each side. These debates are crucial because they thereafter have informed the way the Thai state has conceptualized highlanders as aliens on the national territory, a theme that has been at the heart of Achan Chayan's academic and political engagement with ethnic minorities of northern Thailand. In sum, the history of Khmu labor migration reminds us that migrants did not come into existence against or behind state regulations but were created by them and through them.

1. The documents used for this article come primarily from the archives of the French Embassy in Siam (and its consulates) between 1884 and 1939. These archives were at the time of my research located in Nantes, unlike the colonial archives that can be found in Aix-en-Provence. The file, entitled "Immigration des Khamous" is number 112 in the series "Lois et règlements siamois," but it covers only the period of 1937–39. For earlier periods, I found other relevant documents in the series "Sociétés et Compagnies Commerciales" (file 143) and "Protection des Asiatiques" (file 101) as well as in file 275.

WHEN AND WHY DID THE KHMU START MIGRATING TO SIAM?

Two hypotheses have been made concerning the origin of such migrations, neither of which appears satisfactory. The first one focuses on "push factors" and brings forward disruptions in the native areas of the migrants: wars, rebellions, starvation, endemic poverty, or epidemics would have continuously forced the Khmu to look for subsistence outside of their territory. Indeed, there are several historical records of such migrations inside Thai territory in the course of history. The Khmu living today in Kanchanaburi and Uthai Thani Provinces, for instance, are the descendants of prisoners of war (Suwilai 2002, xxiii). Similarly, the creation of the Khmu villages in Nan Province (twenty-one in total, housing more than 6,800 people— the highest concentration of Khmu speakers settled in Thailand) seems to be related primarily to a history of conflict, starvation, and migration westward involving Mon-Khmer populations around Luang Prabang sometime during the last decades of the nineteenth century, in the wake of the "Haw" invasions (McCarthy 1994, 92). Migration also occurred in the early 1930s, when Khmu highlanders, along with Tai Yuan and Tai Lue villagers, went to Siam to escape the French colonial tax order and the Lao mandarins who benefited from it (Gunn 2003, 172). Finally, in the course and immediate aftermath of the two Indochina Wars, Khmu migrants from northern Laos escaped violence, starvation, and retaliation and arrived in Viang Kaen District, near Chiang Khong, where they created several permanent settlements.[2] There are currently six Khmu villages in this area and three others in the vicinity of Chiang Khong town (including one mixed with Hmong).

However, these population movements were not similar to labor migration: they affected at once a whole village or a group of villages in a specific area; they were collective, permanent, and always were

2. The interviews done with the Khmu villagers of this area point out a period of "uprooting" which extended over nearly one century, with multiple causes: epidemics and colonial taxes in the 1930s, consequences of a millenarian conflict in the 1950s, involvement (on one side or the other) in the two Indochina wars, or insecurity created by those wars.

partly brought about by constraint or emergency under specific contexts. On the other hand, labor migration of Khmu from Laos to Thailand (or, in precolonial times, from Lan Xang to Lan Na) involved individuals recruited from different villages over large areas. Most importantly, the vast majority was—and remains—temporary. Therefore, such migration has not led (or only marginally) to the creation of Khmu villages in Thai territory, though in some cases it can contribute to increasing the population of already existing villages. In sum, there were and remain today two different kinds of migration, relying on separate networks. All my interviews show that the majority of the young Khmu labor migrants who come to Thailand today have few contacts with those settled for a long time in the country,[3] and when they meet, it is often in their workplace.

A second explanation focuses more on "pull" factors and attributes the origin of these labor migrations to the surge of the teak trade in northern Siam during the last decades of the nineteenth century. Indisputably, the development of teak plantations seems to have been a major incentive for Khmu migrants. As the yearly administrative reports of the British consulate in Chiang Mai make clear, Khmu laborers (and this was true also for Rmet) were a crucial source of labor for the (mostly)[4] British companies at that time, and the available numbers of Khmu men regularly fell short of meeting their needs. They were much prized both for their ability to accomplish hard forestry work and to live for long periods of time in remote areas. Tai laborers from northern Siam were recruited in smaller number, not so much because they demanded higher wages but because they remained under the control of the local rulers (*chao*), for whom they had to perform agricultural work as well as statute labor—implying, by

3. There are nonetheless some exceptions. The migrants often mention their contacts with members of two Khmu villages, one in Chiang Rai Province and the other in Lampang Province. They can also meet Khmu individuals living in Thai cities for a long time but this is far from systematic and such contacts usually do not precede migration.

4. In 1902, there were eighty-three timber companies in Chiang Mai, Lamphun, and Lampang, among which fifty-nine were British and twenty-two Thai (Vatikiotis 1984, 90).

contrast, that the relation of the highlanders to the lowland rulers was much more flexible. The possibility of importing labor from India and Burma was regularly discussed during this period, though never implemented.

The teak boom does not provide an entirely satisfactory answer though. Other highlanders, such as the Karen and the Lawa, for instance, could have been employed as easily as the Khmu. Being settled in the borderlands of Thailand and Burma, they were located closer to the teak plantations and came under British influence sooner in the course of history. Some of them were indeed recruited as mahouts, but wage labor did not develop among them as systematically or as early as among the Khmu and Rmet from Laos. Therefore, the question remains what the original incentives of such temporary labor migrations were, specifically among these two ethnic groups—albeit with substantial variation at local levels.[5] Older involvement in trans-Mekong networks, for the acquisition of metal, for instance, may have played a role, but we do not yet have any way of precisely assessing their influence. A more pragmatic argument could be that it was more desirable for British or Siamese foresters to hire Khmu and Rmet rather than Lawa or Karen because, being so far from their native village, they would have had fewer tendencies to be absent, and the turnover of the labor would have been more manageable for their employer.[6]

Frank Lebar (1967, 77–78) hypothesized that these labor migrations may find their origin in ecological factors, the Khmu being supposedly settled in a disadvantaged area for agriculture. That is not true at least for the Nam Tha area, where most of the migrants come from, which has long been "the granary of Luang Prabang" (Lefèvre-Pontalis 2000,

5. Karl Gustav Izikowitz (1951, 347–52) noticed that among the Rmet, labor migration to Siam occurred primarily among those he called the Upper Rmet. Similarly, I observed among the Khmu that migration could be more prevalent among some localized subgroups (*tmoy*) than others (Evrard 2007 and 2010), though here again, the situation could vary greatly from one village to another, and besides, my observations related mostly to the period around the 1930s–1970s, before huge resettlements considerably lessened the localized nature of the *tmoy*.

6. Thanks to Ian G. Baird and Paul T. Cohen for pointing out this argument to me during our discussion at the Thai Studies Conference in Sydney in April 2014.

180) where lowland Lao peddlers came to obtain rice from the highlanders in exchange for crafts and iron. The Khmu village economy was in many respects similar to those of Karen or Lawa villages in the Chiang Mai region, involving both swidden agriculture in the uplands and periodic trade in the lowlands or at the main river confluences to obtain ironware and salt. The main difference is that the former did not develop an economic specialization beyond rice cultivation and the collecting of forest products (e.g., benzoin, cardamom, stick lac, wax, and buffalo and tiger skins) while the latter were, at certain stages and in certain places, involved in slave and cattle trade, in the case of the Karen (Ratanaporn 1989, 132), or in iron production, in the case of the Lawa (Grabowsky and Turton 2003, 232).

The economic context was much more favorable, at least during the last decades of the nineteenth century, along the Siam-Burma border, which was connected to the Moulmein and Bangkok networks, than in northern Laos, where trade with Yunnan, Siam, and Vietnam had nearly collapsed by the 1880s in the wake of the "Haw" invasions. In 1884, the French consul in Bangkok, Alexandre de Kergaradec, reckoned that commercial roads between the Luang Prabang region and Annam were abandoned because of insecurity and banditry,[7] while a few years later, in 1895, the British consul in Chiang Mai noted that "trade with the newly acquired French territory on the east side of the Mekong is as sluggish as ever and there is so far no prospect of any improvement in that direction" (Foreign Office 1895, 4). Almost two decades later, in 1913, the trade with the "French Lao States" was still inconsiderable and "mostly confined to purely local trade along the border" (Foreign Office 1913, 12). An aggravating factor was also that both upland and lowland areas had been at some points depopulated in northern Laos in the course of the nineteenth century—the former by rebellions, starvation, and outmigration; the latter by the campaigns of the Siamese armies, for instance in Xiengkhuang and in Namtha, disrupting commercial networks and breaking down

---

7. "Utilité d'un vice consulat à Louang Prabang," note by Alexandre de Kergaradec, 22 July 1884, file 275, Bangkok collection, Archives of the Ministry of Foreign Affairs, France.

traditional highland-lowland relationships.[8] This combination of historical and geographic factors made it difficult for the Khmu and Rmet highlanders to develop sustainable commercial specializations in their native areas and gave them an incentive to turn toward wage labor instead.

Beyond this discussion on push and pull factors, it is important to point out that the historical and economic context (stagnation and isolation in northern Laos as well as breakdown of the traditional lowland-upland relationship and, conversely, labor market opportunities in Siam) interacted with the social structure and ideology in the Khmu (Lebar 1967; Evrard 2007) and Rmet villages (Izikowitz 1951; Sprenger 2007). In both populations, acquisition of wealth and its consumption or display during specific rituals (mainly weddings, building of a new house, and funerals) is a way to enhance the status of a patrilineal group and also to ensure that proper relations are maintained with the ancestors on the one hand, and with the wife-givers on the other hand. Inside this "socioeconomic ritual complex" (Lebar 1967, 78), the most valuable goods included rice and buffaloes, but also gongs, silverware, coins, and bronze drums. Interestingly, all of them could be obtained through trade and were kept outside the villages: rice grows in the field and is kept in the barns that lie outside the settlements; buffaloes, often bought with labor in lowland villages (Sprenger 2005) wander in the neighboring forest and stay in a semiwild state most of the time; gongs and silverware are obtained through trade, kept in the barns, and mixed with the paddy since they are said to please its soul; bronze drums are also obtained outside and thereafter buried in the old forest which surrounds the settlement, near the graveyards. In sum, goods crucial to the ritual reproduction of society (perpetuation of the links between wife-givers and wife-takers and between the living and the dead) also imply relations with the outside, and, for some of them such as the bronze drums, with relatively distant places or peoples. The

8. Mike Dwyer (2011, 40) convincingly analyzes the breaking down of upland-lowland relationships in the Luang Prabang area as a consequence of the Haw invasions in the 1870s. However, earlier events such as the Siamese military campaigns may also have played an important role.

bronze drums still visible today in Khmu and Rmet villages in northern Laos are of the so-called Heger III type, and villagers refer to them as "Karen drums."[9] However, their ritual use among the Karen is in no way unique in Southeast Asia,[10] and it is unlikely that the Khmu obtained such drums directly from them. Rather, ethnographic and historical evidence tends to show that they were purchased either from neighboring villages or from Khmu middlemen settled in Thai cities.

NAI ROI: KHMU MIDDLEMEN IN NORTHERN THAI CITIES

The labor migrations used to be organized through networks of recruiting specialists from Khmu origin called *nai roi* (a word of Tai origin). For the teak companies, they acted as middlemen by providing them with labor suited to their needs; for the migrants, they were patrons who could give shelter and find jobs for them when they arrived in Siam. Some of the *nai roi* were based in Khmu villages in Laos and they recruited migrants directly in their area. They offered them contracts of one or two years and guaranteed their return at the end of the period. For compensation, they would keep the first month of salary of the migrant as well as a percentage on the other months' pay. Each year at the beginning of the dry season, they would lead groups of fifteen to twenty men to Huay Xai and then Chiang Khong. The migrants would then work in Chiang Khong or be dispatched to other destinations such as Lampang or Chiang Mai. In those bigger cities, other *nai roi* took care of the migrants upon their arrival and ensured they reached their destination. These urban *nai roi* were sometimes called *big nai roi* (Lebar 1965, 9); they were permanently settled in the city, often married to Thai women, and they usually worked for the teak companies. They also acted as traders and sold to

9. The word for such bronze drums among the Rmet (*klo*) is the same as among the Karen; as for the Khmu, they use the word *yaan*, which seems to point out to *yang*, an exonym for Karen in Thailand.

10. Bronze drums and gongs are important ritual artifacts in many highland cultures throughout Southeast Asia. For instance, in 2008 UNESCO inscribed the Space of Gong Culture in the Central Highlands of Vietnam on the list of intangible cultural heritage (see chapter 7 in this volume).

migrants the prestige goods they were looking for just before they returned to their villages at the end of their contracts.

Such networks were not rigidly organized over long periods of time. They could last for a person's lifetime, or sometimes two or three lifetimes, but many were also short-lived. They often depended on the personality of one Khmu migrant who decided to stay in Thailand and who was asked by his employer to provide more workers. By the time he retired, or died, another Khmu migrant that he had recruited would succeed him. His children, if any, were unlikely to become *nai roi* like their father because they usually tended to adopt their mother's culture and language and never went to Laos. In Chiang Mai for instance, a famous *nai roi* in the first part of the twentieth century was known under the name of Nai Kham Ai and lived near Wat Ket, a temple on the Ping River. This area was the hub of the city's economy and included notably the fluvial port and the local branch of the Borneo Company (opened in 1889),[11] which employed many Khmu migrants. Nai Kham Ai accommodated them upon their arrival, found them work, and sold them gongs or bronze drums before their return. He married a northern Thai woman and with her had three children, who were given a Thai family name, Phanthusin (Voravimone 2006, 158–60). Their house, located near Wat Ket, used to be an antique shop and has now become a guesthouse.[12]

The existence of such recruiting specialists points out that the labor migrations among the Khmu were substantial both in number and in duration, though they were not comparable to the large-scale migrations of Chinese or Indian laborers (Kaur 2004 and 2009). In

11. In 1939, the last manager of the Borneo Company in Chiang Mai, William Bain, bought the house and the compound from his employer. The house was inherited by his son, Jack Bain, as well as by an adopted Khmu child, Nai In. The house, known as the "137 pillars house," has since been turned into a luxury hotel.

12. This information was collected during an interview with Somwang Ritthidet, the curator of the Wat Ket temple museum. His father, a Khmu man from Laos, came to work in Thailand in 1939 and never went back to his native area. The day I was interviewing Somwang, Darunee Panthusin, the granddaughter of Nai Kham Ai, coincidently showed up, arriving from Bangkok. It was the first time Somwang had seen her in forty years.

1932, the French consular agent in Chiang Rai, Michel Bréal, estimated that there were "an average of 4,000 to 6,000 Khmu people working in northern Siam."[13] The turnover was important (most of them were staying only one year, sometimes two) and there was also sharp variation from one year to the other in the flux of migrants, but on the whole, the numbers seem to have remained relatively constant. Earlier documents however gave higher estimates: a letter sent to the résident supérieur of Laos in 1906 mentioned that the Siamese and English have "around 30,000 Khmu workers in their plantations."[14] The same year, the résident supérieur of Laos wrote a letter to the governor of Indochina in Hanoi indicating the commandant supérieur of Upper Laos, Mr. Vacle, had told him that "25,000 Khmu were emigrating to Siam each year."[15] Since these numbers were not based on precise surveys, they must be considered with caution. As I show in the next paragraph, the fear of losing a precious labor force may have led some administrators to overestimate the magnitude of these migrations in the first years of the colonial regime in Laos. Conversely, it is also possible that the migrants were much more numerous in the early twentieth century, when the Siamese and the English companies needed their labor, than in the 1930s, when the Siamese authorities started to close their borders to migrants coming from Laos.

These migrant networks also contradict the still-prevailing image of a powerless and marginalized group whose members have for long looked haphazardly for jobs in the lowlands to escape poverty. Indeed, the interviews I did with Khmu migrants who ended up settling permanently in northern Thailand show that some of them acted as cultural intermediaries between their foreign employers and the Thai

13. Letter from Michel Bréal to the French ambassador to Siam, 10 April 1932, file 112, series "Lois et règlements siamois," Bangkok collection, Archives of the Ministry of Foreign Affairs, France.

14. Letter from Mr. Lussan on the difficulty of recruiting Kha coolies who emigrate to Siam because of Laotian mandarins, 27 March 1906, Central Archives of French Indochina, Aix-en-Provence, France.

15. Letter 63 from Mr. Mahé, résident supérieur in Laos, to the gouverneur général of Indochina, Hanoi, 27 March 1906, Central Archives of French Indochina, Aix-en-Provence. Thanks to Oliver Tappe, who sent me a copy of this document.

authorities. They could even become the right-hand men of their employers and be granted official documents (Thai identity card, driving license, etc.) that many northern Thais could not obtain easily at that time. Today, these customary recruiting specialists have disappeared, replaced by village headmen (Lao or Khmu) of border localities in Laos or by Thai entrepreneurs in Thailand, who legally or illegally employ migrants from Laos without paying much attention to their ethnicity. It is tempting to link the end of the *nai roi* system to these transformations of the social, economic, and technological contexts in which labor migration from Laos to Thailand now takes place: it involves a wider range of population (in terms of both ethnicity and gender), destinations, and activities, and it also relies on new and quicker means of transportation and communication. However, most of these transformations started to occur only after the 1960s, while it is the Second World War that, according to the Khmu themselves, marks the end of the *"nai roi* period" (*samai nai roi*). Indeed, the transformation of the structure of the Khmu migration networks is primarily the consequence of the colonial history—external in the case of the Lao banks of the Mekong and internal on the Siamese (and thereafter Thai) side. New notions of borders emerged during that period, which profoundly reshaped long-established trans-Mekong connections.

KHMU LABOR IN THE TEAK ECONOMY: COLONIAL ANXIETIES

By the time the first European administrators and diplomats had begun to travel and live in what is today northern Thailand and Laos, the labor migration of the Khmu was already a well-established trend. During his explorations of the Upper Mekong basin in 1893–94, Pierre Lefèvre-Pontalis ([1902] 2000, 146) for instance witnessed in Chiang Khong "the important exodus of the Kha from Luang Prabang and from M. Pou Kha which have been attracted by the exploitation of the teak forests on the side of Xieng-Mai for many years, without ever failing to return to their home." A few years prior, James McCarthy (1900, 92) had already noticed that the teak trade in Siam was relying heavily on the labor of Khmu from Laos. These migrations soon became a political issue between France and Siam when the French colonial authorities used them as an argument for expanding their control on the western side of the Mekong. They feared that this situation could deprive their newly acquired Lao colony of a much-needed labor source at a time when they held the ambition to build new roads to link Laos with the Gulf of Tonkin and with the Mekong Delta. Besides, they lacked information on the exact nature of such migrations, and some administrators, either by ignorance or dishonesty—unlike Lefèvre-Pontalis—were quick to associate them with slave trading or with systematic attempts at depopulation of the Lao territory on the part of the Siamese, who had conducted massive resettlement campaigns in the Lao lowlands in the earlier decades of the nineteenth century. Finally, geopolitical and commercial arguments also played a role; the French were eager to extend their colonial influence as far as possible on the western bank of the Mekong to counter British influence and to benefit directly from the teak trade.

Following the 1893 treaty with Siam, France not only annexed some of the territories west of the Mekong but also obtained the right to establish consulates in Siamese territory "wherever it was considered necessary to protect the interests of the populations under its jurisdiction" (article 8).[16] In the North, two consulates were created, in Nan and in Chiang Mai, the two major nodes on the routes of Khmu migrants at the end of the nineteenth century. Later on, Nan lost its economic importance and the consulate was moved to Lampang, while another was opened in Chiang Rai. Interestingly, agreements already existed between the kingdoms of Luang Prabang and Siam concerning the Khmu laborers. While working in Siam, they became French protégés; they

> were keeping their quality of subjects of the Luang Prabang kingdom, whose sovereign was a vassal of the Siamese king. The king of Luang Prabang had the right to send his mandarins into the upper Siamese

16. The peace treaty signed on October 3, 1893, between the French diplomat Le Myre de Vilers and the foreign minister of Siam, Prince Dewawongse, included an article (8) which stipulated that the French authorities would have the right to open consular posts wherever they would judge it necessary for the interests of their citizens, "especially in Khorat and Mueang Nan."

region where they could act as consular attachés so to speak, to protect them and to solve the conflicts which could occur between them.[17]

The French consuls were therefore seeing, rather opportunistically, their action as a continuation of the role played historically in these regions by the envoys of the king of Luang Prabang.[18] The new colonial context meant, however, that the previous hierarchical nature of the relations between Luang Prabang and Siam disappeared and that, simultaneously, the migration of the Khmu protégés became an argument for territorial control and economic competition, which was not the case in previous years.

The consular agents' duties were to register the migrants coming from Laos—nearly all of them Khmu—to ensure that proper work contracts were established between them and the timber companies and to settle any conflicts they might have with the Siamese authorities. They had to oversee these migrations and even stop them if necessary to ensure that they were not detrimental to their newly acquired territories on the eastern banks of the Mekong. The French ambassador in Bangkok summarized this idea when he wrote in 1898 to the French Ministry of Foreign Affairs:

> Over the last years, the emigration of the inhabitants of the left bank of the Mekong has considerably increased and the English are successful in recruiting a lot of these precious workers and sending them to their forests in the Burma and Siam border area. It is essential that we get information and that we stop this emigration of the Khmu toward where they would be lost forever for our colony and our influence in the North.[19]

17. Letter from Mr. Lugan, consul in Nan, to the ambassador in Bangkok, 15 September 1910, file 101, series "Protection des Asiatiques," Bangkok collection, Archives of the Ministry of Foreign Affairs, France.

18. The first envoy of the French colonial authorities in northern Siam in 1895, Raoul Hardouin, took with him two Lao princes, Chao Si Song Say and Chao Som, to assist him in his relations with the Khmu and with the Siamese authorities. Later on, he sent Chao Si Song Say to Chiang Mai to open a branch of the Nan consulate.

19. Letter from the French ambassador in Siam to the minister of foreign affairs,

These worries never entirely disappeared from the diplomatic mail and they resurfaced periodically until World War II. They were mirrored, at least during the first years, by symmetric concerns in Siam, where the actions of the French colonial authorities rapidly impacted the availability of Khmu labor for the teak companies.

In 1896, the British diplomatic and consular reports on trade in Chiang Mai mentioned "Forest coolie labor is becoming more and more scarce, the immigration of Khamus [Khmu] from the east bank of the Mekong having greatly decreased. Wages are at least 25 per cent higher than they were a few years ago" (Foreign Office 1896, 5). The 1899 report mentions the same problem and gives interesting details. The Khmu laborers who were engaged by the foresters often stayed in Siam longer than what was initially planned in their contract because their employers delayed the payment of their wages and induced them to remain at their service. When the French colonial authorities set up regulations requiring labor contracts to be registered by the consulate, they

> brought pressure to bear on defaulting foresters to pay arrears. Many Khamoos [Khmu] finding themselves suddenly wealthy in the possession of 100 or 200 rs [rupees], at once returned to their homes, and only the few who had taken to themselves wives and settled down in the country village remained behind. This exodus soon began to affect the supply of labor, and during the last two years this has been accentuated by the much smaller number of men returning coming down, and the majority of time-expired men returning to their home. (Foreign Office 1899, 6)

The procurement of cheap labor was a crucial issue for the teak industry, which was worth around two million British pounds in the Chiang Mai region at the end of the nineteenth century (Foreign Office 1899, 7). It was also a very critical topic for the local Siamese authorities, who got an important part of their incomes from the teak sector, through the duties, bribes, and presents paid by the representatives of the foreign

---

Mr. Louis Delcassé, 29 July 1898, file 275, Bangkok collection, Archives of the Ministry of Foreign Affairs, France.

companies. Ratanaporn Sethakul (1989, 131), for instance, writes, "In 1875, income from the timber trade totalled 200,000 rupees in Chiang Mai with bribes or presents at about 150,000 rupees." The question of Khmu labor was at one point so serious that schemes for importing labor from India and China were discussed by the British. However, the crisis was short-lived, and in 1901 the number of Khmu laborers increased again. The 1901 report notes that

> the supply of Khamu [Khmu] coolies, which had fallen off considerably owing to the restrictive measures introduced by the French authorities, was inflated by the entry during 1901 of some 1,700 men from the eastern bank of the Mekong. Prices accordingly fell from 110 rs and 120 rs to 80 rs and 90 rs per annum, with food added on a two-year contract. (Foreign Office 1901, 6)

The same problem resurfaced briefly in 1907, but on the whole, the timber sector was thereafter able to get sufficient numbers of Khmu laborers from Laos. This was probably partly due to the lower demand of the timber companies since some of the teak forests had become depleted, especially in the Nan watershed area (Foreign Office 1912, 17). More importantly, however, this was also due to the fact that the French were never able to efficiently limit or control the migration of Khmu from Laos, for several reasons.

FAILED ATTEMPTS AT CONTROL

First, and most obviously, the geographic context and the small number of French officials in these regions were serious obstacles. Registering all the migrants was an impossible task, mainly because most of them were staying outside of the cities and worked for British or Siamese employers, who, for the reasons mentioned previously, had no interest in facilitating their registration at the French consulates. Groups of Khmu migrants were, for instance, reported to be avoiding the city of Nan in favor of Phrae, where there was no French consulate. Others left the main northern caravan roads linking the Mekong to Chiang Mai and followed the valley of the Mae Wang down to

Lampang[20] to work on the plantations there. Under such circumstances, and with very limited staff, the French consuls could only rely on their relations with the few Khmu middlemen settled in the main centers and on long and difficult tours of inspection in the countryside to identify and register as many Khmu migrants as possible. As a symbol of these difficulties, the first demand for statistics, formulated in 1910 by Henri Ponsot, the then French ambassador in Bangkok, was met only in 1936 in a report prepared by the French consul in Chiang Rai, Mr. Goenaga. It asserted that an average of only 560 new Khmu migrants were registered in Chiang Rai, Nan, and Lampang each year between 1932 and 1936, but his document shows big variations from one year to another and does not include data from the Chiang Mai consulate.[21] Besides, his numbers do not match those given two years later by the French résident in Huay Xai, Mr. Turquet de Beauregard, who said that only 394 Khmu registered with the Chiang Rai consulate in 1934, 1,031 in 1935, and 1,194 in 1936—without giving the reasons for such variations but announcing a sharp drop for the year 1937.[22]

Second, the economic environment was also working against the French colonial authorities. Their attempts to develop their own timber industry with Khmu labor in the Chiang Khong area were short-lived, as the Mekong did not provide a convenient waterway for the logs, which could take as long as two years to reach Saigon. (Khmu laborers were employed from Pak Tha to Nong Khai for rafting services.) Consequently, between 1896 and 1925, only 3 percent of the teak harvested in Lanna was floated down through the Mekong, against 81 percent through the Chao Phraya and 16 percent via the Salween (Suphawat and Takeda 2007, 126). Besides, the concessions

20. Letter from the French ambassador to Siam to minister of foreign affairs Mr. Louis Delcassé, 29 July 1898, file 275, Bangkok collection, Archives of the Ministry of Foreign Affairs, France.
21. Letter from Mr. Goenaga, French consul in Chiang Rai, to Mr. Henri Ponsot, French ambassador to Siam, 7 July 1936, file 101, series "Protections des Asiatiques," Bangkok collection, Archives of the Ministry of Foreign Affairs, France.
22. Letter from Mr. Turquet de Beauregard, résident de France in Huay Xai, to the résident supérieur in Laos, 28 June 1937, file 112, series "Lois et règlements siamois," Bangkok collection, Archives of the Ministry of Foreign Affairs, France.

obtained from the Siamese were only for fifteen years and were much smaller than those granted to the British,[23] leading to a quick depletion of the teak forests under intensive exploitation. The letter sent in June 1912 by Pierre Lefèvre-Pontalis, the then French ambassador in Bangkok, to the French prime minister (*président du conseil*), Raymond Poincaré, illustrates these problems. Pontalis was writing in support of a French timber company (the French Asiatic Company) in Chiang Khong that needed new teak concessions in this area. While he estimated (probably optimistically) the profitability threshold for this company to be as low as four thousand logs a year, he also conveyed that only two thousand logs had been sent downriver in 1911.[24] As a comparison, the Danish East Asiatic Company was sending 188,000 logs to Bangkok via the Chao Phraya in 1922, out of which 168,000 were exported (*Bangkok Times*, August 5, 1922).

More generally, the economy was much more dynamic in Siam than in Laos throughout the first half of the twentieth century. Even after the 1929 crisis and the progressive depletion of the teak resources, the contrast between the two sides of the Mekong remained high. In 1934, the French ambassador to Siam, Roger Maugras, observed (in response to a letter from the governor of French Indochina, alarmed by accounts of emigration of the Khmu from Laos) that "Siamese Upper-Laos has developed a lot in the course of the last few years" and he mentioned the construction of rail and new roads toward Chiang Rai, Chiang Mai, as well as Nan,

which was until then completely remote and slowly depopulating. These new communication means have transformed the country; they made trading and supplying easier. Trucks have become of frequent use; big villages have been created; land value increased. In this entire region, the peasant feels at ease. Besides, the weight of the central power is not much

23. The French were granted concessions in the lower part of the Ing River basin from 1909 to 1925 and in the Kok River basin from 1925 to 1940.

24. Letter from Pierre Lefèvre-Pontalis, French ambassador in Bangkok, to Raymond Poincaré, président du conseil, 28 June 1912, file 143, series "Sociétés et Compagnies Commerciales," Bangkok collection, Archives of the Ministry of Foreign Affairs, France.

felt: there are fewer administrators than in the central regions, taxes are collected more gently and military recruitment reaches fewer people.[25]

By contrast, the concession-based economic development in colonial Laos was a failure and simultaneously corvée labor tended to fall more heavily on highlanders than on ethnic Lao in the northern part of the country. All these factors therefore fueled the labor migration toward the western banks of the Mekong and certainly conspired to give to Siam a romantic charm in the mind of many Khmu and Rmet young men, who saw it as the "land of possibilities" (Izikowitz 1951, 351).

Finally, a third reason for the failure of the French to both control and limit the labor migration of the Khmu throughout this period is to be found in the constant debates and lack of unanimity among the French colonial administrators themselves concerning the positive or negative nature of such migration for the French colony. I have already mentioned the French colonial concerns expressed as early as 1898 by some administrators in the letters they sent to the Ministry of Foreign Affairs. In the following years, they remained a constant issue and were the topic of many of the reports regularly sent by the French consul in Nan, Mr. Lugan, to the French embassy in Bangkok. A member of the Pavie mission in Laos between 1889 and 1895, Lugan was sent in 1896 to Nan, where he ended his career. A tireless traveler, he undertook regular tours of inspection between Nan and Chiang Mai, registering Khmu migrants and recording their complaints to discuss with the Siamese authorities. He was also an administrator profoundly attached to Laos (he had been the head of the consular post in Luang Prabang for three years before being sent to Nan) and he considered the labor migration of the Khmu with mixed feelings of fatalism and rejection. Unlike Pierre Lefèvre-Pontalis, who participated with him to the Pavie mission and who, right from the start, insisted that these migrations were not a threat because they were always temporary, Lugan considered that they led to depopulation in the northern

25. Letter from Mr. Roger Maugras, French ambassador in Bangkok, to the General Governor of French Indochina, 26 July 1934, file 112, series "Lois et règlements Siamois," Bangkok collection, Archives of the Ministry of Foreign Affairs, France.

regions of Laos and thus deprived this region of "labor force much needed to build new roads between the Mekong and the Tonking Gulf."[26]

Lugan's position echoes the "physiocratic perspective" (Dwyer 2011) in vogue at that time among the French colonial authorities. They constructed the old kingdom of Lan Xang as a resource-rich landscape left largely fallow by "lazy" Lao. It was therefore necessary to exploit it rationally using more "industrious" outsiders—mainly Vietnamese labor, as well as those highland populations like the Khmu who were considered diligent workers and who, in the Upper Mekong area at least, had been supportive of the first French explorers. Under this conceptual framework, the "French colonial authorities translated the idea of 'rule with nature' (physio-cracy) into the social and physical landscape that confronted them. Race, demography and resource development figured centrally in their efforts" (Dwyer 2011, 28). The constant efforts deployed by Lugan in his letters to convince the French ambassador in Bangkok to strictly limit this migration were directly derived from such a perspective. An additional paternalistic stance and the idea of being responsible for the well-being of the Khmu protégés made him also emphasize the troubles encountered by the Khmu in Siam, especially after the 1907 treaty (more on this below), and the obligation of France to grant them the same rights and protection as its own citizens. His complaints, however, were met by skepticism in Bangkok, where the French ambassador, Henri Ponsot, considered this issue a minor one and was unsympathetic toward the Khmu workers who often did not register in the consulates. In his letter dated October 18, 1910, he wondered, "What would be the advantage for France to recognize as French subjects people who have neglected to claim this status when the opportunity was given to them?" He added, "We would need annual statistics on the numbers of French subjects recorded in the North of Siam. It would help to

26. Letter from the consul in Nan, Mr. Lugan, to the French ambassador in Bangkok, 15 January 1908, file 101, series "Protection des Asiatiques," Bangkok collection, Archives of the Ministry of Foreign Affairs, France.

settle the practical interest of this question."[27] As we have already mentioned, his demand was not met before 1936, revealing the incapacity of the French consuls in the North to efficiently control these migrations, and the question of Khmu laborers vanished from the diplomatic mail during the next two decades.

The debate resurfaced in the mid-1930s and took on a more alarmist tone. In 1934, the governor of French Indochina expressed his worries to Roger Maugras, the then French ambassador in Bangkok, about the "increasing emigration from Luang Prabang to Siam."[28] He was referring to the information given by the French résident in Luang Prabang concerning the movement of many villages, Khmu as well as Lue, who left the area of Pakbeng and Pak Tha to settle on the Thai side of the Mekong in 1932 and 1933 in the wake of protests against the colonial tax order (Gunn 2003, 172). These movements of villages were different from the labor migrations that occurred on a regular basis among the Khmu highlanders, but they were misinterpreted as part of the same phenomenon. The French authorities then became (once again) worried about the possible loss of manpower for the colony, and some administrators believed that Siam encouraged them. In his reply, Roger Maugras first insisted on the positive consequences of temporary labor migration for the French colony. He then wrote that Siam did not take any special decision to favor these migrations and pointed out that economic development, rather than politics, was the main factor fueling them. His letter seemed to have temporarily reassured the authorities of French Indochina, but two years later, concerns about these migrations were expressed again, and this time directly from within Thailand.

In May 1936, the French consul in Chiang Mai, Camille Notton, wrote to his ambassador in Bangkok to express his deep concerns about

27. Letter from Henri Ponsot, French ambassador to Siam, to Mr. Lugan, French consul in Nan, 18 October 1910, file 101, series "Protection des Asiatiques," Bangkok collection, Archives of the Ministry of Foreign Affairs, France.

28. Letter from Roger Maugras, French ambassador to Siam, to the governor of French Indochina, 26 July 1934, file 112, series "Lois et règlements siamois," Bangkok collection, Archives of the Ministry of Foreign Affairs, France.

the migration of Khmu from Laos to his city, which he likened to child trafficking. He was especially alarmed by the recent arrival of

> very young Khmu from Laos coming from the province of Upper Mekong [split into two new provinces in 1983, Luang Namtha and Bokeo] who are engaged by recruiters at the age of 10 to 14 years old and are paid very low wages from 15 to 20 rupiah per year. They contract bad habits that make them lazy or even wicked.[29]

Notton reckoned that there were also older migrants between eighteen and twenty-five years old, but those had more difficulty finding work than in the past because the teak companies needed less labor and for shorter periods. Consequently, "their salaries are lower than in the past (40 to 60 ticals against 80 to 100 previously) and they all live illegally in Siam." Notton estimated the total number of migrants at four hundred to five hundred per year in Chiang Mai and was convinced that most of them were not planning to go back to Laos. He believed that the situation was even worse in Chiang Rai, which, according to him, offered fewer job opportunities. Notton sent his letter to Marcel Ray, the French ambassador to Siam, who replied by asking figures and numbers. Notton then said that such figures could not be collected because most of the Khmu working in Chiang Mai did not have any official documents at all and came to the consulate only when they were in serious trouble. "The recent immigrants don't bother to register with us," he wrote, "only the oldest see an advantage in doing so. They also do not bother asking for work contracts from their employers because they want to be able to leave at any time."

The French ambassador then asked the French consul in Chiang Rai, Goenaga, if Notton's observations were true for Chiang Rai and Lampang. Strikingly, Goenaga's report contradicts Notton's on every point. To him, these migrations to Siam were primarily driven by poverty in Laos. The Khmu who arrived each year in March or April

---

29. Letter from Mr. Camille Notton, French consul in Chiang Mai, to Mr. Marcel Ray, French ambassador in Bangkok, 22 May 1936, file 101, series "Protection des Asiatiques," Bangkok collection, Archives of the Ministry of Foreign Affairs, France.

in northern Siam were favorably received because their wages were lower than those of the locals and they were more productive. They were also well treated in general by the employers and usually better nourished than in Laos. He mentioned that they came in groups with recruiting agents called *nai roi* and had contracts for six months to one year. At the end of their contract, they left for Laos again with their recruiting agent, who had promised to their relatives to send them back home. They were paid forty to sixty ticals in 1935, but prices rose in 1936 because French authorities were at that time preventing them from going to Siam in order to use them for the construction of roads in Laos. Goenaga insisted that the Khmu were "absolutely not jobless since there are never enough of them to fill up all the jobs which are offered to them; I have never seen wandering Khmu laborers unable to find work."[30] He also mentioned that around 5 percent of the Khmu migrants were between ten and fourteen years old. These kids followed their parents but did only light work for their employers, who were friendly toward them. Finally he pleaded for the colonial administration to take a positive approach to this migration:

Not only is this a good thing for Laos because it prevents the inescapable poverty created by overpopulation in the mountains, but it is also in Siam one of the main sources of wealth of the northern region. Any measure aiming at forcing the Khmu to stay in their country would have disastrous consequences on both sides of the border.[31]

The résident in Huay Xai, who was asked by the colonial authorities to send a report on this topic, supported entirely Goenaga's conclusions from the other side of the Mekong. He insisted that 95 percent of the migrants were coming back to Laos at the end of their contract and he estimated the income related to these migrations for the whole country at a minimum of twenty thousand piasters per year. He also remarked

30. Letter from Mr Goenaga, consular agent in Chiang Rai, to Mr. Marcel Ray, French ambassador in Bangkok, 15 June 1936, file 101, series "Protection des Asiatiques," Bangkok collection, Archives of the Ministry of Foreign Affairs, France.
31. Ibid.

ironically in conclusion that France had never offered to these people such opportunity to enrich themselves.[32]

These debates show that there was not a single voice among the colonial administrators but a plurality of perspectives; some of them were proposing to get benefits from this migration while others kept a more protectionist and paternalistic attitude that was deeply embedded in a physiocratic approach to the development of French Indochina. Another interesting aspect relates to the time frame of these debates: they were especially intense during the last years of the 1910s and again during the 1930s, two key periods in the history of nationalism in Siam. The first period comes nearly a decade after the end of the extraterritorial status of the French and British Asiatic protégés living in Siam. The second one coincides with the rise of a Thai military regime and the implementation of anti-immigration policies. In both cases, the new legal frameworks identified the migrants as objects of suspicion on the Siamese (and thereafter Thai) side and they also profoundly disturbed their networks, making any form of control even more difficult on the French side. In the next section, I examine successively these two important periods in the history of Thai nationalism and I show how they affected the Khmu migration networks.

FROM PROTÉGÉS TO ILLEGAL IMMIGRANTS: THE RISE OF SIAMESE NATIONALISM

After the 1907 Franco-Siamese treaty, registering with the French consulates became useless for Khmu migrants and even went against their own interests. With this treaty, Siam ceded the provinces of Battambang, Sisophon, and Siem Reap (art. 1) and received the port of Trat and the territory of Dan-Sai (art. 2). Most importantly, France relinquished the extraterritorial status of its Asiatic protégés and agreed that those registered after the treaty date (March 23) as residents in Siam would fall under jurisdiction of ordinary Siamese

32. Letter from Mr. Turquet de Beauregard, French résident in Huay Xai, to the résident supérieur in Laos, 28 June 1937, file 112, series "Lois et règlements siamois," Bangkok collection, Archives of the Ministry of Foreign Affairs, France.

courts. Article 12 of the treaty mentioned that the French Asiatic protégés (either Khmu, Lao, Vietnamese, Cambodian, or Chinese) registered in Siam would be exempt from military services but subject to taxes and ordinary services, such as corvée labor. During the following years, the French consuls in northern Siam complained bitterly about the situation this treaty had created. In January 1908, the French consul Lugan mentioned that the Khmu living in northern Siam considered that France had "completely abandoned them," and the French consul feared that "the obligation to participate in the portage corvée may put them off the French authorities and discourage the new emigrants from registering."[33] The tour of inspection Mr. Lugan did with his deputy, Mr. Roy, at the same period somehow confirmed his fears:

> Mr. Roy has not received any visit from our protégés although they are many of them in the region he crossed and in the settlements he stayed. While the same abstention did not occur with me, the number of Khmu who spontaneously came to see me has been smaller than usual and my extended stay in Phrae allowed me to meet only less than half of those who are living in the outskirts of the city.[34]

However, further reports show that the situation varied according to the region, the relations of the local authorities with Bangkok, and their interpretation of the treaty. In Lampang, for instance, where the French claimed to have fifteen hundred protégés in 1908, few problems occurred. Mr. Lugan attributed it to "the wise administration of the khaluong [chao mueang]" as well as "the greater cohesiveness of our protégés who are established here."[35] He also pointed out that most of the Khmu laborers were living far from the main center and were

33. Letter from the consul in Nan, Mr. Lugan, to the French ambassador in Bangkok, 15 January 1908, file 101, series "Protection des Asiatiques," Bangkok collection, Archives of the Ministry of Foreign Affairs, France.

34. Ibid.

35. Letter from consul in Nan, Mr. Lugan, to the French ambassador in Bangkok, 17 February 1908, file 101, series "Protection des Asiatiques," Bangkok collection, Archives of the Ministry of Foreign Affairs, France.

therefore less likely to be recruited for corvée labor. Conversely, in Chiang Mai, the Khmu migrants were subjected to various taxes and requisitions from the local authorities. In Doi Saket for instance, "where many of them are established,"[36] they were recruited more than sixty days per year to perform portage corvée (sixty-three days between April 1906 and April 1907); they also had to pay a tax in order to escape military service[37] and to accept requisition of rice at 50 percent of its value.[38] Besides, Lugan also noted that the Khmu were in contact in this region with British Asiatic protégés who had kept their extraterritorial rights, a situation which, by contrast, was adding to their resentment.[39] During the following years, the French could never obtain guarantees from the Siamese that the Khmu laborers would get the same privileges as the British protégés and be exempted from corvée work, which they assumed to stem from the desire of the Siamese to lessen the French influence on the west bank of the Mekong.

The Siamese authorities persisted in turning down the claims of the French regarding the status of their Khmu protégés. An exchange of letters between the French consul in Chiang Rai, Michel Bréal, the French ambassador in Bangkok, Roger Maugras, and the Siamese authorities in 1931 illustrates this matter well. Bréal had earlier transmitted to the embassy the complaints received by Mr. Chao Chan, the consular agent in Nan, from Khmu villagers who had registered with the consulate and asked to be exempted from corvée labor. The French ambassador relayed the matter to the Siamese Ministry of Foreign Affairs, which, somewhat ironically, replied through its British adviser, R. B. Stevens. He argued that the conventions

36. Letter from Mr. Lugan to the French ambassador, 17 February 1908 (see note 33 above).

37. Sixty ticals per village. The sum was given to a slave who, in exchange of this sum and his freedom, agreed to serve as a soldier or policeman for two years.

38. In Phrae during that same one-year period, corvée work amounted to 24–32 days per year; the number of days lost by the coolies was actually double since these numbers did not take into account the time they lost to go back home after serving as coolies for Thai administrators.

39. Letter from the consul in Nan, Mr. Lugan, to the French ambassador in Bangkok, 20 February 1908, file 101, series "Protection des Asiatiques," Bangkok collection, Archives of the Ministry of Foreign Affairs, France.

signed by Siam with France, unlike those signed with England (on July 14, 1925), did not include any specific clause concerning the exemption from corvée labor of their protégés. He also pointed out that corvée labor existed in Indochina and that the Siamese subjects living in the French colonies were not exempted from it.[40] He finally remarked that these issues should be solved in the framework of a more general agreement on transborder mobility on both sides of the Mekong.

The situation grew worse in the 1930s with the implementation by the Siamese of policies against immigration—mostly Chinese[41]—of which the Khmu migrants were, so to speak, collateral victims. In 1931, a certificate of residence became necessary for the foreigners who wanted to work in Siam, and it cost thirty ticals to obtain it. This measure proved inefficient, and in 1933 the tax was increased to one hundred ticals and a few years later even to two hundred ticals. The French consul in Chiang Rai, Michel Bréal, expressed his worries in several letters to the embassy in Bangkok. He wrote that such policy would go against the interests not only of the Khmu migrants (the taxes amounted to more than their annual salary) but also of the companies (foreign or Siamese) that employed them and could not pay such taxes, "especially in a context of a depressed teak market."[42] At first, Siamese authorities, through Prince Devawongse, assured the French ambassador that while the law was in theory applicable everywhere in the country (except in the territories located less than twenty-five kilometers from the border of Indochina), in practice there was no immigration post in the North, and the Siamese government did not plan to create any. In 1937, however, two immigrations posts were created in Mae Hong Son and Chiang Rai (*Phra Muang*, May 27, 1937)

40. Letter from Mr. R. B. Stevens, advisor to the Ministry of Foreign Affairs in Siam, to the French ambassador in Bangkok, Mr. Maugras, 2 December 1931, file 101, series "Protection des Asiatiques," Bangkok collection, Archives of the Ministry of Foreign Affairs, France.

41. The growing nationalist discourse among the Thai leaders went along with an admiration for Japan and with a growing resentment against the Chinese immigrants.

42. Letter from Michel Bréal to the French ambassador, 10 April 1932 (see note 13).

and new regulations started to be applied strictly and indiscriminately to all Asian foreigners.

In 1938, two hundred Khmu engaged by British American Tobacco in Chiang Saen were arrested and sent back to the eastern side of the Mekong.[43] The same year, problems were reported in Lampang,[44] with Khmu workers suffering harassment on the part of Siamese officials, including excessive taxes, fines, refusal of identification cards, jail, and many cases of deportation to Laos.[45] Registration did not help in those cases and could even make the situation worse by giving Siamese authorities easier access to the migrants and an argument to require the payment of taxes they could not afford. As noted by Camille Notton in 1936, the new migrants therefore "neglected the registration or the establishment of work contracts, presenting themselves at the consulate only in extreme cases."[46] The consular authorities themselves ended the practice, considering their efforts useless. In 1938, the consular agent in Lampang, noting than more than thirty Khmu had already been deported to Laos that year, wrote, "If the Siamese government acts in a such way toward our Khmu, why bother registering them then?"[47]

43. Letter from the French consul in Chiang Rai, Mr. André Decamps, to the French ambassador in Bangkok, July 15, 1938, file 112, series "Lois et règlements siamois," Bangkok collection, Archives of the Ministry of Foreign Affairs, France.

44. Series of letters dated 1–6 September 1938, by consular agents as well as foreign staff of a French-owned teak company (unreadable signatures), file 112, series "Lois et règlements siamois," Bangkok collection, Archives of the Ministry of Foreign Affairs, France.

45. These events must be seen also in the wider context of the anti-Chinese stance adopted by Siamese government. Between mid-1937 and mid-1938, more than 44,000 Chinese entered Thailand following the war between Japan and China (44,143 according to the statistics given by the *Bangkok Times* on August 3, 1938). Thailand deported 3,000 of them back to China and raised the immigration tax from 100 to 200 ticals per year. New regulations were also adopted which limited foreigners' access to jobs.

46. Letter from Camille Notton to the French ambassador, 22 May 1936 (see note 29).

47. Letter from the consular agent in Lampang to the consular agent in Chiang Rai, Mr. André Decamps, 17 October 1938, file 112, series "Lois et règlements siamois," Bangkok collection, Archives of the Ministry of Foreign Affairs, France.

These political developments not only discouraged Khmu migrants from registering; they also tended to disrupt the organization of their networks, thereby further undermining the efforts of the French consulates to keep track of them. As early as 1908, the French consul Lugan predicted that the new regulations included in the 1907 treaty concerning corvée labor in Siam would hit

the most interesting of our protégés: those who have settled near the main administrative centers and engaged in agriculture or small trade; among them are the "nai roi" who play the role of intermediary between the consulate and all those dispersed in the countryside.[48]

Twenty years later, at the climax of the anti-immigrant policies implemented by the Siamese, several reports echoed Lugan's prediction. A letter from the consular agent in Lampang dated September 6, 1938, and sent to the French consul in Chiang Rai mentioned the case of the *nai roi* called Nai Dong, who was jailed for trying to bring back to Laos the Khmu he had placed in Lampang the year before. In April 1939, the same consular agent reported, among other cases, the story of a Khmu middleman living in Lampang, Ai Kham Keut, who was deported to Laos despite being a "well-established trader and married to a Thai woman."[49] Other letters also mentioned the presence of new kinds of intermediaries who "try to earn their living at the expense of our protégés, . . . placing them without work contract and also encouraging our Khmu to quit their employers."[50] These reports are fragmentary but nonetheless consistent with the views of the old Khmu migrants I interviewed in Laos and Thailand, who all said that the Second World War marked the end of the *"nai roi* period" (*samai nai roi*) and the

48. Letter from Mr. Lugan to the French ambassador, 15 January 1908 (see note 26).

49. Letter to the French consul in Chiang Rai, dated 9 April 1939 in Chiang Mai, signature unreadable, file 112, series "Lois et règlements siamois," Bangkok collection, Archives of the Ministry of Foreign Affairs, France.

50. Letter to the French consul in Chiang Rai, 6 September 1938, signature unreadable, file 112, series "Lois et règlements siamois," Bangkok collection, Archives of the Ministry of Foreign Affairs, France.

development of more individualistic, less structured forms of labor migration. Urbanization, the improvement of transport infrastructure, and the diversification of the activities of foreign companies beyond the teak sector certainly played key roles in this process. However, the colonial experience, both external in Laos and internal in Siam, was also instrumental in shaping a new geography and vocabulary about migration in the Mekong basin. Modern conceptions of borders and sovereignty turned professional recruiters (*nai roi*) into smugglers and Khmu coolies or mahouts into illegal immigrants. In so doing they constructed the migrants as an object of debate and a source of anxiety.

CONCLUSION

At the end of 1939, the French Ministry of Foreign Affairs proposed to the Siamese authorities a convention framing the conditions of transborder movements between Laos and Siam in order to facilitate customary mobility and simplify administrative control in this area. A first draft of the convention submitted to the Siamese Committee of Border Circulation, presided over by Prince Varnvaidya, proposed a twenty-five kilometer zone on each side of the Mekong allowing free circulation for a maximum of thirty days. The extension of this area to some localities or some categories of migrants was to be defined in consultation with Siam. In particular, the draft contained a special appendix proposing to exempt Khmu foresters from taxes for 240 days per year when they worked in teak plantations.

This attempt to settle the question of the Khmu labor migrants was the final act of a nearly fifty-year-long diplomatic struggle between the French and the Siamese that saw the position of the two parties reversed during the 1930s. The former were first hostile to the migration of their protégés and unsuccessfully tried to restrict it until they became convinced of its positive impact on their Lao colony and then attempted to facilitate such migration. Conversely, the Siamese, who initially considered the Khmu laborers a much-needed input for the regional economy and who relied on precolonial agreements with the kingdom of Lan Xang to regulate their mobility, finally adopted a strong anti-immigration stance and started to arrest and deport Khmu workers and middlemen back to the Lao side of the Mekong. It is through this twisted history that Khmu migrants became an object of debates on both sides of the Mekong. Siamese nationalism and suspicions in the 1930s mirrored in a distorted way the French colonial anxieties of the end of the nineteenth century. Later on, the Cold War period further fueled the fear of migrants as potential threats to the Thai nation.[51] It also led to an a priori conceptualization of all ethnic highlanders as immigrants and to the implementation by the Thai state of a policy of "selective citizenship" (Chayan 2005; Pinkaew 2014), an issue that has guided Achan Chayan's engagement in favor of ethnic minorities throughout his career.

REFERENCES

Chayan Vaddhanaphuti. 2005. "The Thai State and Ethnic Minorities: From Assimilation to Selective Integration." In *Ethnic Conflicts in Southeast Asia*, edited by Kusuma Snitwongse and Scott Thompson, 151–66. Singapore: Institute of Southeast Asian Studies.

Dwyer, Mike. 2011. "Territorial Affairs: Turning Battlefields into Marketplaces in Postwar Laos." PhD diss., University of California, Berkeley.

Evrard, Olivier. 2007. "Interethnic Systems and Localized Identities: The Khmu Subgroups in North-West Laos." In *Social Dynamics in the Highlands of Southeast Asia: Reconsidering Political Systems of Highland Burma by E. R. Leach*, edited by François Robinne and Mandy Sadan, 127–59. Leiden: Brill.

———. 2010. "Oral Histories of Livelihoods and Migration under Socialism and Post-Socialism among the Khmu of Northern Laos." In *Moving Mountains: Ethnicity and Livelihoods in Highland China, Vietnam, and Laos*, edited by Jean Michaud and Tim Forsyth, 76–99. Vancouver: University of British Columbia Press.

Foreign Office, Great Britain. 1895–1914. *Diplomatic and Consular Reports on Trade and Finance: Reports on the Trade of Chiang Mai*. London: Harrison and Sons.

Grabowsky, Volker, and Andrew Turton. 2003. *The Gold and Silver Road of Trade and Friendship: The McLeod and Richardson Diplomatic Missions to Tai States in 1837*. Chiang Mai: Silkworm Books.

Gunn, Geoffrey C. 2003. *Rebellion in Laos: Peasants and Politics in a Colonial Backwater*. Bangkok: White Lotus.

51. Frank Lebar's study on Khmu migration to Siam was undertaken in such a context. Conceived primarily as a scholarly contribution to the Human Area Files at Yale University, it was also funded by American and Thai authorities to help evaluate the risk of communist infiltration in Thailand among immigrant populations from Laos (Lebar 1965, 17–18), a concern which echoes those expressed, but for different reasons, by the French and the Siamese in the prewar period.

Izikowitz, Karl Gustav. 1951. *Lamet: Hill Peasants of French Indochina*. New York: AMS Press.

Kaur, Amarjit, 2004. *Wage Labour in Southeast Asia since 1840: Globalization, the International Division of Labour and Labour Transformations*. New York: Palgrave Macmillan.

————. 2009. "Labor Crossings in Southeast Asia: Linking Historical and Contemporary Labor Migration." *New Zealand Journal of Asian Studies* 11 (1): 276–303.

Lebar, Frank. 1965. "The Khamu." Final report to the National Research Council, Bangkok. New Haven: Human Relations Area Files, Yale University.

————. 1967. "Observations on the Movement of Khmu into North Thailand." *Journal of the Siam Society* 55 (1): 61–79.

Lefèvre-Pontalis, Pierre. (1902) 2000. *Travels in Upper Laos and on the Borders of Yunnan and Burma*. Bangkok: White Lotus.

McCarthy, James. (1900) 1994. *Surveying and Exploring in Siam*. Bangkok: White Lotus.

Pinkaew Laungaramsri. 2014. "Contested Citizenship: Cards, Colors, and the Culture of Identification." In *Ethnicity, Borders, and the Grassroots Interface with the State: Studies on Southeast Asia in Honor of Charles F. Keyes*, edited by John A. Marston, 143–62. Chiang Mai: Silkworm Books.

Ratanaporn Sethakul. 1989. "Political, Social and Economic Changes in the Northern States of Thailand resulting from the Chiang Mai Treaties of 1874 and 1883." PhD diss., Northern Illinois University.

Sprenger, Guido. 2005. "The Way of the Buffaloes: Trade and Sacrifice in Northern Laos." *Ethnology* 44 (4): 291–312.

————. 2007. "From Kettledrums to Coins: Social Transformation and the Flow of Valuables in Northern Laos." In *Social Dynamics in the Highlands of Southeast Asia: Reconsidering Political Systems of Highland Burma by E. R. Leach*, edited by François Robinne and Mandy Sadan, 160–185. Leiden: Brill.

Suphawat Laohachaiboon and Shinya Takeda. 2007. "Teak Logging in a Transboundary Watershed: An Historical Case Study of the Ing River Basin in Northern Thailand." *Journal of the Siam Society* 95:123–41

Suwilai Premsrirat. 2002. *Dictionary of Khmu in Thailand*. Special publication, vol. 5 no. 1. Nakhon Pathom: Mon-Khmer Studies, Mahidol University.

Vatikiotis, Michael R. J. 1984. "Ethnic Pluralism in the Northern Thai City of Chiang Mai." PhD diss., University of Oxford.

Voravimone Chairat. 2006. *Ban Ta Wat Ket* [House at the Wat Ket pier]. Chiang Mai: Chomphu Editions and Tai Ekasan.

A Mat-Weaving Cooperative and a Military Coup: The Challenges of Fieldwork in the 1970s in Thailand

Katherine A. Bowie

When I began fieldwork in northern Thailand in the wake of the military coup of October 6, 1976, I faced an extremely polarized political climate. Following the ouster of the long-entrenched military dictatorship on October 14, 1973, Thailand had experienced a three-year civilian interregnum during which students, workers, and villagers began organizing to a hitherto unprecedented degree. The growing strength of the left wing in Thailand catalyzed a conservative backlash. With the collapse in 1975 of the US-supported governments of Vietnam, Cambodia, and Laos, rightist organizations such as Navaphol, the Red Gaurs, and the Village Scouts became increasingly active. From April to August of 1975, twenty-one leaders of the Farmers' Federation of Thailand (FFT) were murdered, more than half of them in the North. The FFT was pressing for land reform and control of land rent; the organization had strong links to the Socialist Party of

Having already agreed to write this essay about the mat-weaving cooperative to recognize the many conversations Chayan and I held as we each did our fieldwork during this difficult time, I had been looking forward to reminiscing with the cooperative's founder, Narong Mahakhom. Unfortunately Narong died November 15, 2014. A kind man, Narong saw many a debt go repaid, but perhaps this article will at least acknowledge the huge debt of gratitude I owe him for the forty years we debated Thai politics. I will miss his *kaeng bon*, a symbol of his pride in being a northern villager. In addition to Narong, this article also owes a huge debt to Kongchan Mahakhom and the founding eight mat-group leaders—Pho Sunthon (Tun) Srikham, Lung Huean Phokaew-Wiriyasitthikun, Ai Ma Khamta, Pho Pankaew Sanglawan, Ai Bun Sitthimun, Ai Sriniam Duangthip, Pho Paeng Cha-ai, and Chai La Rueanmun—and their stalwart wives and families.

Thailand. In February 1976 Dr. Boonsanong Punyodhyana, the party's secretary-general, was himself assassinated.

Villagers already had a long history of distrusting outsiders, recalling royal attendants conscripting youth into corvée and military service, carrying young women off as royal concubines, and confiscating chickens, water buffaloes, and oxen for royal feasts (Bowie 1988). Furthermore, in the face of significant economic insecurity, most villagers were involved in activities deemed by government authorities to be illegal, from fermenting rice wine and gambling to logging teak and transporting opium. The government only added to their suspiciousness with stories about communists distributing penis-shrinking potions and kidnapping old people to make them into fertilizer. Villagers were told to watch out for communists, blood-sucking vampires (*phi dut lueat*), and other strangers.[1]

Every anthropologist faces challenges. One of mine was overcoming villagers' distrust. Northern villages had internal class divides ranging from landed villagers to tenants and wage laborers. Of the 310 households in the village where I conducted my early fieldwork in San Pa Tong District of Chiang Mai Province, 43 percent were completely landless and worked primarily as agricultural wage laborers; weaving bamboo mats was their primary alternate source of income.[2] This early fieldwork had two distinct phases, paralleling two different host families. My initial host family facilitated access to the village elite but complicated my access to the village poor. After my relations with this family collapsed, I moved in with another village family. Together we began a mat-weaving cooperative that involved eight subgroup leaders and one hundred landless families.

This essay, divided into three parts, describes my difficulties in finding a village and host family willing to accept an outsider, my involvement in the challenging process of forming the mat-weaving

1. For more on this period see Morell and Chai-anan 1981; Bowie and Phelan 1975, 1997; Haberkorn 2011; Turton 1978.
2. Data gathered by Narong Mahakhom in a government survey in 1978 also concluded that 11 percent were tenants, 18 percent owned less than 5 rai, 19 percent owned 5-10 rai and only 7% owned 11 rai or more. For discussions of neighboring villages in San Pa Tong District see Cohen 1981 and Anan 1984.

cooperative (*klum sat*; central Thai, *klum suea*), and my growing understanding of the reasons underlying the deep distrust of the poor. The cooperative, which lasted nearly twenty years, enabled me to bridge internal village divides and gain greater insights into the challenges facing everyone in the village. In the process, I forged friendships that provided the foundations for my subsequent career and have enriched my life to the present.

I. FINDING A VILLAGE: MEETING THE ELITE

My own situation was already complex when I began to search for a village in which to conduct fieldwork. In the two years preceding, I had lived in Bangkok. After studying Thai in an intensive language program, I worked as a research editor of a yearbook on Thailand and began writing articles for the *Bangkok Post* as a freelance journalist. One of my earliest articles focused on a by-election in Chiang Mai (Bowie 1975). In the course of interviewing the candidates, I met Dr. Boonsanong.[3] Another article, which I cowrote with Brian Phelan, focused on the assassination of the FFT leaders (Bowie and Phelan 1975). Many of those assassinated had name cards of Dr. Boonsanong in their pockets when they were killed, so I again contacted Dr. Boonsanong for further information about this movement. I had decided I wanted to write my dissertation about this movement. The FFT was particularly strong in the North. Dr. Boonsanong, himself a northerner, helped facilitate meetings. As a result of these meetings, I was able to make arrangements to live in Doi Saket District with the mother of Sithon Yotkantha, who, following the assassination of Intha Sribunruang, was the newly elected northern leader of the FFT. When a bomb was thrown at his home and someone who apparently looked like him was shot, Sithon went underground. I also received a death threat during this period.[4] It was becoming clear that I would not be able to pursue a dissertation on the history of the FFT.

---

3. Lert Shinawatra also ran in this election.

4. The American embassy also learned of this threat but had initially misfiled the report under Barry.

I decided any village would be fine for my fieldwork so that I could at least learn something about village life. I asked various people in Chiang Mai about who might be able to help me in finding a village. Several people mentioned Surasinghsamruam Shimbhanao. He taught Thai literature at the Chiang Mai Teachers College and oversaw students doing their practice teaching in village schools. In addition to teaching, he also wrote for *Jaturat* magazine and served as adviser to the student council. He was one of five teachers at the college who were targeted as "dangers to society" following the coup of October 1976.[5] Since I was American and rumors were circulating that I was a CIA agent, a French friend who knew Surasingh doubted that he would be willing to meet me. However, Surasingh agreed to meet with me and offered to help me find a village. He asked the various school principals who oversaw his student-teachers if anyone in their respective villages might be willing to take me into their homes.

A school principal in a *tambon* (subdistrict) in San Pa Tong initially said I could move in with the *tambon* health officer; she was herself single and living alone in the *tambon* health station. Excited to have finally found a village, I moved in. However, a few days later I received word that I was to report to the district officer. Since it was a weekend, I thought that meant I should wait until Monday, but everyone said that I was to report right away. So Sunday morning the health officer took me on the back of her motorcycle to see the district officer. He was having breakfast at the time. He was very nice, but informed me that it was not going to be convenient for me to remain in that village. He did not explain why, but said that there were many other villages that would be fine for me to live in. I subsequently learned that this village had many involved in the illegal teak trade who were worried that I might learn of their illegal activities.

The search for a village resumed. I went back to see Surasingh. When I told him the names of the villages that the district officer had suggested, he assured me that he also knew people in many of these villages and would make inquiries on my behalf. One of the school principals Surasingh worked with was Narong Mahakhom. Narong's

---

5. For more on Surasingh, see Samruam Singh (1998) (his pen name).

father-in-law was also the *kamnan* (subdistrict head). So after some internal village consultations, I learned that I could live with the deputy *kamnan* and his family.

I moved in with this family in mid-December of 1976. My new host family lived in one of the village's largest teak houses and appeared to be one of the wealthiest in the village. They had two daughters, but I only saw the older daughter occasionally as she had married into a neighboring village. My Thai father was the head of the underground lottery; each month police would appear for their regular payoffs. Because of my Thai father's status, I was able to meet many of the village elite who routinely stopped by at night to drink and talk.

Hints of class divides in the village appeared early in my research. Shortly after my arrival, I was out in the fields with my new younger sister. The villagers were sowing soybeans, so I asked if they would teach me how to plant. As I spent the next few hours helping the women planting, my sister sat in the shade of a tree at the edge of the paddy. As I left to go back home, the women commented, "Katherine has only been in the village a short time, but she has already planted more soybeans than Nong." That evening, when my father came home, he scolded me. I could take photographs and interview people, but it was inappropriate for me to actually be working in the fields.

Because I spent most of my time in the first year with the village elite, I learned about anticommunist initiatives such as the Village Scouts but little about the political views of poor villagers. FFT leaders had been shot in the districts of Hang Dong, Saraphi, and even San Pa Tong itself. In the last national election, villagers had voted for the Democrat, Social Action, and the socialist-leaning New Force parties. Village youths had thrown rocks at the visiting student-teachers' dormitory at the village school. A drunken police officer shot three villagers at a village festival but never faced charges. Police conducted raids in the village for cock-fighting, gambling at funerals, and making moonshine. One village girl with a knitting machine had a picture of Che Guevara on her wall.[6] But rather than politics, villagers preferred discussing whether the stories about man landing on the moon were true.

6. Although some thought perhaps he was a rock star or film idol, she noted

I spent my time visiting with neighboring families, practicing the northern Thai dialect, and learning as much as I could about traditional anthropological elements such as kinship and rituals. I gradually learned that my host family was not as wealthy as they pretended, owning no paddy land; indeed my Thai mother and sister also spent most of their time splitting bamboo and weaving mats. My mother came from a poor family and had a biting sarcastic wit that I enjoyed. Villagers were just as curious about me as I was about them. The term "anthropologist" was not meaningfully translatable. There were various rumors circulating that I was a CIA agent, a Christian proselytizer, a communist agent, and—most inexplicable to me—owner of a small silver revolver. When villagers discussed these rumors with me, it also became clear that these terms connoted "badness"; even corrupt government officials and police were "communists." But the rumors themselves did not impede my initial fieldwork.

My relationship with my host family fell apart in December 1977. My father had been active with the Village Scouts in those later months and was often coming home drunk. Besides with his wife, he had gotten into arguments with various neighbors, such that several were no longer coming over to the house to visit. There were rumors of a minor wife, unpaid debts, discontent with the older daughter who refused to move home with her husband, and other problems. One evening I was invited to join a group of neighbors who were going to be threshing their fields. My mother and sister had no objection; they were sleeping over at the home of a relative who just died, and they gave me keys to lock up the house. My father was not home to ask, but I thought that since the girl inviting me was also the daughter-in-law of the *kamnan*, it would not be a problem if I joined. I was wrong. The following morning, I could feel tension in the air. I learned when my father returned home and found I had gone threshing, he became furious. He had been drinking and ended up throwing a large clay water pot on the ground, shattering it. My mother remarked that no one was enjoying living with Father these days. On December 23, their older daughter's husband got into an accident with the taxi car (*rot*

---

quietly that Che was a revolutionary.

doisan), for which my father was the guarantor. Fearing the blowup about to occur, she thought I should best find somewhere else to live.

I was devastated. Although I had lived in the village for just over a year, I still had not found a topic for a dissertation. With a timing poignantly redolent of earlier generations of people in search of a home for Christmas, I went over to see the school principal and his wife, Kongchan, whom I visited fairly regularly. Narong said he had long thought it was a mistake to have me living with the deputy *kamnan*'s family, adding that he had initially thought to have me live with his family. However, on the day that Kongchan first met me, I was wearing jeans with a matching jean jacket. She mistook me for a man and was worried about having a foreign man staying in her house while her husband was away. She also was worried that I might not eat sticky rice, and she did not know how to make bread. Narong and Kongchan forthwith invited me to move in with them.

The next problem to be solved was that of saving face for everyone involved. Kongchan and her mother were worried that they would be accused of having "stolen" me, and perhaps I should move into town first and then return to the village. Narong felt he could talk to my original family and smooth the transition without me having to move twice. I told my mother and she was relieved that a solution had been found. On Christmas Eve I informed my father that I would move. My father was surprised and began protesting, but then Narong arrived. Narong suggested that it would be good for me to learn about not just how villagers live, but also how government officials live. Furthermore, his family had an extra room and was happy to take me in. Likely relieved, my father accepted Narong's explanation and then proceeded to give me cautionary advice to be careful of my possessions since there had been several recent thefts in the village.

II. FOUNDING THE MAT-WEAVING COOPERATIVE: MEETING THE POOR

On Christmas Day in 1977, I moved in with Narong, Kongchan, and their two young sons. I could not have been happier. Narong even made a small bookshelf for my room. Because Kongchan's father was the *kamnan* and her mother ran the village ricemill, there were lots of people stopping by to visit. Narong and Kongchan had the most luxuries of any village home. They had electricity, the only TV set in the village, chairs, a desk for me, and even a refrigerator, which sat in the living room but was never plugged in until my parents came to visit the following year.

Inevitably, villagers began speculating on the causes of my seemingly sudden move. One of the strangest rumors was circulated by my former family; evidently intended to counter speculation that they had been less than hospitable themselves, they alleged that Kongchan was using water left over from steaming the rice to make coffee for me in the morning. This rumor upset both Kongchan and me since it implied that Kongchan was a bad hostess and that I was lazy. Furthermore both of us knew the rumor was false since I boiled my own coffee water on the coals after Kongchan had steamed the rice. In the days and weeks that followed, I learned much about how villagers viewed my original family. Illustrative is a story one villager told: My mother had asked the villager to buy some rice for her. When she delivered it, my mother said in a loud voice, "Oh, you have come to repay the rice I loaned you." Rather than admit that she had run out of rice, my mother instead humiliated this villager.

The rumors gradually dissipated. I settled in to a happy routine of doing my morning household chores of sweeping, doing dishes, and fetching water while Kongchan went to market and made breakfast. My days were spent talking with villagers, many of whom came over to our house. Kongchan was both a village beautician and seamstress. By day there were always women coming over to have their hair dyed or cut, brides having their makeup done, or villagers who wanted her to sew their clothes on her fancy treadle sewing machine. Evenings were spent talking with Narong, Kongchan, and whomever came by to visit; while Narong split bamboo or finished government reports, Kongchan wove bamboo mats or sewed, and their sons did homework or watched TV. Fridays I often went into town, and Saturdays I would escape to a neighboring villager's home because our house was full of men watching boxing on the only TV set in the village.

Narong was the perfect teacher, comfortable in both central and northern Thai. He had been born into an aristocratic family in

Lamphun, but the father's alcoholism had left his family penniless. He died when Narong was only two years old and the family moved to San Pa Tong. The youngest of six siblings, Narong ordained as a novice in Kileluang. He then transferred to Wat Phrathat Haripunchai's prestigious Rongrian Methi Wuthikon and completed high school. Facing an uncertain future, Narong had enough money to either buy a bowl of noodles or a lottery ticket. He bought a lottery ticket and won 2,000 baht. He used this money to attend the Chiang Mai Teachers College, graduating with a teaching certificate. He became a school teacher and married Kongchan, herself considered a young beauty at the time. Over time he rose to become the school principal.

Because he recognized how close he had come to not being able to continue his own education, he had a particular sympathy for the poor in the village. We often talked about what could be done to help village communities. Narong lamented that the top students in school often came from poor families who could not afford to send their children on for an education. I was shocked by what seemed to be a high rate of suicide and growing heroin addiction. We discussed forming some kind of youth group. On the night of February 16, 1978, some villagers brought mats to sell to Kongchan. As we observed the financial transaction taking place, Narong mentioned that he had thought it would be a good idea to establish a mat-weaving cooperative. At present, middlemen in the village would buy up mats throughout the year and sell them during the harvest seasons, which came twice a year. During the low season mats sold for as low as 8 baht; during the harvest season they retailed for 15–22 baht. There were two major mat merchants who had become quite wealthy in the process.

In the days that followed, Narong and I began discussing this idea with various villagers. My former family cautioned me not to get involved with this project because it would fail and then I would be subject to criticism. To safeguard relations with the village mat merchants, Narong went to talk to them to explain our plan. They agreed the cooperative was a good idea because it would help poor people, but they did not think we would be successful because poor people had so many debts; one of the merchants agreed to serve as an advisor to the cooperative. Other villagers we talked to were enthusiastically in favor of forming a cooperative, particularly a landless but always opinionated carpenter named Pho Tun.

THE PROBLEM OF LOANS AND COLLATERAL

Our first challenge was finding the initial capital. Friends in Chiang Mai put me in touch with Mel Blitzer at the YMCA, an organization that had funds to loan for rural development projects. With Mel's encouragement and with some optimism because I knew several members of the YMCA's advisory board, Narong and I decided to apply for these funds. The night of Friday, February 24, we began discussions in earnest about forming the cooperative. Drawing on the village's seven temple subgroups that sent food offerings to the monks on different days of the week, we discussed who might be best suited to help with the planning and invited them to join the brainstorming. Various problems were discussed. Because mats had been used in harvests for decades, everyone was also confident that the market was stable. Everyone was also confident that we would have no problems storing the mats because even mats that developed mold were sold. A proposal began to emerge. We would request a loan of 36,000 baht from the YMCA. The cooperative would buy mats from members at the low-season rate and resell them during the high season, using the profits to build up a share of 500 baht per member. Once the shares were accumulated, the cooperative would be able to return the money to the YMCA. What could possibly go wrong?

The first public meeting of the cooperative took place the next morning. By the end of the meeting, sixty-seven villagers had signed that they wanted to join, and by the end of the day, over eighty villagers had signed. The following day, even more villagers wanted to join. We decided to cap the membership at one hundred, at least for the first year. As we studied the list of names and the possible subgroup leaders, we ended up with eight groups, each centered in different parts of the village. With a draft proposal and the list of members neatly typed up by Narong, I headed back into Chiang Mai.

The YMCA sent two women to visit us on March 8. This meeting, attended by the group heads and some prospective members, did not go well. Evidently steeped in the myth of the subsistence economy in which everyone owns their own land (see Bowie 1992), the YMCA wanted collateral for their loan, ostensibly as a way to ensure that villagers were seriously committed to the project's success. Of the one hundred people who had signed up for the co-op, over ninety were tenants or wage laborers. In frustration, I finally said that the YMCA was being hypocritical in their claim to want to help poor people; perhaps they should be honest and admit that they only planned to help middle-class landed villagers. When we informed the other members that our meeting had not gone well, one remarked, "So they are like central Thais. They want collateral before they will give out loans."

Pho Tun decided he wanted to talk to the YMCA representatives again, so he accompanied me into town on Friday, March 10. As we walked into the YMCA together, Pho Tun pointed at a sign posted on the wall that read, "If you give a man a fish, he eats for one day. If you teach a man to fish, he eats for a lifetime." He agreed with that philosophy and felt optimistic. As it turned out, the YMCA had just sent a telegram requesting a meeting of the full membership the next day. In addition to collateral, they were concerned about the extent of members' commitment to the group (they had earlier given funds to an abbot who defrocked as soon as he received funding). Pho Tun spoke eloquently about his belief in the merits of this cooperative. The most dramatic moment came when Pho Tun said that he had nothing to offer as collateral other than his word and his life, but he was willing to put his life on the line. For every month the group defaulted on the loan, the YMCA could shoot one of the subgroup leaders, beginning with him.

THE MAT-WEAVING COOPERATIVE BEGINS

The next meeting with the YMCA's representatives, at 4:00 p.m. on March 11, went better. The members arrived early. The group heads had met Friday night and worked through more details about where the mats would be stored (at each subgroup leader's home), the accounting system (three accounts, one account booklet in the hands of the individual members, a second in their name kept by the subgroup head, and a third set kept at Narong's house), and compensation (25 satang per mat according to the number of mats each head stored, and 25 satang per mat to Narong as accountant). Members discussed how the money should be dispersed, concluding they preferred to receive their money at the subgroup leaders' homes when they delivered the mats, as it would be more convenient than having to walk to two locations. Next the discussion turned to determining whether mats should be bought at or above the current village price, the group voting for the market price to maximize profits. Each of the subgroups met to formally elect their subgroup leaders; the results were as anticipated.

After the YMCA's representatives left, discussions continued. Narong was extremely concerned that if there were eight sub-groups each with 500 baht in cash, he would be responsible for 4,000 baht that was no longer under his control. The subgroup heads reached a consensus that the co-op funds would remain with the central accountant, many expressing relief that they would not have to have the responsibility of keeping the cash at their homes. Discussion then followed about the rules for membership—specifically over whether we would include "middle-class" villagers who owned land or would limit the group to the poor. In the end, the decision was to focus on the landless; there was concern that otherwise the poor might not be able to keep up (*bo tan khao*). They felt strongly that this group should make decisions based on their needs, adding as an aside that the poor rarely spoke at village meetings because they didn't have the money to give their opinions weight. I raised the issue of whether we should be concerned about being labeled communists. One leader replied, "If anyone says that, I will tell them that if it weren't for this group, everyone would become a communist!"

Following the March 11 meeting, events developed rapidly. On March 21, Khun Pornthip came from the YMCA to inform us that our request had been approved. After summoning the group heads, she explained the accounting system she had designed. The next afternoon Narong went into town to buy paper. He then typed up and mimeographed the various account forms. We spent the rest of the night folding and stapling the account booklets together.

Wednesday, March 22, we called a mandatory meeting of all the members for 3:00 p.m. Excitement was so high that one member ran off to join even though she was in the middle of having her hair done with Kongchan. The threefold accounting system was explained.

Everyone would have their own booklet which they were to bring with them every time they brought mats to their subgroup head; the head would record the number of mats they had delivered, sign their booklet, and record the information in their copy of the member's booklet; they would then bring their booklet to Narong's house where Narong, Kongchan, or I would dispense the cash. Members were to sign in the third booklet for receipt of the money. We would hold periodic checks to make sure the number of mats and the amounts of money tallied to ensure transparency. Narong also explained that the mats would need to be the same size. Discussion was held to finalize the buying price; the consensus was 10 baht per mat, the going rate of the village merchants at the time. The next morning Mel Blitzer and others from the YMCA arrived with the check for 36,000 baht. The cooperative agreed to repay the loan with an annual interest rate of 50 satang per 100 baht. After the photos were taken, Narong and the three group heads who were designated as cosigners went to the bank to open an account and deposit the check.

With the arrival of the check and the distribution of the members' booklets, we thought our problems were solved. We now learned they were only beginning. We had expected a deluge of mats, but in the subsequent days only a few members sold mats to the co-op. Given that many members and three of the group heads were illiterate, Narong and I wondered if, despite our practice sessions, the accounts were causing confusion. But literacy was not the problem. The group heads had been practicing writing their names and numbers; furthermore, all the group heads had other family members who were literate, particularly daughters who were most likely to be at home at the time any member delivered their mats.[7] As we visited the subgroups, we learned group heads were rejecting some mats because they were smaller than the group's specifications or sloppily woven. But the immediate reasons the cooperative received fewer mats than

7. Indeed one of the illiterate group heads had the best-kept records of the entire cooperative. Amusingly, one elderly woman wanted me to check if she was writing the numbers correctly. I assumed she wanted to check her mat accounts, but instead she was learning to place bets in the underground lottery!

we expected were the problems of preexisting debts and a shortage of bamboo. Each was fraught with controversy.

ADVANCES AND ANGER

Because the members of the cooperative were poor, they were nearly all in debt to various mat merchants already and in need of advances. The case of one woman who wanted to borrow 100 baht is indicative: she had to repay her earlier debt of 22 baht for bamboo, 20 baht for rice (about four liters), and 12 baht for pig feed—plus she needed some money to live on while she wove the next set of mats. We considered repaying creditors on behalf of members but quickly realized sorting out their debts would be a nearly impossible task. We agreed to allow members to carry a debt load of 50 baht if the subgroup head approved. Some heads were overly authoritarian and others overly permissive. Some heads refused to sign approval for advances unless the member had bamboo at home. Others signed because they trusted the member to be responsible, or because they felt sorry for the member and wanted to help them out, or because they simply wanted to avoid unpleasantness. In one case where the head refused to authorize an advance, the member became enraged and withdrew her membership.

When we checked the tally of mats at the group heads' homes against our central records in the initial weeks of the cooperative, we found a shortfall at several homes. We then learned that a system of advances off the books was developing. Many heads found themselves being pressured to approve private advances within official advances. Having already received their official advance from the cooperative, members begged their heads to sign that they had already delivered 10 mats in order to receive an additional 100 baht cash; in fact none of those mats had been delivered. One member did not want a cash loan recorded because she was embarrassed to have Narong or me know that she was in debt; she had begged to keep it a private matter. Tension then arose between the group head and the member when they disagreed on the number of mats the member had repaid.[8]

---

8. Internal specialization also developed in which a member split bamboo but hired others to weave the mats; the splitter paid the weaver 10 baht for every three mats

Furthermore, the heads were liable for the shortfall. Further complicating the mat tally, we found that two of the group heads had awarded themselves private mat advances, one because he was short of rice and another because he had hospital bills to pay when his son developed malaria. The heads felt that they were responsible for any missing mats anyway, and hopefully their compensation as group heads would cover their shortfall. When this pattern continued, we were forced to ask two heads to find replacements for themselves, leading to awkwardness and hurt feelings that lasted for several years.[9]

The problem of debt was further compounded when the cooperative began buying bamboo. Given the need of the cooperative to distribute all the bamboo it purchased and the need of its members to have bamboo to weave mats, the cooperative soon found itself with villagers with advances both in cash and in bamboo. When two members took bamboo from the group but did not send any mats to their group head, the group head, with the agreement of the other heads, expelled them. These expulsions also created considerable tension. As the enraged husband of one expelled member exclaimed, "This group is just going to lead to people killing each other" (*kha kan tai*).

THE BAMBOO PROBLEM

In addition to problems of indebtedness, we faced problems in obtaining, delivering, and distributing bamboo. Unfortunately, at the time the cooperative began, most villagers were out of bamboo. There are many kinds of bamboo; the kind of bamboo needed for weaving these mats had very long sections and only grew in certain forests. Poorer villagers often cut bamboo for their families' use and for sale, but this species of bamboo was becoming scarce in the nearby forests in Mae Win. Other villagers depended on the periodic truckloads brought in

woven and claimed the credit for the woven mats. Not including the time involved in splitting bamboo, a weaver working full-time could finish about two mats in a day.

9. For most group heads, their total compensation rarely covered the shortfalls. One group expected their head to stop by their homes to pick up their mats, as merchants had done. In addition to recording and storing mats, heads were involved in the distribution of bamboo. Over time, compensation was increased to 50 satang per mat and two bundles of bamboo for each shipment.

from Chiang Dao by a village merchant. Each truckload was typically two hundred bundles of bamboo (three to five lengths totaling forty sections per bundle). Technically, all the bamboo villagers wove was illegal. With the government becoming stricter about illegal forest logging, obtaining it involved various backchannels to enable shipments to pass numerous district police stations unimpeded. Three group heads decided to travel to Chiang Dao and succeeded in negotiating a purchase price of 8 baht per bundle. Since bamboo typically sold for 11–13 baht per bundle in the village, we began envisioning profits.

Unfortunately, the first bamboo shipment's arrival on April 5 coincided not only with the New Year (Songkran) preparations but also with the time when poor villagers earned more money harvesting soybeans. So rather than making a profit from the bamboo, the co-op found itself with seventy-nine bundles of drying bamboo that no one wanted to buy. The bamboo was piled at the home of one the heads; some 100 baht was needed to at least recoup the cost of the shipment. One suggestion was to force any member who had not yet purchased bamboo in this shipment to do so. This idea provoked serious resistance from members whose husbands cut their own bamboo in the forest and from those who were busy harvesting soybeans. In the end, each group head contributed 20 baht to cover the shortfall and divided up the remaining bamboo. When group heads initially balked at buying the dried bamboo themselves, one group head chastised the others for being selfish, adding to the tension among the heads themselves.

Subsequent shipments were no less problematic, sometimes delayed by rains and other complications and sometimes coming in rapid succession. On one occasion the cooperative underwrote a group of members to go into the nearby forest in Mae Win to cut bamboo for two weeks. That proved to be a debacle. We hired the *kamnan*'s truck for 500 baht, but it broke down. The driver told us he needed 700 baht for repairs, but only paid for the parts and not the labor; he instead gambled the rest of the money away. This disaster led to conflicts among Narong, Kongchan, and her parents (her father was the *kamnan*). Over time, the cooperative developed more reliable contacts, bringing bamboo in from Chiang Dao, Fang, and later Mae Tha in Lamphun Province.

Developing a system for distributing bamboo was also complicated. Some shipments contained scraggly bamboo no one wanted, and other shipments had beautiful bamboo that had nonmembers putting pressure on members to get them bundles. We eventually developed a system in which the bamboo was unloaded and divided into lots. Members then drew lots, joking about how they had no doubt drawn the worst lot.

MARKETING PROBLEMS

As the cooperative accumulated more mats, we faced the challenge of finding markets. Rice was generally being harvested twice a year: the main harvest and a secondary harvest (*khao do*) in early June. Our village did not use these mats in their own rice harvest.[10] Villagers as far away as Fang District used our mats, but we had no links to them. We were starting to panic that the mats would grow moldy. Furthermore, the homes of the group heads were already about to collapse from the weight of the stored mats; several could barely get into their bedrooms for all the stockpile of mats. A solution presented itself when one of the former village merchants approached us about buying seven hundred mats from us for 13 baht per mat. Some Fang villagers came and bought a couple hundred mats. With a monopoly on the mats remaining in the village by early July, we raised the price to 15 baht. However, we were also realizing that at the time we began the cooperative, this traditional market for mats was declining, replaced by fertilizer bags and plastic mats.

Fortunately we were finding new markets. In early April, a wealthy teacher-entrepreneur contacted Narong about weaving one thousand mats per month for export to Japan.[11] This agreement also had the advantage that we did not have to worry about storage or transportation. Because these mats were smaller than the mats used for the harvest, the cooperative bought them from members for 8 baht each and sold them to him for 10 baht apiece (the price was soon renegotiated to 12

10. Our village prepared a hard surface for threshing by mixing buffalo dung with mud; others used large woven baskets.
11. Khru Somboon in Tambon Nongtong.

baht). Because he wanted the mats sprayed with insecticide, he agreed to pay the group heads an additional 20 satang per mat for their labor. But the headaches soon followed. The mats had to meet exact size and quality specifications, so heads rejected undersized or poorly woven mats. In May it rained for several days nonstop, so many of the mats developed mold. This contract met its demise when the teacher-entrepreneur found that the mats he shipped to Japan developed mold en route as well.

A new market was also emerging in the production of bamboo plywood used in the growing construction industry and in the production of furniture. The cooperative began shipping mats to a new business called Northern Enterprise, located in the newly forming industrial zone in Lamphun (see Glassman 2004). In part because of the cooperative's deliberate decision to slow down production, the price of mats increased gradually. By November 1984, the price of mats had risen to 24 baht each (buying from members at 19 baht; the price of bamboo had risen to 4½–5 baht per length of bamboo; five lengths was enough for three of these mats. Agricultural wage rates had risen to 30–40 baht a day). The bamboo plywood industry became the stable market for the remaining years of the cooperative's existence.

THE RICE SHORTAGE

As the cooperative got off the ground, the price of rice was skyrocketing. Villagers normally eat sticky rice, but the price of *khao chao* (literally "lord's rice," or nonglutinous rice) was traditionally higher. Consequently, landed villagers were increasingly planting enough sticky rice for their own needs and planting the remainder of their paddy lands with *khao chao*. In 1978 there was a shortage of sticky rice, and its price more than doubled, from 2 baht per liter to 5 baht per liter. Villagers were having to eat *khao chao*. Even *khao chao* was hard to come by since it was typically exported out of the village to the national and international markets. As a sign of the times, in July a truck in Chiang Rai was stormed by angry villagers thinking it was transporting rice, only to learn it was carrying soybeans.

Group heads and members had been speculating about the possibility of the cooperative selling rice at cost. When we sold our first load of small mats in early July, we were ecstatic. We sold thirteen hundred mats, making a profit of 5,100 baht. On July 9 the mat group voted unanimously in favor of buying rice. Of ninety-seven members, only eighteen had rice, and their supply would soon be exhausted. Members were already stretching their sticky rice by only eating it in the morning and eating *khao chao* in the evening. However, after a few days, we found we were short about 300 baht for sticky rice. When we measured out a *thang* of rice, instead of 20 liters, we got 19½ liters, necessitating further adjustments. The cooperative's venture into rice ended as that year's rice harvest began, but it was an effort that members appreciated.

III. OVERCOMING RADICAL DISTRUST

By far the biggest challenge in that first year proved to be overcoming a lack of trust. Many members continued to sell their mats to village merchants rather than the cooperative. Initially, we thought that members were repaying preexisting loans, but in July we calculated that from six loads of bamboo that had already been delivered, we should have at least 3,000 large mats or 6,000 small mats; we had instead only 1,600 large mats and 1,800 small mats. Almost half of the mats were being sold outside the group. The outflow contributed to continual frustration among the cooperative leadership, group leaders alternately demanding expulsion or pleading compassion for errant members.[12] It gradually became clear that this outflow to the village merchants was also the result of members' fear of the consequences of disloyalty to their former mat buyers or of incurring the disapproval of their landlords or other members of the village elite from whom they might need a loan to buy medicine for a sick child or to cope with some other emergency.

One mat buyer sold vegetables from her cart; she was formidably resourceful. As soon as she heard the mat cooperative was getting off the ground, she began giving generous cash advances. She refused

---

12. After the first three members were expelled in the early weeks of the cooperative, there were no more expulsions. Instead the cooperative refused to allow errant members additional advances until they repaid their earlier loans.

repayment in money for any advances she made in food or in money, insisting that her loans be repaid with mats. She then began buying mats for 11–12 baht each. When she learned that members caught selling to her would be expelled, she deliberately left mats in front of the homes of members, hoping to implicate them. For a time, even though it involved a detour, she would deliberately walk in front of Narong's home as if to taunt him and force him to expel members.

When we held meetings with various members to ask them why they were selling their mats to her or other buyers, a common reply was that they had longstanding bonds of dependence (*kin kap puean muen*). The group heads retorted, "Well, they have depended on you for many years. You built their houses for them." Several members expressed their fear that if the cooperative failed, the former buyers would exact their revenge on them for their disloyalty (*cha klaeng hao*), by refusing to buy their mats or ever give them loans again. Fear of the group's collapse led to many members hedging their bets, selling mats to both the cooperative and their former buyers.

Also contributing to the outflow of mats was the steady barrage of disparaging remarks made by many of the village elite maligning the motives of the group heads and attacking members for being idiots to join a cooperative that was not going to last (*mueng ngao, khao klum thi bo pen hup*). Although I could understand why the village mat merchants might hope for the cooperative's collapse, it took me some time to understand both why villagers whose income was not affected denigrated the cooperative and why members appeared to defer to their opinions.

A member of the village elite I shall call Naan provides an illustration.[13] Despite being widely disliked, he seemed remarkably influential. Naan repeatedly told members they were being used and that the group heads were making money at their expense (*suea non kin*, "tigers eating while resting"). Although his wife and some other of his female relatives also wove and stockpiled mats for resale, Naan's income came primarily from rent paid by tenants on his family's

---

13. Naan was also a close relation of the abbot of the village temple, where several cooperative members' sons were novices.

relatively substantial landholdings. Many of his tenants lived in a section of the village where there was a significant outflow of mats. Naan had a reputation for abusing his control over land and money to have sex with women in this part of the village and obtain other favors. One group leader, himself a tenant, described a minor incident which occurred after he had planted a mango tree which was about to bear its first fruit. Naan came by and saw the ripe mango, and took it. The head was so angry that he cut the tree down, figuring he would never be able to eat any of its fruit anyway. As I came to learn, his tenants felt they had no choice but accept his abuses because they feared losing their tenancies.

In retrospect, the outflow of mats under these circumstances is less surprising than the courage it took for tenants and wage laborers to even dare to join the cooperative. The elite were able to influence the landless poor in large part because tenants and wage laborers were vulnerable, fearing their participation in the cooperative might jeopardize their access not just to their former mat buyers but more broadly to land to rent or work and to loans in times of emergency. But Naan and other landowners who relied on tenants to farm their land were likely worried that the cooperative was a harbinger of a resistance movement among the poor once represented by the FFT. At a minimum, it raised the possibility that their former dependents might become more independent.

The swirling fears of communism, terrorism, and foreign imperialism also worked their magic, further contributing to the outflow of mats. With the growing presence of an active communist guerrilla movement in nearby Mae Win Subdistrict, San Pa Tong District, the government had classified San Pa Tong as a "pink" zone (red indicating zones under communist control). A young woman from a nearby village was known to have joined the guerrilla movement. The dramatic escalation in the price of rice in 1978 only fueled rural discontent. Pressure was growing on *kamnan*, village headmen, school teachers, and Village Scouts to collect and report information on leftist activities. The village had already had a Village Scout training session and had several active scouts. School teachers had been assigned the task of gathering information about landholdings in each village. In August, local *kamnan* attended a ten-day training session in Phitsanulok at which two former communists described how people plowed the fields without water buffaloes in Cambodia.[14] The *kamnan* were instructed to hold meetings of their villagers to explain to them how bad communism was and to keep an eye on any of their village headmen with leftist sympathies. Furthermore, they were to make sure no villagers sent food or supplies to the communists. Shortly after I left in March 1979, Sawat Nupong, a villager from San Pa Tong District, was gunned down near the YMCA for alleged communist activity.

In this surreal mix of suspiciousness, villagers were afraid to be unwitting stooges to some plan they did not fully understand.[15] The rumors that the cooperative was a front for communism intensified, leading to tensions within the cooperative at every level, as members and group heads worried about the consequences of such rumors for them personally. One poor villager who refused to join explained that he was afraid he would be seen as some sort of rebel.

For Narong, as a government official, the situation became increasingly difficult as rumors suggested he must be a communist organizer or seeking private profit.[16] One day when he was buying cigarettes at the village store, a villager upset him by suggesting he was probably making a fortune from the percentage he was getting from the co-op. Another scurrilous rumor suggested that Narong was using cooperative money to host feasts for the group heads. No less upsetting was the night when a member, denied an additional advance because he had not paid for the past two shipments of bamboo, saw Narong at a

14. Interestingly, *kamnan* were told that although the military dictators Thanom and Praphass had faults like everyone else, they were basically good men and were unfairly criticized by the students in Bangkok. Furthermore the *kamnan* were told that Thailand almost went communist on October 14, 1973, but fortunately enough Thais still loved the nation, the religion and the king to save the country.

15. One left-wing teacher spread rumors that I was probably a CIA agent and that the cooperative's funding came from the CIA. Another villager told a group head to be careful of me because I was clever and my motives were hard to fathom.

16. Narong was a longtime supporter of the Democrat Party and later of the Yellow Shirt movement.

funeral and cursed him in front of everyone present (*ai ha*). More dangerous was the rumor that an anonymous letter was being sent to his superiors in the district office that he was using official time for private business (although he scrupulously avoided cooperative activities during school hours). He began considering withdrawing from his role as central accountant, but there was no one else yet capable of filling this role in his stead.

One sign of the mounting toll of this pressure came in mid-May when mat weavers in adjoining villages approached Narong about joining the co-op as another subgroup. Noting her worries about the libelous letter and rumors of communism, Kongchan objected forcefully. She noted that the traditional village merchants were still buying mats in these surrounding villages. One of these merchants was already so upset with us that his wife and daughters no longer came over to visit. If we were not more careful, we would end up getting shot (*don luk puen*).

For me personally, the toll from these rumors came one night in early June. That night Narong, the group heads, and I had gotten into a particularly heated discussion over how to handle members who were selling mats outside the cooperative, some siding with Narong over the need to enforce rules and others siding with me on the need for compassion. One of the heads who agreed with Narong got angry and was about to stalk out. Kongchan, already very worried about all the enemies she and Narong were creating, got upset that everyone was arguing with each other. Crying, she said to me that it was fine for me to work on this cooperative as I could leave at any time, but she and Narong had to stay in the village. I was single and had no family responsibilities. But she and the children were dependent on Narong for their income and she only had a fourth-grade education. If I went overseas, I would not even know if anything happened to them. Then she added, "If Narong gets killed, I will hate you for the rest of my life."

One of the heads tried to calm us all down, saying that I was a *farang* (foreigner), so I couldn't fully understand the pressures they faced. Tired of being a farang, I snapped back, "That's right. I'm just a farang, not really a human being, but some strange species of animal." I left the house in tears myself. No sooner was I out the door than I found myself surrounded by all the heads of the mat-weaving group. They said it was dangerous for me to be walking down the road in the dark; there were too many ghosts. I retorted that I was a farang, so I wasn't afraid of ghosts. But then one said I had to return to the house or Narong, Kongchan and the entire group would lose face. That argument resonated. I certainly did not want to subject them to the village rumor mill. I calmed down and went back inside. Everyone went home to sleep.

In the morning, the magnitude of my outburst hit me. I waied (a form of bow) Narong and Kongchan, apologizing for having become emotional and making things even more complicated than before. After Kongchan left for the market, Narong complained that he had made a mistake in marrying Kongchan. He understood the pressure she was under, but she didn't understand his values at all. After Narong left for school, Kongchan and I talked; it was clear she understood her husband well but was worried for his safety. Meanwhile, word spread like wildfire through the village that I had been crying; they were amazed to learn that I cried just like a Thai. Oddly, that night was a breakthrough.

We persevered. Finally the day came when the cooperative began generating profits and was finally able to hold its first meeting in which enough members had built up their 500-baht shares and could have cash paid out to them. That meeting served to silence many of the cooperative's skeptics.[17] As the members came to trust the cooperative's survival, the outflow of mats diminished. As the price of mats gradually rose and the market stabilized, members began to speak of depending for their living on the cooperative (*kin kap klum, kin kap sat*). In an ironic reversal, nonmembers began selling their mats to the cooperative through its members. In addition to the meager additional income it provided, it gradually empowered its members, creating a new group of leaders among the poor villagers. Many of the original mat-weaving leaders have died, but several of their sons and daughters are active in village affairs today.[18]

---

17. The cooperative repaid the YMCA on time, with the agreed-upon interest.

18. Kongchan served as president of the village housewives association. Other members have served as volunteer health officers, tambon council members, vote canvassers in election campaigns, and the like.

CONCLUSION

Fieldwork is always challenging. The mat-weaving cooperative enabled me to overcome distrust and develop a wide network of friendships throughout the village that have lasted to the present. In the process, I came to understand more about the ever-changing challenges facing all villagers, from those farming or running businesses to those going into the forest to search for bamboo.

The mat-weaving cooperative lasted nearly two more decades. In the final years, nearly all the group heads were women; Kongchan, despite her fourth-grade education, became the central accountant.[19] Each year tens of thousands of mats and hundreds of thousands of baht flowed through the cooperative, successfully returning profits to its members. As the years went by, the younger generation found jobs in agroindustry and construction; only the old people continued weaving because they had no other sources of income at home. As somewhat-better-paying piecemeal work assembling artificial flowers or deseeding longan fruit came along, they too gradually stopped weaving. When the decision to disband the cooperative was made, the 500-baht shares were returned to each of its members (minus any outstanding advances). One group head continued buying the remaining mats from the few remaining weavers, but after a couple of years, she also stopped. No one in the village currently weaves these mats.

Thailand experienced its most recent military coup in May 2014. However, the situation in Thai villages today is radically different. After the 1976 coup, a growing number of villagers believed the armed guerrilla movement was the only avenue for change; the populist policies of the Thai Rak Thai Party have done much to reinforce northern villagers' beliefs in the electoral process. If poor villagers were once afraid to intimate any critical political opinions, today they are more open. Yellow Shirt sympathizers can be found among the village elite, but Red Shirts comprise the majority of northern villagers. Villages now have a growing middle class and a stronger civil society.[20]

---

19. Narong became school principal at a different school, where he went on to develop a school lunch program to counter malnutrition.
20. For an excellent discussion of these changes, see Walker (2012).

Most village children today attend high school; a growing number
have university degrees. Recent decades have seen a radical change in
the expectations of villagers. Rather than the former expectations that
villagers serve the state, villagers now expect the state to serve them.
The military coup of 2014 has not changed that expectation.

REFERENCES

Anan Ganjanapan. 1984. "The Partial Commercialization of Rice Production in
Northern Thailand, 1900–1981." PhD diss., Cornell University.
Bowie, Katherine. 1975. "Testing the North's Political Mood." *Bangkok Post*, June 29.
———. 1988. "Peasant Perspectives on the Political Economy of the Northern Thai
Kingdom of Chiang Mai in the Nineteenth Century: Implications for the
Understanding of Peasant Political Expression." PhD diss., University of Chicago.
———. 1992. "Unraveling the Myth of the Subsistence Economy: The Case of
Textile Production in Nineteenth Century Northern Thailand." *Journal of Asian
Studies* 51 (4): 797–823.
———. 1997. *Rituals of National Loyalty: An Anthropology of the State and the Village
Scout Movement in Thailand*. New York: Columbia University Press.
Bowie, Katherine, and Brian Phelan. 1975. "Who is Killing the Farmers?" *Bangkok
Post Sunday Magazine*, August 17.
Cohen, Paul. 1981. "The Politics of Economic Development in Northern Thailand,
1967–1978." PhD. diss., University of London.
Glassman, Jim. 2004. *Thailand at the Margins: Internationalization of the State and
the Transformation of Labour*. Oxford: Oxford University Press.
Haberkorn, Tyrell. 2011. *Revolution Interrupted: Farmers, Students, Law, and Violence
in Northern Thailand*. Madison: University of Wisconsin Press.
Morell, David, and Chai-anan Samudavanija. 1981. *Political Conflict in Thailand:
Reform, Reaction, Revolution*. Cambridge: Oelgeschalter, Gunn and Hain.
Samruam Singh [Surasinghsamruam Shimbhano]. 1998. *Voices from the Thai
Countryside: The Necklace and Other Short Stories*. Edited and translated by
Katherine Bowie. Revised edition. Madison: Center of Southeast Asian Studies,
University of Wisconsin Press.
Turton, Andrew, Jonathan Fast, and Malcolm Caldwell, eds. 1978. *Thailand: Roots
of Conflict*. Nottingham: Spokesman Books.
Walker, Andrew. 2012. *Thailand's Political Peasants: Power in the Modern Rural
Economy*. Madison: University of Wisconsin Press.

Revisiting Ethnic and Religious Factors in Thailand's Southern Discomfort

Christopher M. Joll

INTRODUCTION: VIEWING THE SOUTH FROM THE NORTH

Anyone familiar with the career of activist-intellectual Dr. Chayan Vaddhanaphuti will be aware that Thailand's northern ethnic minorities have been his primary ethnographic subjects. This is not surprising for someone hailing from the North, which is the most ethnically diverse region in a kingdom whose linguistic and ethnic homogeneity has been much overstated. Thai citizens of Chinese descent are widely regarded as the kingdom's largest, most prosperous, and most successfully assimilated ethnic minority. Approximately 85 percent of the population of the southern provinces of Pattani, Yala, and Narathiwat Provinces are Malay Muslim. Malays also constitute 50 percent of the Thai province of Satun and 30 percent of Songkhla, which border the northwestern Malaysian states of Perlis and Kedah (Parks 2009). Thailand's third-largest ethnic minority are the one million Khmer who live in southern Isan along the Cambodian border. Peter Vail (2007) has referred to these Buddhist Khmer as "invisible."

As for northern Thailand, Chayan mentions that a census of northern hill tribes conducted between 1985 and 1988 estimated their numbers at half a million. Its conclusions can be considered flawed for the following reasons: Ethnic groups such as "the Shan, Yunnanese Chinese and Burmese" were not classified as "hill tribes" (Thai, *chao khao*)—a new term coined in the early 1960s—but "ethno-regional groups" (Chayan 2005, 156). Although the state surmised that minorities had settled in the North at the beginning of the twentieth century, the Karen, Lua, T'in, and Khmu had occupied upland areas before this. The state system of classification reflects its view of "minorities in the context of national integration and development." Also discriminated against were northern Yuan, Mons in central Thailand, and the Lao-speaking Tai, who—although a national minority—are a regional majority in Thailand's northeast, the area commonly referred to as Isan (Chayan 2005, 152, 153, 155).

On the basis of the policies promulgated by them, Thai bureaucrats appear to have been contaminated by a highly suspect pop anthropology whose analysis of "race" and "religion" trades in essentialized clichés. Discernable in Chayan's approach to ethnic politics in Thailand is both that (1) ethnographic enquiry must also be attentive to historical processes, and (2) most "ethnic" problems develop for more than one reason. I argue that monocausal myths must be replaced by approaches attentive to multicausality. Consider the issue of geographic distribution: ethnic minorities geographically concentrated near international borders are "more likely to develop secessionist movements" (Keyes 2003, 203). Nevertheless, there need to be economic and political advantages—real or perceived—to "separatism." While few northern Khmer living in Isan advocate joining Cambodia, many southern Malays who have missed out on the benefits of Thai modernity compare their circumstances to the political power and economic prosperity enjoyed by Malays in Malaysia. Such factors explain the nonexistence of Shan, Mon, or Karen separatism in Thailand and the presence of Malay separatism.

Although to my knowledge Chayan has never explicitly made mention of multicausality, his analysis identifies the agency of the following processes: (1) the abandonment of the Siamese cosmopolitanism that flourished during the Ayutthaya period (ca. 1351–1767); (2) the exploitation of northern Thailand's natural resources, most notably its teak forests; (3) a perusal of policies representing the internal colonization of ethnolinguistic and ethnoreligious minorities to combat the expansion of British and French colonial interests during the late 1800s; (4) the impact of aggressive assimilation policies pursued by military rulers beginning in the 1930s; (5) the identification of ethnic minorities as threats to national security during the period of communist expansion; and (6) the denial of Thai citizenship to members of ethnic groups residing in Thailand's northern forests, which is related to the state's desire to exploit their natural resources (Chayan 2005).

When I first began working with Dr. Chayan in late 2012, I (in retrospect mistakenly) assumed that my ten years of living in the Malay-speaking Muslim far south would be only marginally relevant in my new academic environment. I soon discovered that local seminars addressing issues of ethnicity in Thailand often broached topics that had caused resentment or angst among minorities. As with southern Malays, these topics included chauvinism and discrimination by government officials, widespread educational underachievement, and language loss among academic achievers. This chapter explores how Chayan's approach to conflicts involving ethnic minorities in northern Thailand might be applied to those in its far south. While I can't claim to make an exhaustive catalogue of all causal factors, I begin by identifying some of the most important that have both initiated and subsequently sustained the decade-long insurgency in the Thai provinces of Pattani, Yala, and Narathiwat. Having claimed the lives of six thousand people (Srisompob 2014), this insurgency represents ASEAN's deadliest ongoing subnational conflict (Parks et al. 2013). My specific interests are to scrutinize the ethnoreligious characteristics of this conflict that Imtiyaz Yusuf (2007, 19) conceptualizes as involving a clash between the two chauvinistic ethnoreligious worldviews of Thai *satsana* and Malay *agama*. These are the Thai and Malay terms both (crudely) translated as "religion."

My essay attempts to move beyond the pedestrian and predictable rounding up of the usual suspects, who in southern Thailand are Malays committed to violent resistance against Bangkok's political legitimacy and cultural program. Anthony Johns (2001, 6) described the interrogation of the usual suspects wherever such violence occurs as a routinized exercise. Interrogators possess an exhaustive repertoire of ways to make people talk, and words are often placed in the mouths of people being interrogated. This chapter attempts to move beyond the habitual by revisiting assumptions about Muslim agency and examining other suspects by reconsidering the importance of Islam in the actions of Muslims and providing details about violent elements within the Thai Buddhist community. I refer below to violence advocated or perpetrated by Buddhists (not Buddhism) and Muslims (not Islam). This point relates to concerns that are central to this chapter; after all, it is *people* who commit violence. Notwithstanding religious identity—whether individual or communal—being important to some, it may be peripheral to others. For the former, religion informs daily rhythms and weekly routines, whereas for the latter religion does no more than determine their final resting place. Furthermore, most faith traditions possess some version of "just war" theology (Fisher et al. 2010; Kelsay et al. 1991). I argue that within the highly ethicized forms of (Malay) Islam and (Thai) Buddhism embodied in Thailand, incivility exists that both the Thai state and traditional religious authorities are incapable of controlling. In line with my wider objective of interacting with Chayan's approach to "ethnic" issues elsewhere in Thailand, I preface my analysis of ethnicity and religion with a prolegomenon to the relationship between the state, ethnicity, and religion. It is both misguided and imprudent to blame all the problems that exist in places like Sri Lanka or Myanmar on Buddhism. The parallel argument is true for states such as Pakistan, Syria, and Iraq, where Muslims constitute the majority. Sectarian violence and subnational conflicts occur wherever there are weak states. Assertions that either Buddhism or Islam plays no role in violence, or that it lies at the heart of it, are equally erroneous (McCargo 2008b, 12). Let us now reconsider the role of the state, ethnicity, and religion in conflict.

RECONSIDERING STATE AND RELIGION

Emily Tripp (2014) is one of a number of scholars (see also Ruane et al. 2010) who have revisited assumptions about the role of the state, language, and religion in subnational "ethnic conflicts." She asserts that it is impossible to assess whether "states divided by religion are more prone to conflict than those divided by language" (para. 1). More important than the relative effect that religious or linguistic divisions have on "ethnic" conflicts, Tripp calls for increased attention to the state and the elite-led group interactions within it. Furthermore, assessments of "religious or linguistic division(s)" are only capable of understanding conflicts "in the context of how the state, and those acting in relation to it, internalise their control" (para. 1).

Tripp identifies assumptions that she evaluates as highly problematic: (1) religious or linguistic divisions lead to conflict; (2) religious or linguistic identities are fixed; and (3) religious or linguistic conflict exists primarily between—rather than within—groups. Many of these are influenced on primordial conceptions of identity associated with Clifford Geertz (1963, 1994, 1996), which have been critiqued by interlocutors formulating constructivist alternatives (Bayar 2009; Brubaker et al. 2000). Tripp argues that Geertz advocated the agency of societal structures "independent of objective realities." Ethnicity might not be arbitrary, but neither is it fixed or independent of language and religion. The actions of ethnic groups are influenced by state structures that contribute to the construction of ethnoreligious cleavages. Furthermore, religious or linguistic rights are sometimes only peripheral concerns of political elites who manipulate conflicts. These dynamics are frequently missed in the analysis of conflicts between ethnic groups. Commentators conceptualizing conflicts along religious or linguistic lines unknowingly or intentionally perpetuate isolationist narratives. These narratives in turn exacerbate boundaries, which become their subject of analysis. Primordial positions more than overlook such divisions. They exacerbate the agency of ethnic fault lines exploited by elites, which Tripp refers to as motivated by perceived threats of "homogenizing state movements" and "self-perpetuating cultural discourses" (Tripp 2014, para. 5).

Tripp examines the phenomenon of "ethnic defectors": individuals voluntarily joining organizations thought to be opposing the "perceived aspirations of their own ethnic group." Citing Stathis N. Kalyvas, she points out that constructivists accept that "ethnic allegiance has the potential not only to be solidified but also to be dissolved" (para. 7). Although accepting that ethnicity is both based on preference and is fluid, such choices are affected by interactions with the state. Particularly during periods of weakness and instability, it is the state—rather than either ethnoreligious or ethnolinguistic divisions—that is the most important causal factor. Anyone familiar with Thai politics will appreciate the utility of this observation. Unstable states frequently emphasize ethnic boundaries or divisions, or claim that these are fixed. While interactions between individuals and state structures are significant for a number of reasons, for Tripp, the most important is that they "[exacerbate] linguistic or religious fault lines" and affect "the definition of boundaries" (final para.). Wherever there is instability of this nature, differentiations must be made between frequent, convoluted debates about the (contested and notoriously vague) concept of identity and the specific analysis of ethnic conflict. Included in the long list of divisions potentially leading to violence are political elites bent of exploiting ethnic boundaries.

As Chayan has pointed out, Thailand's southern Malays are not the country's only ethnic minority to have suffered from ill-conceived state intervention during chapters of political instability. One way to demonstrate the complexity of conflicts ascribed to "religion" is to draw a comparison with state interventions in the northeastern region of Isan, where Lao-speaking Buddhists form the ethnolinguistic and ethnoreligious majority. In the last decades of the nineteenth century and first decades of the twentieth, Siam embarked on an ambitious and aggressive policy of modernizing its antiquated infrastructure and administration. This program included dramatic changes to the educational system and the bureaucratic organization of Buddhism. The medium of instruction in state schools was central Thai, and the Buddhism advocated by the sangha differed in a number of respects from the ritual and doctrinal idiosyncrasies of Buddhists in Isan. It was therefore not surprising that Bangkok's new policies were violently resisted there. Between 1947 and 1973, members of parliament from Isan were assassinated for leading protests against discrimination and interference by Bangkok. The most notorious incident occurred in 1949 during Field Marshal "Plaek" Phibunsongkhram's second tenure as prime minister (Kobkua 1995). In what is referred to as the Kilo 11 incident, four MPs were killed by the police. Two others were subsequently (unsuccessfully) charged on separatism charges (Parks 2012, 245, 247). Worth noting is that this occurred around the same time that southern Thailand's most famous political activist, Haji Sulong, disappeared after being summoned to the Songkhla police station in 1954 (see Chaloemkiat 2004; Ockey 2011).

Space does not permit a discussion of the controversies surrounding Bangkok's attitudes toward Isan residents who speak Lao (Alexander et al. 2014) or Khmer (Vail 2006, 2007; Vail et al. 2013). Among the scholars who have examined minority language policies in Thailand (Keyes 2003; Kosonen 2008; Suwilai 2005; Rappa et al. 2006; Smalley 1994) is Suwilai Premsrirat (2008; 2012, with Uniansasmita), who has explored the role that language rights for Pattani Malay might play in peace building. How has Thailand's political environment helped sustain violence? One of the most authoritative commentators on this conflict cites the chaotic condition of the Thai state (Askew 2007a, 2007b, 2008, 2009, 2010a, 2010b, 2011). Duncan McCargo, a seasoned commentator on Thai politics, considers the root cause of violence in southern Thailand to be its crisis of legitimacy (2008b) that began with the failure of the (ill-conceived and ultimately unsuccessful) policy of co-opting Malay political elites. The main targets were the Muslim members of the Wadah faction who were courted by General Chavalit Yongchaiyudh to join his New Aspiration Party. McCargo also draws attention to the role played by Thailand's "monarchy network" (2006), which dominates the Privy Council and upper echelons of the army and is incapable of entertaining any form of regional autonomy (Srisompob et al. 2008, 2010a, 2011, 2012).

I have previously drawn attention to Bangkok's initiatives to assimilate its southern Malays, an effort that roughly coincided with the rise of a number of modernist and reformist movements (Joll 2011, 35–50). To reiterate, these movements resemble those that impacted Thailand's northern and northeastern ethnic minorities, as described above. Through the Anglo-Siamese Treaty negotiated at the end of King Chulalongkorn's fifty-year reign in 1909, Siam retained the territories of the Malay sultanate of Patani. Chulalongkorn's successor, King Vajiravudh (r. 1910–25), presided over the new project of emphasizing the nation, the monarchy, and the Buddhist religion. In 1921, the Compulsory Primary Education Act required all Malay children to attend Siamese primary school for at least four years. In 1932, the absolute monarchy was replaced with a constitutional monarchy. The provinces of Pattani, Yala, and Narathiwat replaced Monthon Pattani, Saiburi, Yala, and Narathiwat, and the (already marginalized) Malay princes were made redundant.

The military government, led by Plaek Phibunsongkhram before World War II, not only sought to enforce the 1921 Compulsory Primary Education Act but also promulgated the Thai Custom Decree (Rathaniyom). As the decree forbade designations other than "Thai" (Malays were considered Thai Muslims) and aggressively promoted the use of the central Thai language and "modern" and "Thai" dress and customs, it widely impacted southern Malays. In 1945, the Patronage of Islam Act established the king of Thailand as the patron of Islam, mandated the creation of Islamic committees under the Ministry of Interior, and established the position of Chularatchamontri (Yusuf 1998 and 2010), who was appointed by royal decree. The template of this initiative was the government's oversight of Buddhism through the Sangkharat, leading Surin Pitsuwan (1985, 103) to argue that control rather than patronage was Bangkok's primary purpose. And finally, between 1960 and 1971 traditional *pondok* schools were forced to register as Private Schools Teaching Islam and teach the Thai national curriculum alongside the traditional Islamic curriculum. Although by no means limited to the far south, Muslim refusal to cooperate with these initiatives was strongest there, because more than merely providing religious education, *pondok*s constructed and maintained Malay identity and language as well as performing a range of social and religious functions. Given that the new policies coincided with the advent of Islamic revivalism throughout Southeast Asia, unprecedented numbers of Malays chose to study in the Middle East and South Asia.

REASSESSING BUDDHISTS' AGENCY

The previous section began with a survey of fresh perspectives on how states, religion, and ethnicity contribute to conflicts routinely referred to as "ethnic." It ended with a summary of causal factors involving the Thai state. These range from language policies, political instability, manipulation by elites, and assimilation through legislation. This section seeks to explore the role of actors who have only recently, and on rare occasions, been held up to scrutiny by scholars such as Mark Juergensmeyer and Michael Jerryson. Although Islam and Christianity are commonly associated with violence, a term such as "Buddhist warfare" (Jerryson et al. 2010) sounds oxymoronic to people unfamiliar with violence initiated by Buddhists in Sri Lanka, Myanmar, and southern Thailand (Deegalle 2006; Jerryson 2011, 2013a; Keyes 2007; Suwanna 2013; Tikhonov et al. 2013).

Michael Jerryson (2008, 2009a, 2009b, 2011, 2013b) considers his research on the role played by monks in southern Thailand to offer a timely corrective to misconception about Buddhism representing a mystical and inherently peaceful religion, which has led to the role of Buddhists in a number of conflicts being overlooked. The context for Jerryson's study is the attack in 2004 on nine Buddhist temples (*wats*) in which four monks were killed and two others injured. The most highly publicized of these incidents was the murder of monks and novices at Phromprasit Temple in Panare District, Pattani, in October 2005. Following this incident, the sangha committee of Pattani published a twenty-point declaration that included calls for the abolition of the National Reconciliation Commission (NRC). Although McCargo (2010b, 80–81) claims that this move against the NRC was backed by the military and that the names of certain monks were included without their consent, the Pattani sangha accused the NRC of showing little interest in the plight of local Buddhists. Leading southern monks gave interviews slamming the rhetoric of human rights and lamenting that although all the presidents of the Islamic councils in the three southern provinces had been invited to join the NRC, southern monks had not. This would not be the only controversy the NRC would be involved in. Its recommendations were criticized as amounting to an exoneration of Islam in the conflict.

Between 2004 and 2007, sixteen temples were attacked, leaving five monks dead and seventeen injured (Jerryson 2008, 94). In the most violent districts, these attacks reduced the number of monks making their early-morning rounds for alms, with those continuing to do so receiving military escorts and bulletproof vests (Jerryson 2008, 151). Attacks on southern temples also led to almost all of them being militarized, involving the installation of razor wire and the deployment of armed guards, in spite of opposition by some southern abbots. In addition, many temples functioned as barracks and depots for military hardware (Melvin, 2007; Nilsen, 2013). In some isolated districts of Yala and Narathiwat Provinces without temples serving Thai Buddhist communities, some government schools underwent similar transformations. Understandably, Buddhist temples were increasingly associated with the Thai military by local Malays (Jerryson 2009a, 9, 13).

In addition to militarized temples, Jerryson documents covert "military monks" being assigned to guard southern Buddhist temples and fellow monks (Jerryson 2008, 210–29; 2009a, 13–33). While the ordination of active soldiers is prohibited, and the 1905 Thai Military Service Act exempted monks from military service, Jerryson argues that the Thai Buddhist tradition of temporary ordination created space for circumventing the guidelines for Buddhist soldiers. Soldiers are granted a four-month paid leave for ordination. In 2005, seventy-five soldiers were ordained on Queen Sirikit's birthday. These "military monks," however, were ordained without either putting down weapons or abandoning military duties (see also McCargo 2008a, 74). Like much of the southern insurgency, military monks are shrouded in secrecy. Jerryson (2009a, 24) views Thailand's southern conflict as having activated the "latent tendency for militant Buddhism," similar to what analysts of the conflict in Sri Lanka have observed (see International Crisis Group 2010; Kent 2010).

McCargo, who dismisses suggestions by Charles F. Keyes (1989) that Buddhism has played a positive "civic" role in Thai democracy like Islam in Indonesia (see Hefner 2000), cites Jerryson's findings as demonstrating the uncivil nature of Buddhism in Thailand. The anti-Islamic polemics by the influential scholar-monk Prayudh Payutto has provided (saffron) "robes of respectability" for growing Buddhist intolerance, much of which is online (Phrae 2012). In addition to calling for the abolition of the NRC, some southern abbots furthermore expressed sympathy for the heavy-handed tactics of the Thai military (McCargo 2008a, 63, 69, 71). During the drafting of the 2007 constitution, elements of the sangha advocated that Buddhism be made Thailand's national religion.

Members of the royal family have also become embroiled in religious controversy. One incident involved the establishment of an alternative to the village volunteer initiative known as the *cho ro bo*, which was established by local police and army units in 2004 . During one of Queen Sirikit's stays in the Thaksin Ratchanives Palace in Narathiwat in late 2004, local Buddhists successfully secured her patronage for an additional village defense volunteer system, the *o ro bo*. The International Crisis Group claims that although initially envisaged as an initiative that both Buddhists and Muslims could join, its membership was soon almost exclusively Buddhist. Furthermore, its mandate was the protection of Buddhist minorities (International Crisis Group 2007, 19). Another incident involving the queen occurred around the same time. After two of the Narathiwat Palace's officials were fatally shot, she delivered an emotional speech to an audience of over a thousand people, which was also broadcast on national television. Queen Sirikit declared that Thais were determined to die for their compatriots and urged Buddhists not to be intimidated, to remain in the region, and to take shooting lessons—which she herself undertook to do. While noting the carefully worded speech to police and army officers by the king the next day, McCargo (2008b, 3, 19–20) comments that this was not the sort of "royal intervention liberals had hoped for."

David Camroux and Don Pathan (2008, 91) comment that calls from the queen and senior monks for the defense of Thai Buddhists not only increased the flow of weapons and the number of self-defense organizations and paramilitary groups but also increased the specter— or at least the language—of civil war. Over and above the volunteer schemes charged with the defense of Buddhist and Muslims communities, a number of paramilitary organizations also operate in southern Thailand (International Crisis Group 2007, 14–21). These include the clandestine group Ruam Thai (Thais United), which boasts six thousand members and is led by Police Colonel Phitak Iadkaew. Recruits are trained in a two-day course in private rented facilities. In addition to raising awareness of security risks and providing basic military training (with their own weapons) for self-defense, Ruam Thai also provides commando training, according to Nonviolence International. Some who complete the training are also permitted to work alongside the police wearing police-like uniforms and armed with combat weapons. Accusations of vigilante-style attacks against Muslims by Ruam Thai led to Phitak's transfer out of the area. However, this decision was subsequently reversed following protests by Buddhist residents in Yala.

Not surprisingly, the growing presence of armed Buddhist and Muslim civilians eventually led to increased sectarian violence. Some of the most infamous episodes followed the ambush of a passenger van in Yaha district of Yala Province on March 14, 2007. Although the Muslim driver was spared, the nine Buddhist passengers he was driving were shot at point-blank range. Only one of them survived. Notwithstanding the fact that summary executions of Buddhist civilians had occurred as early as the late 1970s and that—however outrageous—this incident was not the first of its nature, the Buddhist reaction to the ambush was as important as the incident itself. On the evening after the ambush, two attacks against Muslims took place in Yaha. There was a grenade attack on the Almubaroh Mosque in Patae subdistrict. An hour later, a tea shop in Katong subdistrict was attacked, leaving one Muslim patron dead. Later that night, unidentified gunmen drove around the predominantly Muslim village of Kuan Ran (in Bukit Toreng district), firing at random. Three days later, a *pondok* in Pian Subdistrict of Sabayoi (Songkhla Province) was attacked. Grenades were thrown, and huts were sprayed with bullets from shotguns and M16 assault rifles. This led to two fatalities and eight injuries. Muslim villagers accused Rangers (Thahan phran), an auxiliary force of the Royal Thai Army, of perpetrating this attack, and the villagers sustained a protest for over a month. On March 26, local Buddhists staged a two-thousand-strong counterprotest outside the town hall in Sabayoi to demand that the Rangers and Border Patrol Police remain in the village. On May 27, seven bombs exploded in Hat Yai (Songkhla Province), killing one and injuring twelve. The next day, a bomb exploded in the Buddhist section of the market in Sabayoi. This killed four and injured twenty-six. On May 31, 2007, young men sitting opposite the Kolomudo Mosque in Sabayoi's Chanae Subdistrict were fired upon by gunmen from two pickup trucks, leaving five dead and two injured (International Crisis Group 2007, 21–24).

Having previously delineated how initiatives and interventions by the Thai state have exacerbated ethnic insecurities and offended religious sensitivities, I investigated above the role played by Buddhists in southern Thailand and beyond. In the section that follows, I reconsider the role that Islam has played in violence perpetrated by Muslims.

REVISITING THE ROLE OF ISLAM

Malay rebellion in Pattani, Yala, and Narathiwat has changed dramatically from the period immediately after WWII when Gabungam Melayu Patani Raya, the Patani People's Movement, and the Patani United Liberation Organization (PULO) were dominant. Before the acceptance of the amnesty brokered by Prime Minister (and General) Prem Tinsulanonda in the 1980s, the groups employed orthodox guerrilla tactics that operationally relied on the presence of mountains and jungles. Since the early 2000s, operatives have remained in their homes, and, according to Chaiwat Satha-Anand (1987), their organization resembles a network without a core. In the past, Malay nationalism—more than Islam—ideologically drove the struggle (Surin 1985). An anthropologist colleague once related how he had been asked by a former PULO guerrilla to buy a bottle of duty-free gin when returning to Thailand. He commented that Ramadan was just around the corner and that this was a month for fasting and feasting—not partying. While few question that the present insurgency is more religiously motivated than any of its predecessors, it is being countered and conceptualized in the post-9/11 milieu (Abuza 2009; Bond et al. 2009; Gunaratna et al. 2005).

Joseph Liow (2008, 12) has pieced together what he considers to be a "fairly cogent map of some ideological pillars" through his interviews with (past and present) insurgents and analysis of leaflets (see McCargo 2012; Anusorn 2011, 69–72) and the limited number of booklets and pamphlets available such as "Berjihad di Patani" (Anonymous, n.d.; English translation provided by Gunaratna et al. 2005, 118–45). The prominence of jihadi rhetoric is cited by many as proof that a radical Islamist ideology has been grafted onto what was formerly a nationalistic narrative. Wattana Sungunnasil (2006) has analyzed "Berjihad di Patani," which was found at the Krue Se Mosque in Pattani after the attack there on April 28, 2004. Wattana (2006, 123) describes the tract as an "authentic and detailed statement of radical Muslim militant views in the deep South" that restates the struggle in explicitly religious terms. Such claims are questionable for a number of reasons. Chaiwat Satha-Anand's (1987) study of violence in southern Thailand between 1976 and 1981 includes an examination of leaflets produced by PULO at the time. In addition to claiming responsibility for actions, leaflets also mentioned (1) the distinctiveness and superiority of Islam, (2) calls for unity among Muslims (to support their aim of establishing an independent Islamic Patani state), (3) claims that fighting *kafir* is a Muslim obligation, and (4) that anyone refusing to do so is a hypocrite (*munafik*). It cannot be said, therefore, that the views expressed in "Berjihad di Patani" are a post-9/11 or post-2004 development.

A number of rebuttals of "Berjihad di Patani" have been written. The first and only one to have been written in Malay was penned by the influential reformist (Salafiyyah) leader, Dr. Ishmael Lutfi Japakia (Braam 2013; Muhammad Ilyas Yahprung 2014). Intriguingly, a refutation by Thai Islamic authorities followed, but this was written in Thai—not Malay. Lutfi summarizes the document's fundamental misperceptions concerning the role of Islam in the conflict. He emphasizes that only a recognized religious authority is permitted to declare jihad, and that this was only possible after other avenues such as *da'wah* (call to Islam) had been pursued (Ismail Lutfi Japakiya 2005). Is "Berjihad di Patani" a reformist articulation of jihad? This line of enquiry erroneously assumes that this expression of Islam is more prone to religiously motivated violence that Sufism, which has historically influenced traditionalist Islam in Southeast Asia (Woodward et al. 2014). That the coordinated Muslim attacks in April 2004 leading to the Krue Se incident followed all-night group chanting sessions (*zikir*) and involved invulnerability cults precludes the involvement of southern Thailand's reformist constituency. As well as being few in number, most southern reformists are highly educated middle-class Malays. Like PULO leaflets replete with jihadi rhetoric, there is nothing new about the involvement of invulnerability cults, which are mentioned by both Surin Pitsuwan (1985, 251–55) and Hugh Wilson (1992, 52) in their studies of Malay separatism.

As I have argued earlier (Joll 2010), the presence of jihadi *rhetoric* does not prove the existence of a developed jihadi *rationale*. Duncan

McCargo comes to a number of negative conclusions about the role of Islam and jihad in southern Thailand in his *Tearing Apart the Land: Islam and Legitimacy in Southern Thailand* (2008b). References to jihad, the involvement of religious teachers and Islamic schools in recruitment, and the performance of initiation ceremonies and magic suggest the conflict is a religious one. McCargo (2008, 187–88) concedes that Islam might have something to do with it, but "it is not about Islam." Rather, Islam functions as a rhetorical and legitimizing resource and an ideological framework that is selectively and pragmatically invoked. Local jihadi ideology is "simplistic [and] populist," lacking "historical or theological foundations" and ultimately representing attempts to "capitalize on popular global discourse about jihad" (2008b, 176–77). Liow's (2009b, 127–29) analysis of locally produced Malay manuals on jihad notes the absence of differentiation between a general *jihad* and *jihad qital* (armed struggle). There is also silence about whether the latter is an individual responsibility (*fard ain*) or a group responsibility that can be delegated to individuals (*fard kifaya*). Other issues that are neglected include whether parental permission is required by aspiring *mujahideen,* and which religious authorities are capable of mandating *jihad qital.*

Numerous claims and counterclaims have been made about global connections in southern Thailand. Rather than a pan-Islamic caliphate, the goal of the militants is to legitimize the "religious sacred community" of an imagined Malay nation of Patani (Helbardt 2015, 29). Local leadership were suspicious of foreign operatives who visited southern Thailand and rejected proposals to expand operations north of Malay-dominated Pattani, Yala, and Narathiwat (National Reconciliation Commission 2006, 37). Rather than the local presence of global jihadism, Camroux and Pathan (2008, 94) have discerned the "localization of the global." French sociologist Olivier Roy (2002), who coined the term "Islamic neofundamentalism," describes this situation as being simultaneously the product and the agent of globalization, in which unprecedented numbers of Muslims now live outside of traditionally Muslim countries. This has had the effect of deterritorializing Islam and emphasizes its supranational *ummah* that transcends statist politics. Neofundamentalism is also concerned with the protection of the normative Islam dating from the formative first Islamic century from external threats.

There are other reasons for questioning the agency of foreign fighters in southern Thailand. Rather than rank outsiders, it was Patani Malay Muslim veterans, intoxicated by their success against a superpower in Afghanistan, who founded Gerakan Mujahideen Islam Patani (International Crisis Group 2005, 16). Furthermore, most major streams of Islamic thought and practice from the Middle East and South Asia are present in Southeast Asia, although they possess distinguishing features (Bubalo et al. 2005, 16). This is in part due to these ideas having been introduced by mobile and multilingual locals (Joll 2012). Increased disposable income, access to the Internet (see especially André 2012 and 2014), and affordable air travel now perform the roles once played by steamers and printing presses. Training camps have lost their market share, as most Muslims who have become convinced about the legitimacy of violence developed these views from their mobile phones.

Far from a dichotomous analytical choice between internationalist jihadism and Malay ethnonationalism, Sascha Helbardt (2015, 232) claims that both these elements coexist. Liow adds that despite appropriating a range of religious metaphors and making claims about it being a religious conflict, insurgents in the far south are motivated by past grievances that have been repackaged for its consumers. While a range of uncivil interpretations of Islam have local currency, the conflict remains rooted in historical grievances and insecurity over ethnic identity. It cannot be denied that certain *pondok*s have been involved in indoctrination and recruitment. This is explained by their function as conduits for disseminating local histories that emphasize Patani's oppression and colonization at the hands of the Siamese. Religion has animated Malay ethnonationalism by injecting further meaning and intelligibility into the drive for self-determination. I finally note that the "geographical footprint" of the armed insurgency has remained unchanged for over one hundred years. Apart from occasional actions in Hat Yai, violence continues to be restricted to the Malay-dominated far-southern provinces of Pattani, Yala, and Narathiwat (Liow 2009a, 75, 79, 80, 92, 94).

CONCLUSION

Anthropologists viewing Chayan's embodiment of his discipline as potentially paradigmatic for impacting the public sphere may well share my concern for responding to essentialized clichés about the role of religion and ethnicity in conflicts. The conceptual eddies which these create are lethal whenever they inform state responses to subnational conflicts, and weak states frequently exacerbate ethnoreligious dynamics. Although ill-conceived policies are often based on a highly suspect pseudoanthropology, conducting research in contexts such as southern Thailand presents a number of challenges to both local and foreign anthropologists. I have argued above that on certain topics ethnographic enquiry must be particularly attentive to historical processes. Such an approach provides fresh perspectives on problems referred to as "ethnic," which are assumed to possess one root cause. Monocausal myths should be replaced with multicausal remedies. By reassessing Buddhist agency and revisiting the role of Islam, I have drawn attention to the presence of highly ethnicized forms of (Malay) Islam and (Thai) Buddhism in the South of Thailand. Assertions that either Buddhism and Islam play no role in violence or, alternatively, are central to it are equally questionable. Uncivil elements exist in both communities, which neither the Thai state nor traditional religious authorities appear capable of confronting or controlling. Activist academics critical of how "religion" and "ethnicity" have been misapprehended in conflicts have a part to play in ameliorating complex conflicts. It is as misguided as it is imprudent to ascribe all problems present in Sri Lanka, Myanmar, Syria, and Iraq to their religious majorities, and neither can Thailand's southern discomfort be explained in strictly religious terms.

REFERENCES

Abuza, Zachary. 2009. *Conspiracy of Silence: The Insurgency in Southern Thailand and Its Implications for Southeast Asian Security.* Washington, DC: United States Institute of Peace Press.

Alexander, Saowanee T., and Duncan McCargo. 2014. "Diglossia and Identity in Northeast Thailand: Linguistic, Social, and Political Hierarchy." *Journal of Sociolinguistics* 18 (1): 60–86. doi:10.1111/josl.12064.

André, Virginie. 2012. "'Neojihadism' and YouTube Patani Militant: Propaganda Dissemination and Radicalization." *Asian Security* 8 (1): 27–53.

———. 2014. "The Janus Face of New Media Propaganda: The Case of Patani Neojihadist YouTube Warfare and Its Islamophobic Effect on Cyber-Actors." *Islam and Christian-Muslim Relations* 25 (3): 335–56.

Anonymous. n.d. "Berjihad di Patani" [Waging jihad in Patani].

Anusorn Unno. 2011. *"We Love Mr. King": Exceptional Sovereignty, Submissive Subjectivity, and Mediated Agency in Islamic Southern Thailand*. Seattle: University of Washington Press.

Askew, Marc. 2007a. *Conspiracy, Politics, and a Disorderly Border: The Struggle to Comprehend Insurgency in Thailand's Deep South*. Washington, DC: East-West Center.

———. 2007b. "Thailand's Recalcitrant Southern Borderland: Insurgency, Conspiracies, and the Disorderly State." *Asian Security* 3 (2): 99–120.

———. 2008. "Thailand's Intractable Southern War: Reflections on Policy, Insurgency, and Discourse." *Contemporary Southeast Asia* 30 (2): 186–214.

———. 2009. "Fear and Trust in South Thai Villages and Insurgency." *Journal of Southeast Asian Studies* 40 (1): 59–86.

———. 2010a. "Insurgency and the Market for Violence in Southern Thailand: 'Neither War nor Peace.'" *Asian Survey* 50 (6): 1107–34.

———. 2010b. "The Spectre of the South: Regional Instability as National Crisis." In *Legitimacy Crisis in Thailand*, edited by Marc Askew, 235–72. Chiang Mai: Silkworm Books.

———. 2011. "Insurgency Redux: Writings on Thailand's Ongoing Southern War." *Journal of Southeast Asian Studies* 41 (1): 161–68.

Bayar, Murat. 2009. "Reconsidering Primordialism: An Alternative Approach to the Study of Ethnicity." *Ethnic and Racial Studies* 32 (9): 1639–57.

Bond, Christopher S., and Lewis M. Simons. 2009. *The Next Front: Southeast Asia and the Road to Global Peace with Islam*. Hoboken, NJ: John Wiley and Sons.

Braam, Ernesto H. 2013. "Malay Muslims and the Thai-Buddhist State: Confrontation, Accommodation, and Disengagement." In *Encountering Islam: The Politics of Religious Identities in Southeast Asia*, edited by Hui Yew-Foong, 271–312. Singapore: Institute of South East Asian Studies.

Brubaker, Rogers, and Frederick Cooper. 2000. "Beyond 'Identity.'" *Theory and Society* 29 (1): 1–47.

Bubalo, Anthony, and Greg Fealy. 2005. *Between the Global and the Local: Islamism, the Middle East, and Indonesia*. Washington, DC: Saban Center for Middle East Policy, Brookings Institution.

Camroux, David, and Don Pathan. 2008. "Borders of/on the Mind, Borders in Jungles: Islamic Insurgency and Ethno-Religious Irredentism in Southern Thailand." In *Promoting Conflict or Peace through Identity*, edited by Nikki Slocum-Bradley, 81–101. Aldershot: Ashgate Publishing.

Chaiwat Satha-Anand. 1987. *Islam and Violence: A Case Study of Violent Events in the Four Southern Provinces of Thailand, 1976–1981*. Tampa: Department of Religious Studies, University of South Florida.

Chalk, Peter. 2008. *The Malay-Muslim Insurgency in Southern Thailand: Understanding the Conflict's Evolving Dynamic*. RAND Counterinsurgency Study, Paper 5. Santa Monica, CA: RAND Corporation.

Chaloemkiat Khunthongpetch. 2004. *Haji Sulong Abdun Kadir: Kabot rue wiraburut haeng si changwat phak tai*. [Haji Sulong Abdul Qadir: A rebel or a hero of the four southern provinces]. Bangkok: Matichon.

Chayan Vaddhanaphuti. 2005. "The Thai State and Ethnic Minorities: From Assimilation to Selective Integration." In *Ethnic Conflicts in Southeast Asia*, edited by Kusuma Snitwongse and W. Scott Thompson, 151–66. Bangkok: Institute of Security and International Studies; Singapore: Institute of South East Asian Studies.

Deegalle, Mahinda, ed. 2006. *Buddhism, Conflict, and Violence in Modern Sri Lanka*. London: Routledge.

Fisher, David, and Brian Wicker. 2010. *Just War on Terror? A Christian and Muslim Response*. Farnham: Ashgate Publishing.

Geertz, Clifford. 1963. "The Integrative Revolution: Primordial Sentiments and Civil Politics in the New States." In *Old Societies and New States: The Quest for Modernity in Asia and Africa*, edited by Clifford Geertz, 105–57. London: Collier-Macmillan.

———. 1994. "Primordial and Civic Ties." In *Nationalism*, edited by John Hutchinson and Anthony D. Smith, 29–34. New York: Oxford University Press.

———. 1996. "Primordial Ties." In *Ethnicity*, edited by John Hutchinson and Anthony D. Smith, 40–45. New York: Oxford University Press.

Gunaratna, Rohan, Arabinda Acharya, et al. 2005. *Conflict and Terrorism in Southern Thailand*. Singapore: Marshall Cavendish Academic.

Hefner, Robert W. 2000. *Civil Islam: Muslims and Democratization in Indonesia*. Princeton, NJ: Princeton University Press.

Helbardt, Sascha. (2015). *Deciphering Southern Thailand's Violence: Organisation and Insurgent Practices of BRN-Coordinate*. Singapore: ISEAS.

International Crisis Group. 2005. "Southern Thailand: Insurgency Not Jihad." Asia Report no. 98, May 18. International Crisis Group, Brussels.

———. 2007. "South Thailand: The Problem with Paramilitaries." Asia Report no. 140, October 23. International Crisis Group, Brussels.

———. 2010. "War Crimes in Sri Lanka." Asia Report no. 191, May 17, 2010. International Crisis Group, Brussels.

Ismail Lutfi Japakiya. 2005. *Islam Agama Penjana Kedamaian Sejagat* [Islam as the pathway to harmony]. Alor Star, Malaysia: Pustaka Darussalam.

Jerryson, Michael K. 2008. "Sacred Fury, Sacred Duty: Buddhist Monks in Southern Thailand." PhD diss., University of California, Santa Barbara.

———. 2009a. "Appropriating a Space for Violence: State Buddhism in Southern Thailand." *Journal of Southeast Asian Studies* 40 (1): 1–25.

————. 2009b. "Militarizing Buddhism: Violence in Southern Thailand." In *Buddhist Warfare*, edited by Michael K. Jerryson and Mark Juergensmeyer, 179–210. New York: Oxford University Press.

————. 2011. *Buddhist Fury: Religion and Violence in Southern Thailand.* Oxford: Oxford University Press.

————. 2013a. "Buddhist Traditions and Violence." In *The Oxford Handbook of Religion and Violence*, edited by Mark Juergensmeyer, Margo Kitts, and Michael K. Jerryson, 41–66. New York: Oxford University Press.

————. 2013b. "A Path of Militant Buddhism: Thai Buddhist Monks as Representations." In *Buddhism and Violence: Militarism and Buddhism in Modern Asia*, edited by Vladimir Tikhonov and Torkel Brekke, 75–94. London: Routledge.

Jerryson, Michael K., and Mark Juergensmeyer, eds. 2010. *Buddhist Warfare.* New York: Oxford University Press.

Johns, A. H. 2001. "Perspectives of Islamic Spirituality in Southeast Asia: Reflections and Encounters." *Islam and Christian-Muslim Relations* 12 (1): 5–21.

Joll, Christopher Mark. 2010. "Religion and Conflict in Southern Thailand: Beyond Rounding Up the Usual Suspects." *Contemporary Southeast Asia* 32 (2): 258–79.

————. 2011. *Muslim Merit-Making in Thailand's Far-South.* Dordrecht: Springer.

————. 2012. "Islam's Creole Ambassadors." In *The Ghosts of the Past in Southern Thailand: Essays on the History and Historiography of Patani*, edited by Patrick Jory, 129–46. Singapore: National University of Singapore Press.

Kelsay, John, and James Turner Johnson. 1991. *Just War and Jihad: Historical and Theoretical Perspectives on War and Peace in Western and Islamic Traditions.* New York: Greenwood Press.

Kent, Daniel W. 2010. "Onward Buddhist Soldiers: Preaching to the Sri Lankan Army." In *Buddhist Warfare*, edited by Michael K. Jerryson and Mark Juergensmeyer, 157–78. New York: Oxford University Press.

Keyes, Charles F. 1989. "Buddhist Politics and Their Revolutionary Origins in Thailand." *International Political Science Review* 10 (2): 121–42.

————. 2003 "The Politics of Language in Thailand and Laos." In *Fighting Words: Language Policy and Ethnic Relations in Asia*, edited by Michael E. Brown and Šumit Ganguly, 177–210. Cambridge: MIT Press.

————. 2007. "Monks, Guns, and Peace: Theravada Buddhism and Political Violence." In *Belief and Bloodshed: Religion and Violence across Time and Tradition*, edited by James K. Wellman, Jr., 145–64. Lanham, MD: Rowman and Littlefield.

Kobkua Suwannathat-Pian. 1995. *Thailand's Durable Premier: Phibun Through Three Decades, 1932–1957.* Kuala Lumpur: Oxford University Press.

Kosonen, Kimmo. 2008. "Literacy in Local Languages in Thailand: Language Maintenance in a Globalised World." *International Journal of Bilingual Education and Bilingualism* 11 (2): 170–88.

Liow, Joseph Chinyong. 2009a. "Ideology, Religion, and Mobilization in the Southern Thai Conflict." In *Radical Islamic Ideology in Southeast Asia*, edited by S. Helfstein, 74–95. West Point, NY: Combating Terrorism Center.

————. 2009b. *Islam, Education, and Reform in Southern Thailand: Tradition and Transformation*. Singapore: Institute of South East Asian Studies.

McCargo, Duncan J. 2006. "Thaksin and the Resurgence of Violence in the Thai South: Network Monarchy Strikes Back?" *Critical Asian Studies* 38 (1): 39–72.

————. 2008a. "Buddhist Democracy on Trial: Thailand's Southern Conflict." In *Religion and Democracy in Thailand*, edited by Imtiyaz Yusuf and Canan Atiligan, 62–79. Bangkok: Konrad-Adenauer-Stiftung.

————. 2008b. *Tearing Apart the Land: Islam and Legitimacy in Southern Thailand*. Ithaca, NY: Cornell University Press.

————. 2010a. "Autonomy for Southern Thailand: Thinking the Unthinkable?" *Pacific Affairs* 83 (2): 261–81.

————. 2010b. "Thailand's National Reconciliation Commission: A Flawed Response to the Southern Conflict." *Global Change, Peace, and Security* 22 (1): 75–91.

————. 2011. "Informal Citizens: Graduated Citizenship in Southern Thailand." *Ethnic and Racial Studies* 34 (5): 833–49.

————. 2012. "Patani Militant Leaflets and the Uses of History." In *The Ghosts of the Past in Southern Thailand: Essays on the History and Historiography of Patani*, edited by Patrick Jory, 277–98. Singapore: National University of Singapore Press.

Melvin, Neil J. 2007. *Conflict in Southern Thailand: Islamism, Violence, and the State in the Pattani Insurgency*. CIPRI Policy Paper no. 20. Stockholm: Stockholm International Peace Research Institute.

Muhammad Ilyas Yahprung. 2014. "Islamic Reform and Revivalism in Southern Thailand: A Critical Study of the Salafi Reform Movement of Shaykh Dr. Ismail Lutfi Chapakia Al-Fatani." PhD diss., International Islamic University of Malaysia.

National Reconciliation Commission. 2006. *Overcoming Violence with the Power of Reconciliation*. Bangkok: National Reconciliation Commission.

Nilsen, Marte. 2013. "Military Temples and Saffron-Robed Soldiers: Legitimacy and the Securing of Buddhism in Southern Thailand." In *Buddhism and Violence: Militarism and Buddhism in Modern Asia*, edited by Vladimir Tikhonov and Torkel Brekke, 37–53. London: Routledge.

Ockey, James. 2011. "Individual Imaginings: The Religio-Nationalist Pilgrimages of Haji Sulong Abdulkadir al-Fatani." *Journal of Southeast Asian Studies* 42 (1): 89–119.

Parks, Thomas I. 2009. "Maintaining Peace in a Neighbourhood Torn by Separatism: The Case of Satun Province in Southern Thailand." *Small Wars and Insurgencies* 20 (1): 185–202.

————. 2012. "The Last Holdout of an Integrated State: A Century of Resistance to State Penetration in Southern Thailand." In *Autonomy and Armed Separatism in South and Southeast Asia*, edited by Michelle Ann Miller. Singapore: Institute of South East Asian Studies.

Parks, Thomas, Nat Colletta, and Ben Oppenheim. 2013. *The Contested Corners of Asia: Subnational Conflict and International Development Assistance*. Bangkok: Asia Foundation.

Phrae Sirisakdamkoeng. 2012. "Perspectives of Thai Citizens in Virtual Communities on the Violence in the Southernmost Provinces." In *Mapping National Anxieties: Thailand's Southern Conflict*, edited by Duncan McCargo, 160–83. Copenhagen: Nordic Institute of Asian Studies Press.

Rappa, Antonio L., and Lionel Wee. 2006. *Language Policy and Modernity in Southeast Asia: Malaysia, the Philippines, Singapore, and Thailand.* Vol. 6 of *Language Policy*, edited by Bernard Spolsky and Elana Shohamy. New York: Springer.

Roy, Olivier. 2002. *Globalised Islam: The Search for a New Ummah.* London: C. Hurst.

Ruane, Joseph, and Jennifer Todd. 2010. "Ethnicity and Religion: Redefining the Research Agenda." *Ethnopolitics* 9 (1): 1–8.

Smalley, William A. 1994. *Linguistic Diversity and National Unity: Language Ecology in Thailand.* Chicago: University of Chicago Press.

Srisompob Jitpiromsri. 2014. "An Inconvenient Truth about the Deep South Violent Conflict: A Decade of Chaotic, Constrained Realities and Uncertain Resolution." DeepSouthWatch. http://www.deepsouthwatch.org/node/5904.

Srisompob Jitpiromsri and Duncan McCargo. 2008. "A Ministry for the South: New Governance Proposals for Thailand's Southern Region." *Contemporary Southeast Asia* 30 (3): 403–28.

Surin Pitsuwan. 1985. *Islam and Malay Nationalism: A Study of the Malay-Muslims of Southern Thailand.* Bangkok: Thai Khadi Research Institute.

Suwanna Satha-Anand. 2013. "Question of Violence in Thai Buddhism." In *Buddhism and Violence: Militarism and Buddhism in Modern Asia*, edited by Vladimir Tikhonov and Torkel Brekke, 175–93. London: Routledge.

Suwilai Premsrirat. 2005. "Thailand: Language Situation." In *Encyclopedia of Language and Linguistics*, edited by Keith Brown, 642–44. Oxford: Elsevier.

———. 2008. "Language for National Reconciliation: Southern Thailand." *EENET: Enabling Education* 12:16–17.

Suwilai Premsrirat and Uniansasmita Samoh. 2012. "Planning and Implementing Patani Malay in Bilingual Education in Southern Thailand." *Journal of the Southeast Asian Linguistics Society* 5:85–96.

Tikhonov, Vladimir, and Torkel Brekke, eds. 2013. *Buddhism and Violence: Militarism and Buddhism in Modern Asia.* London: Routledge.

Tripp, Emily. 2014. "Evaluating Religious or Linguistic Conflict through the State." *E-International Relations.* http://www.e-ir.info/2014/01/17/evaluating-religious-or-linguistic-conflict-through-the-state/.

Vail, Peter. 2006. "Can a Language of a Million Speakers Be Endangered? Language Shift and Apathy among Northern Khmer Speakers in Thailand." *International Journal of the Sociology of Language* 178:135–47.

———. 2007. "Thailand's Khmer as 'Invisible Minority': Language, Ethnicity, and Cultural Politics in North-Eastern Thailand." *Asian Ethnicity* 8 (2): 112–27.

Vail, Peter, and Panuwat Pantakod. 2013. "The Politics of Script: Language Rights, Heritage, and the Choice of Orthography for Khmer Vernaculars in Thailand."

In *Rights to Culture: Heritage, Language, and Community in Thailand*, edited by Coeli Barry, 135–62. Chiang Mai: Silkworm Books.

Wattana Sungunnasil. 2006. "Islam, Radicalism, and Violence in Southern Thailand: Berjihad di Patani and the 28 April 2004 Attacks." *Critical Asian Studies* 38 (1): 119–44.

Wilson, Hugh E. 1992. "Tengku Mahmud Mahyiddeen and the Dilemma of Partisan Duality." *Journal of Southeast Asian Studies* 23 (1): 37–59.

Woodward, Mark R., Muhammad Sani Umar, Inayah Rohmaniyah, and Mariani Yahya. 2014. "Salafi Violence and Sufi Tolerance? Rethinking Conventional Wisdom." *Perspectives on Terrorism* 7 (December). http://www.terrorismanalysts.com/pt/index.php/pot/article/view/311/html.

Yusuf, Imtiyaz. 1998. "Islam and Democracy in Thailand: Reforming the Office of the Chularajamontri/Shaikh Al-Islam." *Journal of Islamic Studies* 9 (2): 277–98.

———. 2007. *Faces of Islam in Southern Thailand.* Washington, DC: East-West Center.

———. 2010. "The Role of the Chularajamontri (Shaykh al-Islam) in Resolving Ethno-religious Conflict in Southern Thailand." *American Journal of Islamic Social Sciences* 27 (1): 31–53.

Resistance through Meditation: Hermits of King's Mountain in Northern Thailand

Shigeharu Tanabe

INTRODUCTION

As Achan Chayan's academic practices and numerous works have alluded to, one of the crucial aspects of critical scholarship in anthropology is to harness power, knowledge, and life experiences from the oppressed and marginalized peoples we study. In particular, his investigations have often directed scholars to locate and identify the potential of local knowledge put to use in the context of "everyday forms of resistance" among these peoples. One of his seminal works is titled "Phoei rang sang tua ton" (Declaring oneself HIV-infected, constructing oneself) (Chayan 1999). It deals with the ways in which people living with HIV from northern Thailand in the 1990s constructed a new identity, or "subject position," that was resistant to social sufferings and distress, which came through tenacious efforts to redefine meanings of the "HIV-infected" and establish self-help groups and networks in order to increase their potential and power to negotiate their position in a wider social space (also see Tanabe 2008a, 2008b). Achan Chayan's critical scholarship thus continuously provides insight into how people actualize their potential—hitherto covert or dispersed—in difficulties and crises in their everyday lives.

In appreciation of Achan Chayan's critical prospects in anthropology, this chapter tries to clarify how people practice Buddhist meditation to imagine and construct "what they could be" in order to evade complex power structures. Buddhist meditation primarily aims at pursuing nirvana (*nibbāna*), absolute liberation from earthly bondage, but it also seeks this-worldly ends such as healing, fortune telling, protection, invulnerability, and so on. Such pursuit of soteriological ends, particularly for many monks, hermits, and laypersons in northern Thailand, involves ways by which they transform themselves into others, or "become" (*devenir*) somebody or something else,[1] including a Buddha. In other words, the meditator devotes oneself to resistance to a variety of material and spiritual hardships and distress or even insanity in this world. This chapter investigates such resistance through meditation in the ethnographic accounts of the hermits who have recently developed a forest retreat at King's Mountain (Khao Phra Racha) in northern Thailand.[2]

This chapter first examines meditative practices by Phra Pho Pan and his colleagues at the King's Mountain retreat, particularly focusing on their way to meditation, including *samatha* and *vipassanā* methods. It also deals with a variety of their practices in relation to the soteriological ends and with their meditative experiences that lead to their own liberation and an increase of their own potential in this world. Subsequently, it discusses the hermits' experiences of meditation that lead to absorption, higher levels of consciousness through which they attain "becoming" something or somebody else. I examine this phenomenon—in particular, "becoming a Buddha" or an embodiment of a Buddha and *dhamma*—among the hermits on a wider background of traditional meditation technology, which seems to have some connection with the *yogāvacara* (*yokhawachon*) tradition in northern Thailand. Finally, this study tries to situate these meditative experiences and imaginations of the hermits within the context of constructing their own subjects resistant to suffering, distress, oppression, and the rationalized modern knowledge and its associated power structures.

THE WAY TO MEDITATION AT KING'S MOUNTAIN

Meditative Practices among the Hermits

Construction of the forest retreat was started in the mid-1990s by a

---

1. As to the concept of "becoming," see Deleuze and Guattari (1987, 291), and also Tanabe (2013), which deals with "becoming spirits" by spirit mediums in northern Thailand.

2. The historical background of the King's Mountain retreat and details about the practices by hermits and yogis are given in Tanabe (2016).

hermit named Phra Pho Pan. During the 1970s and 1980s, while he was simultaneously a Buddhist novice and a peasant leader, he established a utopian community by introducing the power and order derived from practicing *dhamma*. Having moved to King's Mountain in the late 1990s, he became a hermit to concentrate on meditation together with his colleagues. In early 2014 there were four resident male hermits, Pan, Hot, Smart, and White, who practiced meditation every day at the main hermitage; five resident female yogis recited sutras every evening (*suat mon yen*) before one of the main Buddha statues near the nunnery as well as practicing meditation sporadically.

The meditative practices they have adopted and appropriated consist of two different but practically connected methods: *samatha* (tranquility or concentration) and *vipassanā* (insight). *Samatha* is an extremely tranquil, peaceful, and lucid state of mind attained by strong mental concentration, focusing one's mind on a particular object— mainly one's own breathing. It aims at the attainment of the meditative absorptions (Thai, *chan*; Pali, *jhāna*), high degrees of tranquil concentration by which the meditator liberates his or her mind from impurities and inner obstacles and gives it greater penetrative strength. *Vipassanā*, on the other hand, aims at the attainment of insight-wisdom (*vipassanā paññā*) to expose the truth of impermanence (*anicca*), suffering (*dukkha*), and nonself (*anatta*), or the impersonal and unsubstantial nature of all phenomena of existence. Such insight can lead the meditator directly to stages of purification (*visudhi*); it does not choose any particular visible object of concentration like earth, water, fire, wind, and so on but intuitively makes direct observation of the fundamental nature of all phenomena.

Both tranquility and insight methods are basically not much different from the modern versions widely practiced among monks, novices, and lay followers in northern Thailand. It should be noted, however, that these widespread meditative practices that may be broadly called Lanna-style meditation (*kammathan Lanna*)[3] are

3. For details on Lanna-style meditation, see Swearer (1995), Sombun (n.d.), and Wirot (2014). Also useful is Kitchai's work that compares the practices of *yogāvacara* and the Thammakai meditation (Kitchai 2013). For more on texts for

different from modern meditative styles. The latter have mainly been derived from the modern Thammayut sect in Thailand since the mid-nineteenth century. These styles have also been strongly influenced by the Burmese meditation master Ledi Sayadaw and more strictly follow the fifth-century text *Visuddhimagga* (*The Path of Purification*) by Buddhaghosa (2010), a meditation master in Sri Lanka.

In northern Thailand, monks and laypeople for many centuries have written about the way to meditation (*witthi patibat kammathan*) in texts for practice in *tua tham*, or Lanna script. Therefore, it has been transmitted as discursive knowledge as a part of Buddhist teachings. For practitioners, meditative practices are, however, a type of practical knowledge that is transmitted as "situated learning" within a community of monks through a teacher-disciple relationship. In this sense, it is important to identify who is involved in teaching the meditative methods and how particular methods have been developed and transmitted to disciples and other people. With regard to this situated transmission, we should also note that meditative practices are a kind of technology that an actual practitioner learns through some modification and adaptation in order that each technical element will be appropriate to both mind and body. Bearing these issues in mind, I outline some of the major features of meditative practices currently conducted by Pan and other colleagues at the King's Mountain retreat:

1. Before commencing meditation, the meditator should maintain good mental and physical condition, be dressed neatly, and speak politely. At the liturgical ritual the meditator burns twenty-one incense sticks for the earth goddess (Mae Thorani) and sixteen sticks for the guardian spirit of the place (*chao thi chao thang*) and other guardian gods and devas.

2. Pan recommends that his disciples run around (*wing chong krom*) or walk around (*doen chong krom*) a designated site such as the pagoda or the reclining Buddha statue in the compound

---

meditative practices, inscribing *yan* (*yantra*), and related medical practices in diverse areas other than northern Thailand, see Chai (1936).

before sitting for meditation.[4] The meditation practiced by many *khubas* in the North, especially Khuba Sriwichai and Khuba Khao Pi in the early and mid-twentieth century, stressed the practice of slow circumambulating around Buddhist monuments, statues, and so on. Pan would normally assign his disciples to run around such sites one thousand times so that they can attain the state of absorption quicker or easier than starting to sit immediately for meditation. Normally it would take four hours to complete the running ritual.

3. After running or walking, the meditator sits in front of the Buddha statue and expresses respect for the five gems (not only the three gems in ordinary liturgical occasions): Buddha, *dhamma*, and sangha, plus the meditation subject (such as *samatha*, or diverse subjects in *vipassanā*) and the meditation teacher who supervises the meditator.[5]

4. Sitting in a meditation position, the meditator repeats verses in Pali and then holds the rosary, recollecting the Buddha by reciting (*phawana*): "*phuttho, phuttho*" (Buddha, Buddha), pronouncing "phut" while breathing in and "tho" while breathing out, and counts 108 beads of one rosary.[6]

5. After repeating recollection and counting beads many times, the meditator continues the journey of *samatha* toward the attainment of full ecstatic concentration (*appanā samādhi*). The meditator becomes detached from sensual objects and unwholesome consciousness, and enters the first absorption (*pathom chan*), and subsequently attains the second (*thutiya*

---

4. Buddhist precepts prohibit monks from running on any occasion, but there are a few monks who practice running *chong krom*. According to Hot, Luang Pho Pan at Wat Bang Nom Kho in Ayutthaya has long practiced running *chong krom*.

5. In Phannawong's text translated by Donald Swearer, the meditator prays for encountering the future Buddha, Ariya Mettrai: "May I have the opportunity to see the Maitreya (Pāli, Metteyya) Buddha" (Swearer 1995, 210). Sombun's text also includes prayers to Ariya Mettrai (Sombun n.d.).

6. In place of "*phuttho, phuttho*" the meditator says something like "*yup no phong no*" (breathe in, breathe out) or "*nang no, yuen no, doen no, non no*" (sit, stand, walk, lie down) in modern practices.

chan), the third (*tatiya chan*), and finally the fourth (*chatuttha chan*), which is a state beyond pleasure and pain. In the first and second absorptions, the meditator becomes filled with rapture (*piti*) and joy (*suk*),[7] while from the second absorption onward one gradually begins to gain tranquility, concentration, and oneness of mind through the power of the extraordinary virtue of the Buddha.

6. At the final stage of *samatha* meditation, through the disappearance of rapture, joy, and tranquility, one attains full concentration in the fourth absorption. Furthermore, the meditator can develop the way to *samatha* meditation, attaining the higher spiritual and supernormal powers (*aphinya, abhiññā*) such as magical powers, divine ear, divine eye, and so on.[8] The meditator can also proceed to *vipassanā* meditation, through which one intuitively exposes and gets insights into the truth of impermanence, suffering, and nonself through direct observation of one's own body and mind.

In order to give a concrete picture of the meditative practices, I focus, now, on the experiences of meditation and the associated practices by two practitioners of different generations: Pan and Hot, eighty-two and forty-seven years old, respectively, in 2014.

7. Pannawaong described the attainment of full concentration in his meditation text in the early twentieth century: "'Pervading rapture' fills the body with happiness, pervading the whole body in the same way as water flows into and fills ponds and rivers. Upon the arising of 'pervading rapture,' *upacāra samādhi* [access concentration] emerges. This samādhi suppresses the disorder and unrest of the mind, and the mental faculties function quite slowly. It is a stable, unshakable, and joyful state. The mind will rest firmly and tranquilly on one's chosen contemplation object. . . . Ecstasy trance (*appaṇā samādhi*) [full concentration] will not arise [without it]" (Swearer 1995, 212; brackets in the original).

8. Invulnerability (*kham*) is a protection technology to cope with an enemy's attacks during wars and rebellions. In northern Thailand it has been commonly regarded as a supernormal power gained through meditation in the absorption of *samatha* meditation (see Tanabe 1984; Turton 1991).

Pan: Meditation toward Politics of Loving-Kindness

Pan had long been the head of the hermitage since its establishment in 1997 until early 2014 when he moved to the pasture keeping cows, buffaloes, and horses called the Walled Palace of Cows and Buffaloes (*wang wiang ua khwai*), located in the Ban Mai Sawan, four-and-a-half kilometers southeast of King's Mountain. Pan established this Buddhist project for promoting loving-kindness (*metta*) and compassion (*karuna*) toward animals and enhancing symbiosis with them. His career of meditative practice spans nearly fifty years from the time when he participated at a retreat as a layman in the Huai Phueng Forest near the Huai Manao River area for three years in the mid-1960s. There he began to study Buddhist *dhamma* by himself with special reference to political justice and democracy. Pan was then the chief of irrigation management (*huana mueang fai*) at the Khun Khong System of the Mae Wang River. He then started meditation in the forest to find ways by which *dhamma* could contribute to solving irrigation conflicts among the farmers and, more generally, to relieving rural poverty in part caused by the local administration under the influence of local capitalists and corrupt government officials. Thus, from the beginning, his Buddhist interests and meditative practices were strongly concerned with politics based on *dhamma* and realizing a righteous rule in this world, especially among local peasantry.[9]

He was ordained as a novice for the second time in 1979 at the age of forty-seven at Wat Ban Mai Sawan in the utopian village of Ban Mai Sawan (New Heavenly Village), established by him in 1970. This made him maintain a position of half novice, half peasant leader—farmers referred to him as "wearing yellow, wearing black" (*nung lueang nung dam*) until the early 1990s when he retreated into the hermitage. In 1981, Pan often went alone into the Doi Saphan Yu hills near Ban Mai Sawan for meditation. Thereafter, his meditative experiences deepened and his commitment to involvement in political situations decreased accordingly. One day, during *samatha* meditation at night, he entered absorption and saw, as an image, a strong beam exposing the ruin of Wat Saphan Yu illuminated as a brilliant huge monastery. Pan

9. As to Pan's politics based on *dhamma*, see Cohen (1984) and Tanabe (2004).

interpreted this *nimit* (*nimitta*, a mental image or vision appearing during meditation) as a sign given to him and thus started the construction of a *phra bat* (the Buddha's footprint) and a *phra that* (a pagoda containing the Buddha's relics) at that site with support from the villagers of Ban Lao Pa Fang, in which the Wat Saphan Yu is located (see Tanabe 2004, 103–4).

One of the prominent features of the meditative practices of Pan and his colleagues is to stress the appearance of *nimit* during *samatha* meditation. As far as I know, his experience at Doi Saphan Yu is one of his early *nimit*. This *nimit*-led project has been followed by many others, including the construction of a new forest retreat at King's Mountain in the late 1990s, the recent project of the Walled Palace of Cows and Buffaloes, and so on. These omens and visions appearing during meditation are connected often to the images of various Buddhas and sometimes to the Buddhist structures and landscapes to be constructed or repaired (Tanabe 2004, 195–96; Cohen 2001, 235n35).

More specifically, some of Pan's *nimit* inspired the construction of Buddhist sites such as a pagoda (*phra that* or *chedi*) or monastery (*wihan*) through which he expects loving-kindness and compassion toward other humans and animals can be fostered and enhanced.[10] The construction of monasteries and pagodas during the past few decades at King's Mountain has provided good opportunities not only for merit-making (*tham bun*) but also for meditative practices among hermits, monks, novices, and laypeople involved in the projects.[11] At the site of construction, a community consisting of diverse groups including farmers, craftsmen, merchants, business owners, and different ethnicities from many parts of northern Thailand emerges to give donations and to engage in meditative practices and prayers. Pan always has high expectations for the deep affect of loving-kindness emerging among them, fostered by cooperation in the projects of

10. According to Pan, this should be promoted because Phra Sri Ariya Mettrai was already born into the heart of those who have loving-kindness (Tanabe 2016).

11. Khuba Phan, who succeeded the abbot of Wat Phraphuttabat Huai Tom in Li District of Lamphun from Khuba Chaiya Wong, told me of such experiences during the periods in which many construction projects were carried out by Khuba Sriwichai and Khuba Khao Pi in the early and mid-twentieth century.

construction and repairs. The ideals of loving-kindness and compassion are, for Pan and other hermits in the retreat, not an abstract notion but a social praxis through which the meditator can accept pain and agony of others as one's own. With such centrality of *nimit*-led projects based on meditative practices and of the associated politics of loving-kindness and compassion, the social praxes of Pan and his colleagues can be articulated with the historical figures of the *khuba* (venerable teachers) tradition in northern Thailand, represented by Khuba Sriwichai and Khuba Khao Pi.

Hot: From Patient to Healer

Hot was born in 1967 in the village of Pa Sang District, Lamphun. He had lived in Bangkok and southern Thailand and later moved to work for a few years at a Japanese factory in the Northern Industrial Estate, Lamphun, where he married a worker. Thereafter he learned magical lore (*wicha*) from his wife's father, the leader of laypeople (*achan wat*) of Wat Na Kuam Nuea located in Lampang. However, a few years later he divorced his wife and, in 2005, was ordained as a monk at Wat Na Kuam Nuea at the age of thirty-eight. He commenced meditative practices for the first time with a monk at that monastery. The first meditation was *vipassanā* on "the subject of impurity" (Thai, *asupha kammathan*; Pali, *asubha kammaṭṭhāna*) investigating hair, nails, teeth, skin, and so on of a corpse in order to gain insights into the impure. Later, during meditation he had a *nimit* of traveling by boat to a city near India with a long-haired, white-robed old man.[12]

Around that period Hot was hospitalized twice at a psychiatric hospital in Chiang Mai. After his recovery from his serious illness, he moved to Hot District of Chiang Mai and was diagnosed as having a mental disorder. Tulung Sawat, a senior monk at Wat Phrathat Up Kaeo Chamathewi, then suggested that he stay with Pan at King's Mountain. During the past ten years or so Pan has accommodated many mentally challenged people in the retreat for practicing *dhamma* together, providing an enabling environment for healing.

---

12. Pan later told Hot that the old man must be Khuba Khao Pi.

In 2009, Hot met Pan for the first time and lived in his retreat for eight months. Hot thus entered into the network of Pan, whose intention was to develop social praxes based on loving-kindness and compassion. In the early days at the retreat, he completed running *chong krom* more than twenty thousand times around the two pagodas over several weeks and inscribed sacred formulas (Thai, *yan*; Pali, *yantra*) on cloths for making sacred candles (*thian yan*) for Pan. He also participated in the ritual of "embodying the teacher" (*khrop khru*) conducted by Pan to encourage and give powers to the disciples practicing *dhamma* in the retreat. In this Brahmin rite, some participants trembled with the teacher's mystical power and with joy as Pan covered each one's head with the mask of a hermit (Tanabe 2016). After a few years' absence, in 2014 he returned to King's Mountain and succeeded Pan as the head of the retreat.

Hot is a master of meditation; he gained proficiency in entering absorption very quickly, and he can achieve this state within one or two minutes, like the northern Thai (*kham mueang*) saying, "An elephant folds down the ears, a snake flashes the tongue, a bird drinks water" (*chang phap hu ngu laep lin nok kin nam*). One of his crucial moments through meditation was when he gained the inspiration of a lifelong objective (*kham khuan*) to construct a monastery by tracing the footsteps of Khuba Khao Pi, Khuba Sriwichai, and Chao Mae Chamathewi (legendary queen of Hariphunchai kingdom at present-day Lamphun). It was not *nimit* as a visual image itself but "wisdom" (*paññā*) based on mental development when reaching the stage of full concentration (*appanā*). A *nimit* normally appears in a variety of stages during meditation even prior to absorptions. When one enters the first absorption, its frequency decreases and a *nimit* becomes a true one.[13] In terms of the experiences of Hot, *nimit* at the first, second, and third absorptions are mainly memories about the past; therefore, some meditators see *nimit* concerning their own previous lives (*adit chat*).

13. It is widely said that a *nimit* often appears at the early stages of *samatha* meditation for new practitioners. They should not be obsessed with such a *nimit* but should go further to attain higher levels of absorption. According to Hot, during the first, second, and third absorptions, most meditators see beams or flashes of lightning (*fa laep*), which mostly disappear at the fourth.

At the same time, however, a *nimit* and its associated sign and omen have been significantly connected to social praxes as exemplified in the *khuba* tradition in northern Thailand (Isara 2011; Tanabe 2016).[14]

For Hot, meditative practices and asceticism (*bamphen taba*) have occupied the heart of his life for a decade. His practice of meditation is in part related to coping with his own illness but is, following Pan's path, always articulated for the relief of others. Hot and the other hermits at the retreat hope that meditation leads not only to liberating themselves but also to becoming somebody who works for others. In short, these hermits try desperately to resist "what they are" and to become "what they could be" through meditation and asceticism. Hot explains more articulately that such a transforming process of meditation effectively leads to the solving of the meditator's own problems and is then used to solve the problems of others. Through practicing meditation he has recovered from mental illness and transformed himself into a meditation master. According to him, some *nimit* concerned with past lives were able to reveal the fortunes of others through investigation, and these *nimit* appeared during meditation. In this way, he has used his *nimit* for visitors and patients in fortune telling (*poet kam*) and found ways to cure or reverse fortunes (*kae kam*). This shows a twofold process of "becoming the other" in order to transform himself and "becoming a healer" in order to save others through meditation.[15]

BECOMING A BUDDHA
Embodiment of a Buddha
The Buddhist phenomenon of a sense of unity with a Buddha by meditating practitioners has been less examined in the Theravada tradition though much discussed in cases of its Mahayana counterpart. It is, however, evident that unity with a Buddha or embodiment of a Buddha has been widely observable in the Theravada tradition,

---

14. According to Pan and Hot, the *nimit*s which Khuba Khao Pi and Khuba Sriwichai saw were not at the lower levels of absorption but at the highest level, where they accomplished emptiness (*suññatā*) after having completed their attainments.

15. As to the similar processes of "becoming" in the case of spirit mediums, see Tanabe (2013).

particularly when we look at popular Buddhist practices in northern and other parts of Thailand, Laos, and Burma.

In order to give an outline of the embodiment of a Buddha, let me first cite an instance from the Mahayana tradition referred to by psychoanalyst Carl Jung. The concept and practice of the embodiment of a Buddha have long been developed in Mahayana tradition, as shown in the Buddhist sutra in Chinese "Amitāyur-dhyāna Sūtra" (Sutra of Meditation on Amitāyus, dating from AD 424). In this text the Buddha teaches a queen yoga meditation, which should enable her to attain rebirth in the brilliant Amitābha Land (Pure Land). Jung argues that *samādhi* (concentration) is withdrawn-ness, a condition in which all connections with this world are absorbed into the meditator's inner world (Jung [1958] 1969, 562). The sutra thus says, "In fine, it is your mind that becomes the Buddha, nay, it is your mind that is indeed the Buddha" (Ibid., 563).

As in the meditation on Amitāyus, the embodiment of a Buddha at King's Mountain exclusively relates to meditative processes, especially when the meditator attains absorptions. The meditators see a visual image of a Buddha as *nimit* within their bodies, normally while attaining inner tranquility and oneness of mind in the full concentration (*appanā samādhi*) of the fourth absorption, though in some cases even before such attainment. Hot points out that for the Buddha emerging in *nimit*, one should recite verses properly; while reciting "*phuttho, phuttho,*" counting beads, and closing one's eyes; anybody who sees *dhamma* can also see the Buddha, because the Buddha is within one's body.[16] Pannawong's text in the early twentieth century doesn't refer to the image of a Buddha as *nimit*. He meticulously describes, however, the meditator's inner experiences of embodying a Buddha in full concentration at the fourth absorption:

16. We should also pay attention to the fact that in northern Thailand and elsewhere some practitioners see an image of a statue within their body. Hot gives an instance of a meditator seeing a Buddha statue (Phra Sing Buddha) in his own body, referring to the case of Luang Pho Charan at Wat Amphawan in Singburi.

Fear and anxiety, shame and dread will be overcome as though the meditator were standing before the Buddha himself.[17] He will be unable to do wrong; his body will be a shrine of buddha virtues; he will be as worthy of worship as a reliquary. (Swearer 1995, 213)

We can also find instances of becoming a Buddha in a more material and corporeal fashion. Relevant at King's Mountain is the ritual of "embodying the Buddha" (khrop phut), which has long been performed by Pan. In this rite, like "embodying the teacher," already touched on before, Pan puts a small Buddha statue (Phra Sing Buddha, about twenty-five centimeters high) on the head of his disciples and visitors in order to transmit the virtue and power of the Buddha to their bodies. Another case relates to the changes that occur to the body of the meditator, whose aim is to attain "becoming a Buddha." Hot's experience is a case in point; when he gives blessing to visitors at the retreat, sometimes his voice is shaking, as if Chao Mae Kuan Im (a female Mahayana bodhisattva) is possessing him. When reciting a sutra or giving a blessing the voice of Hot becomes high-pitched or deep depending on the embodying Buddha or other figures (see Tanabe 2016).

In addition to the above cases from King's Mountain, we also pay attention to Thammakai (Dhammakāya) meditation, though there is no direct relation between the two. Thammakai meditation uses a crystal sphere to visualize as nimit, a mental image within the meditator's body, a kind of Buddha-quality, which allegedly exists inside everybody. The Thammakai Foundation has declared that Luang Pho Sot (Phra Mongkolthepmuni) at Wat Pak Nam in Bangkok discovered Thammakai meditation in the mid-twentieth century. He achieved a much deeper and purer level than others who used the crystal sphere visualization technique. According to Rory Mackenzie (2007, 111), Thammakai meditation seems to begin with a samatha method focusing of the mind on a crystal sphere and then gradually

---

17. One of the texts compiled by Wirot (2014, 43) contains a similar description of images of the Buddha appearing above the meditator's head or in front of his or her face.

acquires an inner image (*nimit*) of it as a bright light located within the meditator's body, two finger widths above the navel. In addition to this embodiment of the Buddha-quality, the Thammakai meditation includes a *vippasanā* method in which the meditator proceeds to gain insights into selected topics on the truth through direct meditative observation of one's own bodily and mental processes.

For some hermits and practitioners at and beyond King's Mountain, one of the most significant and celebrated topics concerns Pan himself becoming a Buddha, although he has never acknowledged or spread it.[18] As Hot gains insight, Pan has already become Phra Sri Ariya Mettrai, a future Buddha full of loving-kindness and compassion, or the Corps of Loving-Kindness (*kong thap metta*), which struggles to give relief to sufferers, the disadvantaged, and the oppressed.[19] As represented by Pan, becoming a Buddha is a struggle for transforming oneself into somebody or something else by incorporating a Buddha within one's body. The hermits in the retreat strive to attain "becoming a Buddha" through meditation and asceticism in order to negate the current conditions that determine their life circumstances, including impermanence, suffering, illness, oppression, and even the self (ego). Becoming is a struggle against their identity as poor peasants or laborers, sufferers, and so on, subjugated under the modern massive systems of control, capitalism, and the nation-state as a whole. Becoming a Buddha is not only the attainment of transforming oneself but also a way by which they try to rid themselves of such almost invincible systems, envisaging a terrain for creating their new lives (see Tanabe 2013).

18. In the 1970s and 1980s Pan raised his political idea of nonviolent struggle against "capitalists" (*nai thun*) and corrupt government officials based on Buddhist solidarity and justice among the peasantry. In that period the people around his village used to call him a "bodhisattva on horseback," supporting his nonviolent struggle (Cohen 1983, 106–7; Tanabe 2004, 210).

19. In Buddhist discourse, the "Corps of Loving-Kindness" is a collective force seeking to attain loving-kindness. So here it means that Phra Sri Ariya Mettrai (or Pan) represents such a force.

"Becoming a Buddha" and the Yogāvacara *Tradition*

Kate Crosby, in her recent work based on studies by François Bizot and others, argues that the philosophy and practices of the Theravada tradition in mainland Southeast Asia should be described as what she calls *yogāvacara*, or Lance Cousins's (1997, 185) "esoteric Buddhism," in that it is far removed from the modern rationalistic and monolithic Theravada as long understood by many scholars (Crosby 2000, 141).

Yogāvacara (*yokhawachon*), or "practitioner of spiritual discipline," is not a relic, still living in many aspects of Buddhism in northern Thailand and beyond,[20] some of which constitute a main feature of practices among the hermits of King's Mountain. Within the eleven major features of the *yogāvacara* tradition that Crosby points out, I can identify several prominent ones as directly relevant to the practices of the hermits: first, the creation of a Buddha within through the ritual of placing and recognizing within one's body the qualities of the Buddha, which in turn become the Buddha; second, the use of sacred syllables or phrases to represent a larger entity as exemplified by spells (Thai, *mon*; Pali, *mantra*) and sacred scripts composed of heart syllables (Thai, *yan*; Pali, *yantra*), mostly derived from the names of Buddhas and sutras;[21] third, the significance of the embodiment of a Buddha and the sacred syllables or phrases to both soteriological ends (i.e., the pursuit of nirvana and this-worldly ends, such as healing, longevity, protection, invincibility, and potentially the harming of others); and finally, the importance of *samatha* and *vipassanā* meditation, although these are not interpreted as they are in Buddhaghosa's *Visuddhimagga* (Crosby 2000, 142–43; Buddhaghosa 2010). I have so far discussed all these features recognized among the hermits in some ways, especially diverse forms of the embodiment of a Buddha. In this way, the practices and

---

20. Justin McDaniel, who describes chanting of the protective texts such as *chinnabanchon* (*caiyabengchon, jinapañjara*), argues that *yogāvacara* is a vague and broad term that is generally not found in texts or stated explicitly by most Thai practitioners (McDaniel 2011, 107). However, in many Lanna-style meditation texts in northern Thailand, most sections begin with the address to *yokhawacon*. For instance, see Wirot (2014) and Sombun (n.d.).

21. As to Pan's spells and sacred scripts, see Tanabe 2004 (147–52). The related topics will be dealt with in another paper in preparation.

their background knowledge and philosophy among the hermits are recognizably common to Crosby's *yogāvacara* tradition.[22] This means that techniques related to "becoming a Buddha" as practiced at King's Mountain are not isolated but belong to the wider Theravada tradition that extends to northern and northeastern Thailand and beyond and tends to have been neglected under the domination of the modern and rationalized Theravada Buddhism of the reformist Thammayut movement since the nineteenth century.

RESISTANCE THROUGH MEDITATION
Resistance through Subjugated Knowledge

The meditation practiced at King's Mountain is a means of incorporating *dhamma* and a Buddha into a meditator's body in order to bring about absolute extinction of the life-affirming will and ultimate deliverance from rebirth, old age, death, and suffering, finally leading to nirvana. It is, however, also assumed to enhance the internal "intensity" of bodily and mental resistance to external powers, including enemies, diseases, disasters, evil spirits, and—above all—political repression. This aspect of meditation is often articulated with this-worldly practices of magic, healing, fortune telling, protection, invulnerability, and so on, as I have indicated in the cases of Pan and Hot. Such meditation-related practices, which may be based on the so-called *yogāvacara* tradition, have long been local knowledge struggling against centralized, modernized knowledge and its associated power structures such as the nation-state and the modern state sangha. The resistant aspects of meditation in social contexts could be best exemplified by the social movements in the early and mid-twentieth century led by Khuba Sriwichai and Khuba Khao Pi. Such resistance can be called, to use Michel Foucault's (1980, 81) term, "an insurrection of subjugated knowledge." It is through such meditative practices and the associated absorptions, imaginations, and visions that the

---

22. The hermits (including Pan and Hot) at the retreat have accumulated a variety of knowledge about meditation including those referred to in *Visuddhimagga* or more modernized versions such as that of Piyadhassi's *Vimuttidhamma* (2011). It would be, however, important to note that they still cling to the "traditional" in favor of the *khuba* predecessors.

hermits of King's Mountain could construct and polish their own "subject" resistant to newly developed political and economic environments, such as the flux of global capitalism and rationalized modern knowledge and practices.

This being so, it is worthwhile to locate such subject construction by Buddhist meditation in comparison to the Western tradition, especially in the context formulated by Foucault and Gilles Deleuze. As Deleuze argues, whereas Western meditation or related cultivation practices have focused on the construction of the "subject" resistant to outside powers, the meditative practices in East and Southeast Asia have tried to extinguish self and become nonself (*anatta*). For many scholars, including Deleuze, these seemingly contrasting processes have been obstacles to understanding what Buddhist meditative practices actually accomplish in the end. Here I only cite Deleuze's rather delusive argument referring to such Asian asceticism in relation to Foucault's mode of "subjectivation" (*asujettissement*):[23]

Perhaps the Orient does not present such a phenomenon, and the line of the outside continues to float across a stifling hollowness; in that case asceticism would be a culture of annihilation [nirvana] or an effort to breathe in such a void, without any particular production of subjectivity. (Deleuze 1988, 106)[24]

On the contrary, we should, however, understand that "subjectivation" in the mind and body is attained, in Buddhist terms, through extinguishing obsession with the self (*attan*). My concern here is to clarify the processes of "subjectivation" in the *samatha* and *vippasanā* methods historically and currently practiced by many *khuba*s and hermits in northern Thailand. As such, the "becoming others" and "becoming a Buddha," as observable at King's Mountain and in other cases, is

23. While earlier English works often translated *asujettissement* as "subjugation," now most works translate this neologism as "subjectivation" following Foucault's more positive usage.

24. A note follows: "The question would be: is there a Self or a process of subjectivation in Oriental techniques?" (Deleuze 1988, 148n30). However, Deleuze himself doesn't seem to be able to answer such a question.

exactly a product of "subjectivation," which enables practitioners to resist power structures such as the sangha, the nation-state, and the modern individualization of subjects.

"An Island unto Oneself"

If we devote our attention to the Foucauldian "subjectivation" through meditation, we have to distinguish the two meanings of "subject": the first is subject to someone else by control and dependence, and the second is tied to a person's own identity by conscience or self-knowledge (Foucault 1982, 212). As such, a crucial point here is how the latter emerges through meditation. Meditation is, theoretically, a means to attain the ultimate goal of nonself and nirvana, but it is, more importantly, a means to work on the individual's own ways of life, body, and spirit so as to transform oneself. It is what Foucault aptly called "technologies of the self"[25] as he examines the Western cultivation methods as follows:

> [T]echnologies of the self… permit individuals to effect by their own means, or with the help of others, a certain number of operations on their own bodies and souls, thoughts, conduct, and way of being, so as to transform themselves in order to attain a certain state of happiness, purity, wisdom, perfection, or immortality. (Foucault 1997, 225)

Pan has always activated and manipulated a variety of "technologies of the self" to create his own subject embodying loving-kindness and compassion. His self-knowledge has firmly clung to Phra Sri Ariya Mettrai, a future Buddha, or the ideal of a compassionate bodhisattva (enlightened being) who is, still remaining in this world, exclusively concerned with saving all humans and all living things. According to Pan, Ariya Mettrai has not realized the path of holiness (*arahat*) but attained only the first and second absorptions in meditation because he is much more concerned with saving people by remaining a bodhisattva than by becoming a "holy man" or "living Buddhist saint"

25. What Crosby (2013, 7–8) has called "'technology of transformation" might correspond, in part, with the Foucauldian formulation.

(*arahat*) like Achan Man Phurithatto in northeastern Thailand during the twentieth century. In this sense, through becoming Ariya Mettrai, Pan has created his own active subjectivity by sustaining "pathos"— like Nietzsche's "will to power"—to remain poor, aiming at saving people (see Tanabe 2004, 131–32; also Tanabe 2013, 184).

In the Buddhist context, the "technologies of the self" are definitely connected with the self, which should be extinguished in the processes of "mental development" (Thai, *phawana*; Pali, *bhāvanā*). The Buddha gave the teachings about such processes to his close disciple Ananda toward the end of his life, as narrated in "Mahā-parinibbāna Sutta" (Last Days of the Buddha). The Buddha talked about processes of contemplation on the body, feelings, mind, and mental objects, after having overcome desire and sorrow in regard to this world, and he revealed the way by which a monk would be able to construct his own subject as "an island unto himself":

> [T]hen, truly, he is an island unto himself [*attadīpā*], a refuge unto himself, seeking no external refuge; having the Dhamma as his island, the Dhamma as his refuge, seeking no other refuge. ("Mahā-parinibbāna Sutta" 1998, 34)

In the context of the Buddha's teachings above, nonself (*anatta*) is to be attained through the meditative practices to negate, relieve, and transcend the self (ego) so as to create one's own subject. It is created as "an island unto oneself" or "refuge," enabling one to fulfill all responsibility for one's own conduct and karma (*kam*). In this way, the attainment of nonself is not merely to extinguish one's self or ego in a "culture of annihilation" (i.e., nirvana), but more significantly to construct one's ethical subject to steer one's own conduct toward personal and social objectives in an active and flexible fashion. What should be noted then is the case of hermits. Given that monks within the sangha normally form such a single and unified subject within the monastic order, each hermit of King's Mountain is allowed to constitute even multiple and different subjects. The subject is constructed of multiple parts; it is not an unchangeable, fixed single subject in accordance with a hermit's ever-changing situated position, such as a sufferer, meditator, healer, farmer, political activist, or other role. It is under hermits' privileged and heterodoxical—some might even deem it heretical—position with considerable freedom and seclusion that they are able to pursue their own ways to *dhamma* as a bodhisattva, healer, or farmer.

CONCLUSIONS

One of the major points emerging out of this chapter concerns resistance to the present state of affairs among hermits through meditative practices. Becoming others—particularly, becoming a Buddha—is such an attempt at transforming one's self into something close to the Buddha by incorporating it or its Buddha-quality into one's body. The hermits at the retreat try to attain, consciously or unconsciously, "becoming a Buddha" through meditation and asceticism, hoping to create new subjects governing their own bodies and minds. As a result, such subjects would be capable of negating their deteriorating life circumstances including suffering, illness, oppression, insanity, and even their own selves. For the hermits, becoming a Buddha by meditation is nothing other than resistance to diverse material and spiritual hardships and distress—in short, against the power structures in existential, religious, economic, or political terms in contemporary society.

In this connection, the *samatha* meditation practiced by the hermits is extremely interesting because it brings out one's cognitive potential, hitherto unnoticed, when facing personal and social problems. The *samatha* processes consisting of the intense focus of the mind on a particular object, subsequent emergence of inner images (*nimit*), and full concentration are sometimes articulated with social praxes by the meditator as a newly created subject. In a broad sense, *samatha* is a way of creating, to use the Bergsonian-Deleuzian term, the interior "intensity" of body and mind, which could subsequently be actualized as "extensive" (therefore visible) powers. Such powers could be utilized to solve problems, possibly combined with insights into a variety of personal and social phenomena that are gained through *vipassanā* meditation. Such practical implications of meditation are often emphasized by Pan as well: "King's Mountain is not like ordinary universities, which pursue only progress [*kao*], but a university for cultivating wisdom [*sati pañña*] to work out [*kae*] problems and contradictions that humans could hardly solve before."

The King's Mountain retreat, where meditation and asceticism as knowledge and practice are pursued by the hermits, is a space for fundamental resistance to the present, or moving from "what we are" toward envisaging "what we could be." It is an alternative space to develop a variety of "subjects," where, for instance, Pan materializes politics of loving-kindness and compassion by "becoming Phra Sri Ariya Mettrai" and Hot accomplishes "becoming a healer" after having overcome his own problem. As such, the politics of loving-kindness and compassion is flourishing among the hermits, partly because of a relative autonomy from intervention by the outside monastic order and administrative institutions. But we have to pay more attention to the fact that it has always been connected to the outside world through a fairly large number of visitors and the extensive networks of monks and hermits reaching to other parts of Thailand and beyond.

More than thirty years ago, Charles Keyes described how Khuba Sriwichai's position as a "savior-saint" following a bodhisattva ideal contrasted strongly with another pole—that of Achan Man as *arahat* (Keyes 1982, 156). The politics of loving-kindness and compassion has long been embedded with the *khuba* tradition, as embodied by Khuba Sriwichai and Khuba Khao Pi. Resistance to the present has intrinsically been connected with the politics of loving-kindness in Lanna Buddhism. In focusing especially on the hermits of King's Mountain, this chapter has tried to reveal that such politics is articulated with and activated from meditative practices and other related "technologies of the self."

REFERENCES

Buddhaghosa, Bhadantacariya. (1956) 2010. *The Path of Purification (Visuddhimagga)*. Translated by Bhikkhu Nanamoli. Kandy: Buddhist Publication Society.

Chai Yasotharat, Phra Maha. 1936. *Nangsue phuttharangsi thritsadi yan wa duai samatha lae wipatsana kammatthan si yuk* [A book of *samatha* and *vipassanā* meditation of four eras]. Bangkok: Wat Boromniwat.

Chayan Vaddhanaphuti. 1999. "Phoei rang sang tua ton: Kan khluean wai thang sangkhom khong klum phu tit chuea HIV" [Declaring oneself HIV-infected, constructing oneself: Social movements of HIV-infected peoples]. Paper presented at annual conference of the Faculty of Social Sciences, Chiang Mai University.

Cohen, Paul. 1983. "A Bodhisattva on Horseback: Buddhist Ethics and Pragmatism in Northern Thailand." *Mankind* 14 (2): 101–11.

————. 1984. "The Sovereignty of the Dhamma and Economic Development: Buddhist Social Ethics in Northern Thailand." *Journal of the Siam Society* 72:197–211.

————. 2001. "Buddhism Unshackled: The Yuan 'Holy Man' Tradition and the Nation-State in the Tai World." *Journal of Southeast Asian Studies* 32 (2): 227–47.

Cousins, Lance. 1997. "Aspects of Southern Esoteric Buddhism." In *Indian Insights: Buddhism, Brahmanism and Bhakti: Papers from the Annual Spalding Symposium on Indian Religions*, edited by Peter Connolly and Sue Hamilton. London: Luzac Oriental.

Crosby, Kate. 2000. "Tantric Theravāda: A Bibliographic Essay on the Writings of François Bizot and Others on the *Yogāvacara* Tradition." *Contemporary Buddhism: An Interdisciplinary Journal* 1 (2): 141–98.

————. 2013. *Traditional Theravāda Meditation and Its Modern-Era Suppression.* Hong Kong: The Buddha-Dharma Centre of Hong Kong.

Deleuze, Gilles. (1986) 1988. *Foucault.* Translated by Seán Hand. Minneapolis: University of Minnesota Press.

Deleuze, Gilles, and Félix Guattari. (1980) 1987. *A Thousand Plateaus: Capitalism and Schizophrenia.* Translated by Brian Massumi. London: Athlone Press.

Foucault, Michel. 1980. "Two Lectures." In *Power/Knowledge: Selected Interviews and Other Writings, 1972–1977*, edited by Colin Gordon, 78–108. Brighton, Sussex: Harvester Press.

————. 1982. "The Subject and Power." In *Michel Foucault: Beyond Structuralism and Hermeneutics*, by Hubert L. Dreyfus and Paul Rabinow, 208–26. Brighton, Sussex: Harvester Press.

————. (1994) 1997. "Technologies of the Self." In *Ethics: Subjectivity and Truth.* Vol. 1 of *Essential Works of Foucault, 1954–1984*, edited by Paul Rabinow. New York: New Press.

Isara Treesahakiat. 2011. "The Significance of Khruba Sriwichai's Role in Northern Thai Buddhism: His Sacred Biography, Meditation Practice and Influence." MA thesis, University of Otago, New Zealand.

Jung, Carl G. (1958) 1969. "The Psychology of Eastern Meditation." In *Psychology and Religion: West and East*, translated by R. F. C. Hull. Princeton, NJ: Princeton University Press.

Keyes, Charles F. 1982. "Death of Two Buddhist Saints in Thailand." In "Charisma and Sacred Biography," edited by Michael A. Williams, special issue, *Journal of the American Academy of Religion*, Thematic Studies 48 (3/4): 149–80.

Kitchai Urkasame. 2013. *Samathi phawana nai khamphi akson tham* [Meditation in *tham* alphabet manuscripts]. Sydney: Dhammachai International Research Institute.

Mackenzie, Rory. 2007. *New Buddhist Movements in Thailand: Towards an Understanding of Wat Phra Dhammakāya and Santi Asoke.* London: Routledge.

"Mahā-parinibbāna Sutta: Last Days of the Buddha." 1998. In *Digha Nikaya* 16, Pali Text Society: D ii 72, chapters 1–6. Translated from the Pali by Sister Vajira and Francis Story. http://www.accesstoinsight.org/tipitaka/dn/dn.16.1-6.vaji.html.

McDaniel, Justin. 2011. *The Lovelorn Ghost and the Magical Monk: Practicing Buddhism in Modern Thailand.* New York: Columbia University Press.

Piyadhassi, Bhikkhu. 2011. *Vimuttidhamma: From Chakra to Dhammachakra.* Chiang Mai: Dhamma Publication Fund, Wat Tam Doi Tone. Also available in Thai.

Sombun Kanthasilo, Bhikkhu. n.d. "Nangsue samatha kammathan phawana lae wipatsana" [Book on tranquility, mental development, and insight]. Translated by Phaithoon Dokbuakaew. Palm leaf manuscript held at the Social Research Institute, Chiang Mai University.

Swearer, Donald. 1995. "The Way to Meditation." In *Buddhism in Practice*, edited by Donald Lopez. Princeton, NJ: Princeton University Press.

Tanabe, Shigeharu. 1984. "Ideological Practice in Peasant Rebellions: Siam at the Turn of the Twentieth Century." In *History and Peasant Consciousness in South East Asia*, edited by Andrew Turton and Shigeharu Tanabe, 75–110. Senri Ethnological Studies 13.

———. (1986) 2004. *Nung lueang nung dam: tamnan khong phu nam chao na heang Lannathai* [Wearing yellow, wearing black: The story of a peasant leader in northern Thailand]. Bangkok: Chulalongkorn University Press.

———. 2008a. "Suffering, Community, and Self-Government: HIV/AIDS Self-Help Groups in Northern Thailand." In *Imagining Communities in Thailand*, edited by Shigeharu Tanabe. Chiang Mai: Mekong Press.

———. 2008b. *Chumchon kap kan pokkhrong chiwayan: klum phu tit chuea HIV nai phak nuea khong thai* [Community and governmentality: HIV self-help groups in northern Thailand]. Bangkok: Sirindhorn Anthropology Centre.

———. 2013. "Spirit Mediumship and Affective Contact in Northern Thailand." In *Duai Rak: Essays on Thailand's Economy and Society for Professor Chatthip Nartsupha at 72*, edited by Pasuk Phongpaichit and Chris Baker. Bangkok: Sangsan.

———. 2016. "Hermits of King's Mountain: A Buddhist Utopian Movement in Northern Thailand." In *Communities of Potential: Social Assemblages in Thailand and Beyond*, edited by Shigeharu Tanabe. Chiang Mai: Silkworm Books.

Turton, Andrew. 1991. "Invulnerability and Local Knowledge." In *Thai Constructions of Knowledge*, edited by Manas Chitakasem and Andrew Turton. London: School of Oriental and African Studies.

Wirot Inthanon, ed. 2014. *Bot suat lae withi pathibat kammathan Lanna* [Mantra and methods of meditative practices in Lanna]. Chiang Mai: Department of Philosophy and Religion, Faculty of Humanities, Chiang Mai University.

Part 3

Scholarly Activism in the Greater Mekong Subregion

"Learning Across Boundaries": Grantmaking Activism in the Greater Mekong Subregion

Rosalia Sciortino

INTRODUCTION

This article reflects on "Learning Across Boundaries in the Greater Mekong Subregion," a grantmaking initiative managed by the Southeast Asia Regional Office of the Rockefeller Foundation during the years 2001–7, and its significance for current debates in philanthropy and development. LAB,[1] as the initiative was commonly called, responded to concern that a large proportion of people in the Greater Mekong Subregion (GMS) were excluded from the benefits of regional growth. To foster more equitable development, it funded collaborative efforts to understand transnational processes and address their effects on the poor and vulnerable.

In a short time, LAB acquired a reputation for its innovativeness. It was not allowed to come to full fruition, however, because of changes at the Rockefeller Foundation that, I argue, reflect a general shift among philanthropies away from contextual and socially engaged grantmaking following the rise of the so-called technocratic philanthropists, philanthrocapitalists, or venture philanthropists. These philanthropic individuals and institutions—foremost among them the Bill and Melinda Gates Foundation—take multinational corporations as their model and seek market and technological solutions

---

1. References to LAB are based on annual reports, grant reports, and program documents written by the author at times with her colleagues in the fulfillment of institutional requirements, as well as external evaluations during and after her assignment.

to development problems. In doing so, they have come to dismiss the "humanistic philanthropy"[2] of the 1990s and early 2000s, to which LAB can be considered to belong, and its stress on social and cultural processes, contexts, and solutions. LAB's premature closure thus exposed a paradigmatic tension between development discourses that, as will be explained in more detail below, have been around in various manifestations since the 1950s and remain contentious to this day.

After a brief description of the overall strategy, I will examine three of LAB's core aspects that distinguished it from the philanthropic and development approaches most in vogue today. First, I will highlight LAB's regional scope, which contrasts with the national and global models privileged by international funders. Second, I will show that LAB's aim to understand and address the social impact of inequitable regional integration positioned it as an alternative to a development discourse preoccupied with market-oriented infrastructural and technocratic processes. Third, I will argue that from this LAB opted for social sciences, capacity-building, and academic activism on the side of disadvantaged groups, rather than the focus on natural sciences and academic excellence that has become more common in philanthropy today.

My reflections, though based on primary documents and secondary literature, nevertheless remain subjective, since they are derived from my earlier role as regional director of the Rockefeller Foundation's Southeast Asia Office and as the conceiver of LAB, and to a lesser extent from my experience with the Ford Foundation, Australian Agency for International Development (AusAID), and International Development Research Centre (IDRC), also in Southeast Asia.[3] In the

2. The terms "technocratic" and "humanistic" philanthropy are used in the remainder of the chapter to point to two distinctive paradigms, in line with recent literature and for lack of better nomenclature. It also needs to be noted that the paradigms and the terms associated with them exist alongside each other, but their influence varies at different points in time. As this chapter argues, the technocratic paradigm, which started to emerge fifteen years ago and has become dominant in the last decade, can actually be seen as a rebranding of an older "modernization" paradigm, in spite of its being heralded as "new."

3. More specifically I worked for the Ford Foundation Office in Indonesia and

following, I will not attempt to provide a complete overview or assessment of the program. Rather, I will try to articulate an insider's conviction that to be relevant, grantmaking ought to be responsive to specific geopolitical and developmental contexts and to support alternative visions and voices that would be otherwise ignored.

LAB IN BRIEF

With the hiring of a regional director in 2000, the Rockefeller Foundation signaled its intention to build a presence in Asia. My mandate was to establish a Southeast Asia regional office in Bangkok and to develop, with the assistance of the only senior specialist based there, John O'Toole, a regional program responsive to local realities. Through a year of consultation with a wide range of stakeholders, we learned of their concern with the increasing pace of regionalization and the far-reaching transnational impact it was having on previously isolated countries and communities. At the same time, the required capacity to address this growing interdependency was poorly developed locally, and the few Japanese, European, and US foundations that focused on social development did so in selected countries or without focusing on the GMS as an emerging geopolitical zone. The production of knowledge and the building of capacity to better cope with regionalism were thus identified as a potential niche for the Rockefeller Foundation's Southeast Asia Regional Program, to be managed from Bangkok.

The problematic sketched by the program officers focused on the regionalization process involving countries along the Mekong River—namely, Cambodia, Laos, Myanmar, Thailand, Vietnam, and China's Yunnan Province.[4] Taking advantage of the opening up of socialist countries, in 1992 the Asian Development Bank (ADB) and other donors, in collaboration with the concerned governments, had

---

the Philippines in 1993–2000, was the Rockefeller Foundation's regional director for Southeast Asia in 2000–2007, was senior adviser for AusAID in 2009–10, and served as the IDRC regional director/representative for Southeast and East Asia in 2010–14.

4. In 2005, on request from China, Guangxi Province was also included, although it is not technically in the Mekong River basin.

launched an ambitious regional cooperation program to strengthen the competitive position of what the bank came to call the Greater Mekong Subregion as a trading bloc in the global economy (ADB 2015). The GMS Economic Cooperation Program supported market liberalization and infrastructural development to foster transnational trade, investment, and exploitation of natural resources.

The GMS vision enabled strong economic growth, but—as the foundation's staff argued to the board of trustees in 2002—not everybody benefited from it in equal measure. Relative poverty across groups and countries was increasing, and more than a third of the combined population of roughly 240 million people at that time remained in absolute poverty. Also there was no attention to the profound social changes transforming predominantly subsistence-farming societies into market-oriented ones, with unparalleled degrees of urbanization and industrialization challenging existing lifestyles and cultures. Mounting demands on shared resources were disrupting delicate environments, and lopsided development was creating unprecedented flows of people, diseases, and crime across borders. In particular, communities along the borders, and cross-border migrants, who often belonged to ethnic and religious minority groups, were becoming further marginalized.

To emphasize the confluence of geopolitical and cultural factors in shaping marginalization and poverty, the Rockefeller Foundation's Bangkok office staff focused on the concept of "boundaries" as central to regional programming. The choice of "Learning Across Boundaries in the Greater Mekong Subregion" as the title of the program strategy was meant to suggest that transboundary trends cannot be dealt with in isolation and that a collective process was needed to capture the benefits and mitigate the negative side effects of regionalization. LAB therefore privileged collaborations among institutions and individuals in the region that would contribute to (1) understanding and anticipating cross-border and intercultural challenges arising from regional integration, especially as they affect the poor and excluded; and (2) formulating effective policy and intervention responses directed at improving the welfare of disadvantaged groups and fostering greater equity in the region.

While LAB's grantmaking strategy focused on regional integration in its complexity, it also served as a platform for specific initiatives that leveraged the Rockefeller Foundation's expertise in the thematic areas of health, food security, and culture. More specifically, Cross-Border Health (CBH) was directed at stemming the cross-border flow of diseases (principally AIDS, TB, malaria, dengue fever, and later SARS and avian influenza/H5N1), while enabling protection of vulnerable mobile and ethnic minority populations. Upland Communities in Transition (UCT) aimed to increase agricultural production in upland areas along the borders and to foster access to regional markets in order to improve the lives of upland ethnic minorities. And Bridging Diversity (BD) sought to enhance appreciation of the region's diversity, while aiming to reduce sectarian and discriminatory tendencies against ethnic and migrant groups arising in the context of regional integration.[5]

In operational terms, LAB combined four lines of grantmaking. One line concerned *knowledge building,* with grants that supported the study of regional dynamics through joint projects among institutions in the region. A second line supported *human and institutional capacity building,* with grants that enabled interinstitutional learning, expansion of institutional resources across GMS countries, and establishment of regional centers. Another important line of work focused on *agenda setting,* with grants that fostered the public's and policy makers' awareness of transboundary trends and potential responses. Finally, the fourth line of grantmaking supported *experimentation,* with grants that financed the development and cross-fertilization of alternative program models for more equitable GMS development in the previously described thematic areas of concern.

LAB's expansion was rapid, and by 2007 program staff had increased to four officers who, since the start of the regional program, had managed more than two hundred grants, mostly to local organizations, for a total of over thirty-five million dollars, including contributions from the foundation's thematic programs mentioned above. In the course of programming, our initial insights were confirmed and LAB's

---

5. The internal collaborations were for CBH with the Health Equity program, for UCT with Food Security, and for BD with Creativity and Culture.

critical role in filling a gap was increasingly recognized. The strategy itself had begun inspiring other institutions, including Thai government units and some UN agencies and bilateral donors, to consider transnational approaches to regionalization and to pay more attention to social development challenges and equity concerns. Cross-border health and migration, two of the issues advocated by LAB as requiring a regional focus, came to be seen as priorities for intergovernmental collaboration. More generally, the critical views and voices of those supported by the foundation had started to gain credibility in policy debates.

Some interesting lessons also began to emerge on appropriate governance mechanisms for processes of a regional and transnational nature and on the added value of cross-border and multisectoral collaborations—despite high transaction costs. As indicated by the increasing number and quality of funding requests, visits to the Bangkok office's website, use of publications and audiovisual media produced by grantees, and media reports on grant-supported activities, LAB had managed to raise the Rockefeller Foundation's profile in the region and, most importantly, generated interest in the issues promoted. The attractiveness of LAB as a platform for change was also shown by the increasing number of governmental and nongovernmental organizations wanting to partner with their own resources in LAB-initiated activities and the growing amount of funding "leveraged" from other foundations, aid agencies, and private sponsors.

This promising trajectory was interrupted by a transition at the helm of the Rockefeller Foundation in 2005. The new president's decision to restructure and centralize programming led to the closure of regional programs, both in Africa and Southeast Asia, and to a preference for global initiatives to be applied uniformly across the world. In spite of congratulatory internal assessments, a positive external evaluation commissioned by the new management from an independent US-based philanthropy center, support by leading institutions and experts, and the encouragement of partners, LAB was closed in 2007. To complete ongoing efforts, so-called "legacy" grants were given, with activities ending a few years thereafter.[6] The few selected grantees that continued to be supported had to fulfill prescribed mandates to fit the new global initiatives. With the adoption of a decontextualized, top-down approach characteristic, as I will argue below, of then-emerging trends in philanthropy, there was no longer space for a tailor-made initiative like LAB, grown out of a specific geopolitical context with its unique development challenges.

A REGIONAL VIS-À-VIS A NATIONAL OR GLOBAL GRANTMAKING APPROACH

LAB's premise was that as nations and markets become more interconnected and more complex, development programs ought to take into account regional dynamics, their transnational and cross-cultural ramifications, and their impact on vulnerable groups.

This approach was grounded in principles common to philanthropic institutions in the 1990s but applied them to a different geopolitical unit. During that decade, due to a combination of political and ideological factors, international grantmaking by American foundations had grown rapidly and had become increasingly context-specific (Renz and Samson-Atienza 1997, 3). As funders gained greater access to emerging democracies and a growing civil-society movement globally, they became more diversified and localized, with funding priorities set according to location and in consultation with local stakeholders. Although donor influence is inherent in the unequal grantee-grantor relationship, particularly when it plays out in resource-scarce settings, foundations did make a serious effort to confer widely and to be participatory in formulating context-specific strategies. They also subscribed to the principle of "local ownership of local problems" and sought to fund local organizations with the assumption that they were best positioned to find systemic solutions to complex societal problems (Renz and Samson-Atienza 1997, 3–6).

6. Another external review of all the LAB grants including the legacy grants was conducted in later years when the original staff, including the author, had already left. The findings were again positive but did not reverse the decision to close the regional program. This may raise questions as to the use of evaluation and the much-heralded value of so-called evidence-based accountability.

For those foundations that had field offices abroad—the Ford Foundation foremost among them (CIBA Foundation 1975)—the mandate was to provide on-the-spot attention and to formulate country-based grantmaking strategies centered on selected thematic priorities as shaped by national realities. The field office's role was to facilitate the convening of key actors to identify priority challenges and to support the building of the institutions, capacities, and networks required for context-driven problem solving. Close interaction also served to ensure that the host country and the intended beneficiaries had a direct stake in supported development processes and that programs would be responsive to their needs.

Within the scope of country programs, there were various intervention levels, from the community and village to the provincial and national levels. LAB took this multilevel structure into account but shifted the strategic focus to the higher regional level. The regional-program model it pioneered centered on the emergence of a supranational cooperation area increasingly connected not only by geography but also by socioeconomic, administrative, and political processes. In doing so, the programmatic choice was to target transnational linkages among countries and communities as they became more integrated into a region.

In this respect, LAB differed from regional programs of other international foundations and development agencies, which typically display an aggregated system of parallel country programs connected by some facilitated exchange of skills and expertise. Proximity and logistical necessities most often delineate the scope of these programs, but other considerations may also play a role. For instance, the World Health Organization's South-East Asia Region Office (SEARO) and Western Pacific Region Office (WEPRO) disregard generally accepted geographic definitions because of inconsistently applied and politically tainted criteria set as far back as 1948 (WHO-SEARO 2015). The result is that the GMS countries, despite their being part of the Association of Southeast Asian Nations (ASEAN), fall into two different regions as far as the World Health Organization is concerned. Moreover, regional programming does not always imply total coverage of the demarcated "region." In some cases it may barely concern a couple of countries, such as Indonesia and Myanmar for the Soros Foundation's Southeast Asia program area, or just a few scattered project localities. In these cases, the "region" is more an instrumental construct for "landing" or "grouping" thematic work rather than a critical factor shaping programming, as in LAB's case.

Similarly, some "international" programs de facto only apply to a limited number of countries across the globe selected by donors according to a variety of historical, ideological, geopolitical, or analytical reasons, or simply because of funding opportunities. An example is the international program of the Toyota Foundation, which includes Indonesia, Philippines, Thailand, and Vietnam based on their being close to the home country, Japan, and having achieved a certain economic level (Toyota Foundation 2015). Most often the "international" label refers to theme-driven programs that fund selected countries in more than one continent, like the Packard Foundation focusing its reproductive health program in designated locations in the US, sub-Saharan Africa, and Asia (i.e., India, Pakistan, and Myanmar) (Packard, 2015). This reduction is justified by pragmatic reasons to avoid stretching limited financial and human resources too thin and to ensure sufficient concentration of context-relevant expertise.

Such partial interpretations of "place" in international grantmaking have become even more limited in the last decade with the advent of the technocratic philanthropists. Their rebranded "global" programs, grounded in Thomas Friedman's view of the world as "flat," fail to recognize "glocalization," or the uniqueness of the interaction of the local and the global, which renders development needs and solutions distinctive and place-bound. In the words of a philanthropy expert,

> geography and context are de-emphasized. An effect of this is to work globally, but without regard to differences or nuances of place, language, history, politics, or governance. (Feinstein 2012, 91)

This "universality" harks back to the top-down approaches of the 1950s and 1960s, even though they were long criticized for being ineffective and unsustainable. Now, as then, solutions thought up "at the center" are considered applicable anywhere in the world:

It is as though they were saying, "The developed world will find the solutions for the developing world (whether new vaccines, new seeds, new forms of credit instruments, or better democratic governance structures); these then need only be implemented locally and scaled up." This attitude thus flies in the face of 60-plus years of hard-learned lessons by development practitioners which show that context, culture, and locally "owned" solutions do indeed matter, and that without taking them into account, the best-intentioned technical innovations or trendiest new ideas can be doomed in practice in the field. (Feinstein 2012, 92)

The grant giver, with the input of selected advisers, comes to feel once again in charge of steering development processes. Prioritization of global problems and their responses has been (re)centralized at headquarters and "global" initiatives defined by the leadership are passed down through the increasingly bureaucratic layers of thematic directors and group teams for execution by selected recipients and their subrecipients. Field offices have had to relinquish their function (Feinstein 2012, 91) and when not shut down (as in the recent cases of the Vietnam office of the Ford Foundation and IDRC's[7] Southeast and East Asia Office in Singapore), they have been reduced to logistical support units with little autonomy (as in the case of the Rockefeller Foundation's Southeast Asia Regional Office in Bangkok). Most seriously, local grantees have lost their "ownership." As I noted in a short article a few years ago,

> grant-making strategies are no longer intended as synergic umbrellas, but have become detailed initiative plans with set activities, inputs, and outcomes allocating fixed roles to the grantees. In the process local aspirations, knowledge, and capacity are overlooked, and the grantee is reduced from initiator of social action to a commissioned implementer. (Sciortino 2013)

7. The Canadian IDRC is not a private foundation, being supported with parliamentary allocations, but its grantmaking practices are similar to those of American foundations and are affected by the same trends.

Other than donors directly approaching preferred institutions to execute their "global" initiatives, the modus operandi of choice is through "requests for proposals." Potential grantees, now renamed "clients" (of the philanthropic industry), are no longer expected to define their more pressing local problems and contribute to context-specific solutions but rather to propose interventions that address shared "grand challenges"—in the Bill and Melinda Gates Foundation's (2013) language—as prioritized and framed by donors for the entire world.

Interestingly, this style of grantmaking, which claims to respond to the demands of globalization, neglects interconnectivity and the processes of interaction and integration that are at globalization's very core. The segmented choice of locations ignores intra- and intercountry linkages. Rarely is there a focus on transnational phenomena and flows, and when there is, it is far from comprehensive. As such it could hardly be more diverse than LAB, which addressed transboundary trends as embedded in a particular regional setting—the GMS—and articulated them as an expression of the interface of the global with the local.

A SOCIOCULTURAL, NOT A TECHNOCRATIC AND MARKET-ORIENTED, APPROACH TO DEVELOPMENT

In aiming to contribute to more equitable development in the GMS, LAB proposed a sociocultural approach as an alternative (or at the very least as a complement) to the market- and infrastructure-driven model implemented by the GMS governments with the support of the ADB and other international partners.

As previously mentioned, the GMS Economic Cooperation Program was set up to link and harmonize less-developed economies with more dynamic ones in the grouping through financial and infrastructural integration in order to spur economic growth. More particularly, it aimed to improve competitiveness through regionalization of markets, production processes, and value chains and by facilitating the movements of goods, investment, and labor across borders. In order to do so, connectivity enhancement was prioritized through the building of a transnational infrastructure network of "economic corridors" that would link transport systems, power grids, and markets and make the GMS a vital gateway between China, India, and the other ASEAN countries (Sciortino et al. 2006). A large amount of resources was allocated to infrastructural development, with technocratic projects also funded in selected strategic sectors such as energy, telecommunications, trade, investment, tourism, and agriculture.

The GMS model of regional cooperation, favoring the "hard" side of development in pursuing economic regeneration, was (and still is) common to international banks and financing institutions endorsing a neoliberal market ideology. While being mainstream, this growth-centric outlook was not without its critics. In 1990, the UNDP launched the Human Development Index to emphasize that development not only could be conceived as economic and infrastructural progress but also needed to emphasize improvements in human well-being (especially in health and education). Foundations working internationally were enthusiastic, too, in adopting the notion of sustainable development as a systemic, long-term, and multifaceted approach to improve quality of life in society, particularly for the more disadvantaged (Thompson 2007, para. 3).

> Many grantmaking foundations around the world have embraced this [sustainable development] notion and have invested millions of dollars … in a large number of projects. And there have been some notable achievements in the field of empowerment of communities, self-organization, consciousness-raising, increasing self-esteem and strengthening of cultural identity, all of which are essential as a starting point for moving forward—the so-called "soft" side of development. (Thompson 2007, para. 4)

LAB too subscribed to this counterdiscourse in the realization that poverty is multidimensional and that more than economic interventions or faith in the "invisible hand" of the market were required to effectively tackle inequity, marginalization, and social injustice. LAB further stressed that the social, environmental, or cultural impact of regional integration needed urgent attention. Just to give an example, the rapid expansion of the road network, besides enabling greater economic reach, also facilitated transnational crime (like drug and human trafficking), the spread of infectious diseases, and encroachment of protected natural resources, and it caused disruption to the lives of previously isolated ethnic communities. Reflective of the core values of humanistic philanthropy, to address these multiple repercussions, LAB proposed a broader vision of development as a systemic sociocultural and political transformation process, and invested in building the necessary capacities and institutional mechanisms to realize it. Grantmaking supported the fostering of multidisciplinary knowledge and skills, the creation of multistakeholder venues and networks—inclusive of activists and public intellectuals so often ignored in regional policy debates—and the formation of regional governance systems and social movements to advocate for policy change and bring to public attention neglected, yet pressing, social development issues.

An example is LAB's contribution to the control of cross-border transmission of diseases. While today public health emergencies of international concern are common, at the time global preoccupation was limited to HIV/AIDS, with attention for more traditional infectious diseases, such as tuberculosis and malaria, concentrated in particular locations. Yet, in interaction with experts and practitioners on the ground, staff of the Rockefeller Foundation[8] were quick to identify the challenge posed by new and reemerging infectious diseases for Southeast Asia and Eastern and Southern Africa. Overcoming headquarters' initial resistance to localized initiatives in health, LAB devised the Cross-Border Health (CBH) initiative to establish in the GMS a transnational surveillance system from the community up in anticipation that this region would become a hotspot because of its rapid market integration and the increasing density and mobility of its human and animal populations. Grants were given for three main purposes: One was to optimize institutional capacity for disease surveillance and promoting cross-border collaboration. A second purpose was to foster critical perspectives on neglected health issues related to regionalization, market integration, trade, and the growth of

8. The initiator of programming in disease surveillance was Sarah McFarlane, and after being integrated at her departure into LAB at my initiative, it was eventually entrusted to Katherine Bond.

the livestock industry and to advocate for pro-poor risk reduction and coping strategies. Third, grants were used to build bridges among nongovernmental organizations, civil society groups, academic institutions, and the medical, veterinary, and social science disciplines. CBH's centerpiece was the establishment of the Mekong Basin Disease Surveillance, a collaborative disease-control initiative launched by the GMS governments in 2000, and therefore in time to play an important role in the control of the SARS outbreak in late 2002 and the avian influenza (H5N1) outbreak in 2003 (Rockefeller Foundation 2008). One important outcome was that trust was built among government officials of different countries through regular interaction, as the collaboration allowed for the sharing of information across borders and beyond political barriers—a qualitative element that proved crucial in enabling joint control of epidemics and that would not have been considered a "deliverable" in a technocratic or market-oriented approach. This and other lessons resonate these days with the Ebola virus reminding the world of the risk of regional outbreaks becoming global epidemics if not promptly and comprehensively tackled.

Gradually, activities funded under CBH and LAB's other components succeeded in drawing attention to hitherto neglected consequences of regionalization. The social change agenda that was being set did not go unnoticed, and even the ADB began investing, albeit at a limited level, in some of the "soft sides" of development, adding to its priority projects also human resources, health, migration and trafficking, and the environment. Oddly, it was precisely at that point that the Rockefeller Foundation halted LAB, having jumped on the bandwagon of technocratic philanthropy and having decided to redirect its resources toward market-oriented "innovations."

The then-emerging philanthropic trend entailed, in fact, not only the decontextualization of grantmaking practices, as discussed above, but also a return to the positivist style typical of the 1950s and 1960s, which it should be noted had been criticized in the 1990s for its reductionism. In this paradigm, development is conceived of as "a process of overcoming ignorance and a deficit of technical knowledge," (Pratt et al. 2012, 12) rather than as structural sociopolitical and cultural change. Consequently, grantmaking aims at the discovery and application of "magic bullets" that, if combined with adequate joint investment from foundations and the corporate sector, will deliver "value for money" and solve development problems without requiring holistic or critical approaches. So, for instance, universal health coverage has recently been heralded by major foundations as a panacea to address health inequity. No need is felt to understand the sociopolitical root causes of inequity, let alone to challenge them, in spite of evidence that in itself universal health coverage is insufficient and that inequities could persist or even widen depending on the model of coverage applied (see Rodney and Hill 2014). As one recent review of private foundations in international aid puts it,

> [it seems that] foundations and other "philanthrocapitalists" are focused on finding technical solutions to clearly identified problems. ... Many of the aims of more technical programmes cannot be faulted; who would not want to see a vaccine for malaria or an improved treatment for HIV/AIDS patients? They fill a gap which is clearly there, and a results-based, entrepreneurial focus can help to promote innovation and effective programmes, not dragged down by old bureaucracies. ... However, this perceived preference for technical and vertical solutions has led to an over-reliance on somewhat one-dimensional solutions. We have seen a return to projects merely providing equipment or technology, e.g. vaccinations, new water systems or bed nets. ... This "techno-fix" investment [is at odds with] ... a more participatory, socially embedded approach to development marked by empowerment, ownership, capacity building and sustainability. (Pratt et al. 2012, 11)

More strongly, a scathing essay with the provoking title "The Death of International Development" criticizes "development technocrats" as follows:

> [The apolitical view of poverty as a natural phenomenon] lends itself to technocratic interventions led by "experts" in development "science": take MIT's Poverty Action Lab, for example, or Jeffrey Sachs' now-discredited "millennium villages". On a more popular level this approach manifests as quick-fix fads like merry-go-round water pumps,

deworming campaigns, microfinance and laptops for children—projects that studiously avoid thinking about the political context of impoverishment. This is the stuff of TED talks, and donors love it. It allows people to feel they are fixing the problem of poverty without ever having to confront power, challenge the tenets of the prevailing economic order, or question their own position within the global class system. (Hickel 2015, para. 11)

It is not surprising then that in technocratic philanthropy, civil society is no longer seen as a primary partner, and when it is, NGOs are expected to operate according to "entrepreneurial" principles in seeking "innovations" and "technological fixes." Public-private partnerships and working with the private sector are the preferred modalities. Despite growing doubts about the private sector's claims of dynamism, efficiency, and accountability (Simms and Reid 2013), among foundations there persists the strong belief that "market-driven solutions carried out by private institutions can eliminate the scourges of disease, poverty, and inequity" (Feinstein 2012, 89). A poignant case is a recent call for proposals from IDRC and Canada's Department of Foreign Affairs, Trade, and Development for projects that aim at developing, testing, and applying ways to scale up food security and nutrition innovations, which includes as a condition that "at least one of the key implementing partners must be a private sector organization (private company, business-focused NGO, investment organization, etc.)" (IDRC 2015). Neither the call for proposals nor such criteria would have been thinkable a few years before, when humanistic philanthropy still dominated the discourse—including at IDRC.

ENGAGED SOCIAL SCIENCE AND ACADEMIC ACTIVISM

The advent of technocratic philanthropy has also affected the prioritization of disciplinary support. In the 1990s and early 2000s, at the height of humanistic philanthropy, foundations' appreciation of sociocultural processes was reflected in generous giving for social sciences, and "overseas, funding for arts and culture experienced dramatic growth" (Renz and Samson-Atienza 1997, 3). These days we are witnessing a marked increase in funding for "hard science" and the development of "technical" fields and of commodifiable, market-driven knowledge, while funding for the so-called soft fields is being reduced if not stopped altogether (Feinstein 2012, 95).

The shift is particularly significant since it departs from the historical line of philanthropy, especially insofar as the oldest American foundations are concerned. Although philanthropic efforts have contributed to all kinds of basic sciences, they have played a very significant role in building up humanities and social studies, considered crucial to understanding and addressing societal problems; such efforts often compensate for a lack of governmental and private- sector funding in these fields. Since early in the last century, in the United States funding for social research, education, and institutional building (including the establishment of the Social Science Research Council) has come from the likes of the Rockefeller Foundation, the Carnegie Endowment, and later the Ford Foundation. These three foundations and other smaller American and European foundations also contributed in the past fifty years to the growth of area studies and the internationalization of social sciences. All over the world, grants supported social science research, bachelor's, master's, and doctoral fellowships, academic courses, and publications as well as institutional capacity building. They also made governments aware of the importance of the social sciences in governance and policy processes (Beals 2009).

In line with this tradition and with the philanthropic paradigm dominant at the time, LAB subscribed to the notion that policy and interventions had to be grounded in the understanding of social transformations occurring in the GMS. Knowledge building and knowledge transfer were fundamental to the entire approach and were realized in four main modes.

First, LAB funded collaborative research efforts among GMS institutions to investigate the interconnectivity of regional phenomena and take a critical look at regional development. Outputs include the seminal book *Social Challenges in the Mekong Region* (Mingsarn and Dore 2003) and the publication series "Flying with the Dragon" of the Greater Mekong Research Network,[9] which examined the opportunities

---

9. Both joint research projects involved intellectuals, government representatives,

and challenges posed by the greater integration of GMS countries with China with regard to trade, investment, agriculture, industry, and tourism.

Second, LAB emphasized knowledge exchange and dissemination to create greater public awareness of regional processes, to set a transformative agenda, and to give voice to disadvantaged communities. Grants supported multistakeholder forums, policy briefings, interpretation services, and production, translation, and dissemination of books, newsletters, and audiovisual material on relevant issues. News media were also encouraged to investigate and critically report on regional trends. The "Imagining Our Mekong" Media Fellowship Program supported GMS journalists and photographers to write features and produce photo-essays on pressing transboundary issues, which were later disseminated through various media outlets and a series of publications in English and local languages.[10]

Support for the arts also contributed to raising awareness, enabling the use of "the creative space for learning, artistic expression, social advocacy, and engaging the public to tackle social issues confronting the region" (PETA 2015, para. 3). Performing arts and theater communities through the Mekong Partnership Project (PETA 2015) and visual arts faculties through the Mekong Art and Culture Project (Asiart Archive 2012) were supported to collectively explore development and identity concerns and reflect on them through their art. The resulting performances and exhibits were brought to a variety of audiences, helping to broaden their understanding of ongoing changes in the GMS.

Third, LAB supported the establishment and strengthening of institutional networks and other mechanisms that allowed comparison of country experiences, discussion of regional trends, and planning of joint evidence-based action. For instance, the Hanoi-based Vietnam Museum of Ethnography linked up with similar institutions in Laos, Myanmar, and Thailand to exchange information and artifacts for collective exhibits on issues of shared interest that may not otherwise

---

and activists and were led by the Social Research Institute of Chiang Mai University.
10. The fellowship was led by Inter Press Service Asia and Probe Foundation.

be easily addressed because of political sensitivities such as ethnic diversity, the sociocultural impact of road construction, and environmental transformations along the Mekong River. In the field of migration, LAB supported the establishment of the Mekong Migrant Network (MMN 2015), which brought together research and advocacy organizations to examine migration patterns in the GMS for collective transnational advocacy of migrants' rights and action to protect them. More generally, the Development Analysis Network, consisting of economic research institutions in Cambodia, Laos, Thailand, and Vietnam, studied market integration processes and their ramifications for vulnerable countries and populations in order to inform more equitable policies.

Fourth, LAB had a strong focus on individual and institutional capacity building. Capacity was built in established disciplines relevant to the strategy in countries with weaker education systems through a mentoring system using institutions in neighboring countries. Cross-border scholarships and technical know-how in course production and teaching methods were funded. The program strengthened, among others, agriculture teaching programs in key universities and colleges in Laos and Cambodia by providing fellowships for their faculty members to study at Thai academic institutions. Public-health master's programs were also established in Laos and Cambodia—a first in both countries—with the assistance of Thai and Vietnamese institutions. In the arts and humanities, Silpakorn University in Thailand and the Hue University College of Arts in Vietnam launched an exchange program for their students and staff.

These disciplinary efforts were complemented by multidisciplinary ones through the support of training programs that specifically addressed regional issues from a variety of disciplines. Examples of regional programs that contributed to create a broader understanding of the socioeconomic, environmental, and cultural diversity of the region are the "Weaving the Mekong into Southeast Asia Studies" fellowship program managed by Chulalongkorn University (SEA-Chula 2014) and the bachelor's, master's, and doctoral programs offered by the Regional Center for Social Science and Sustainable Development

(RCSD) of Chiang Mai University, with joint Ford Foundation, Rockefeller Foundation, and Heinrich Böll Foundation support.

RCSD was also funded to undertake the Program for Knowledge and Educational Enhancement in the Mekong Region, which granted visiting scholar and research fellowships to both academics and activists and helped create a pool of public intellectuals from the region (RCSD 2015). Support for RCSD also extended to seminars, publications, and social media that disseminated analysis of development challenges and possible solutions and that built the evidence base for joint advocacy efforts in the interests of disadvantaged groups. Collaborations were also established with the National University of Laos and the Royal University of Phnom Penh in Cambodia to establish masters programs in international development studies with a focus on sustainability, poverty alleviation, and regional development in the GMS. Through these many activities, RCSD developed into a center of academic activism that linked graduate training and research to development advocacy, policy, and practice. Under the visionary leadership of its director, Chayan Vaddhanaphuti, RCSD succeeded in shaping a community of engaged development specialists capable of analyzing, contextualizing, and synthesizing regional development challenges and proposing policies and interventions for a more equitable and sustainable region.

Academic activism, engaged and critical social sciences and arts, and capacity building of local academics, practitioners, and institutions were all elements of a grantmaking strategy that challenged the status quo and aimed to contribute to social change by understanding and addressing the complexity of unfolding development processes. On the other hand, these approaches are unsuitable to technocratic approaches wary of complexity and the "immensurable." In their search for order, the "new" foundations—and the "old" foundations that are following in their footsteps—are looking for the best scientists to provide, in the shortest possible time, technical solutions that will "yield the best metrics" for the entire world (Feinstein 2012, 92). Oblivious to concerns about "academic imperialism," they prefer to fund well-resourced institutes in Western countries touted as centers of excellence. When not acting as implementers, these privileged institutes act as intermediaries, distributing funding to subgrantee institutions in developing countries. In the hierarchical division of labor that thus arises, research formulation and analysis is the prerogative of the "center" while collection of data can be delegated—under supervision—to local researchers in the periphery.

The high quality of outputs and related outcomes resulting from LAB and many other grantmaking strategies of a humanistic brand dispels concerns that funding local institutes and building capacity means foregoing achievements of a high standard. Direct investments have also proven sustainable, and in spite of reduced resources, the institutions and networks established or strengthened with LAB funding, including those previously mentioned, have remained committed and active to this day, as have the students, lecturers, and journalists who have benefited from scholarship programs and have come to constitute a pool of critical expertise on regional issues.

Yet among today's technocratic-oriented foundations there seems to be no appreciation for such results, in spite of their declared faith in "evidence." They show little interest in directly funding research institutes in less-developed countries, with the possible exception of leading institutions most often located in capital cities. Nor do they view as their mandate building such institutions and expertise if they are lacking in situ. They also do not seem concerned, in contrast to LAB, with supporting the strengthening of a locally-owned scholarship, valued by many southern-hemisphere scientists. As Santos writes,

> it should be clear that we are not calling for a wholesale rejection of… Western research and technology. We are rather calling for more balancing with and respect for Southern perspectives, so that the synthesis becomes truly universal or internationalist—"the best that has been created by humanity." For this to happen, there is a need first for Southern academic or intellectual work to achieve true parity, to restore equality and mutual respect vis-à-vis Western academic or intellectual dominance. This too is a challenge to Asian public intellectuals in particular. (Santos Jr. 2012, 57)

LAB, with its support for local academic knowledge and a locally owned scholarship for the GMS, tested the power relations in science as it had contested the power relations at play in the process of regionalization. Paraphrasing the terminology of "academic activism" used to describe the type of efforts it funded, LAB could be described as a form of "grantmaking activism." Or it could be defined as "social-justice philanthropy," a specific brand of humanistic philanthropy that "identifies who benefit (or not) and how" from development, "requires the input of those who stand to gain or lose the most from grantmaking: the grantees and the communities they serve," and shows "a commitment to evidence-based strategy [that does not] ignore the tangible, positive impact—and often the necessity—of influencing public policy" (Jagpal and Laskowski 2000, 1). In this framework, LAB investment in knowledge-making was for emancipatory purposes within the dialogue and praxis of social justice beyond the seeking of technical and entrepreneurial solutions privileged by technocratic philanthropy.

CONCLUSION

Recent literature concludes that humanistic and technocratic philanthropy should not be seen as a dichotomy and that the debate should be reframed with a shift "from an 'either/or' to a 'both/and' perspective" (Connolly 2011a, 135; see also Connolly 2011b). Along with a recommendation for more mutual respect, there is a call to integrate the most strategic elements of each paradigm into a hybrid model:

> As a more technocratic approach to philanthropy has emerged over the past 15 years, it has been seen as the opposite of humanistic philanthropy. Rather than a dichotomy, these approaches are on a continuum. The best tools from each approach can and should be brought to bear, including the well-thought out and disciplined strategies and results orientation of technocrats and the values base, intuition, responsiveness, and flexibility of the humanists. (Connolly 2011a, 120)[11]

11. Some of this characterization needs to be contested as "rational" qualities such as "well-thought out and disciplined strategies" are also common to humanistic

While appealing from a normative perspective, this win-win situation that would take advantage of the "dynamic energy" between the humanistic and the technocratic approaches to philanthropy may prove an unrealizable utopia. As the case of LAB shows, the paradigmatic tensions are significant and real, and, what is more, they translate into diverse funding priorities and approaches. As resources are always finite, the impact is great when it comes to decisions on what gets funded and what doesn't. Moreover, it may be difficult or even impossible to selectively blend specific elements since, as this review shows, they are tied together by different conceptualizations of the functions and aims of grantmaking as well as by different socioeconomic and political perspectives of development and development processes.

Contrary to the syncretic view, this article argues that the emergence of the technocratic approach has had devastating consequences for humanistic and, especially, social-justice approaches. As a case in point, LAB could not survive as the institutional conditions changed radically under the transition and the directed shift in paradigms and derived practices from humanistic to technocratic philanthropy. It speaks volumes that a recent Rockefeller Foundation book of its work in Thailand fails to showcase LAB, its Thai partner organizations, and the wide impact of the projects (Rockefeller Foundation 2013). Consequently, for similar approaches to emerge again, another paradigm shift will have to occur. This is not unthinkable considering the history of alternating paradigms in philanthropy and the increasing criticisms that are being raised against technocratic philanthropy (as many of the quotations in this article also indicate).

Moreover, while in the current climate LAB's model of social-justice philanthropy may not be in vogue, this does not imply that it has become irrelevant. On the contrary, with the acceleration of economic integration brought about by the impending launch of the ASEAN Economic Community in 2015, questions of equity and holistic development are even more pressing in the region. It testifies to the value of LAB that, as said before, its partners are continuing

philanthropy. Here the quote is merely used for the purpose of illustrating the emerging call for integration of the two approaches.

their work, even if with reduced funding, and that a few donors have followed suit with regional programs in the GMS. Foremost, USAID launched in 2009 the Lower Mekong Initiative to promote "greater cooperation in the Mekong sub-region" in "shared responses to the most pressing cross-border development challenges" (USAID 2015), some of which, like those in health and agriculture, are the same as those anticipated by LAB. Still, the need remains for greater support as the issues will only become more complex as integration proceeds, and critical voices and transformative interventions are not necessarily accommodated by the new programs. Beyond the GMS, a LAB-like grantmaking approach is also very much needed, as the global community is faced with a widening income gap (Elliot and Pilkington 2015), increasing ethnic and religious tensions, poorly governed migration, and transnational spreading of diseases, just to name a few of the cross-boundary issues LAB raised ahead of their time and requiring urgent attention today.

From this perspective, it can only be wished that the pendulum does swing back and that more humanistic and social-justice approaches emerge. May this chapter extend the activism that LAB showed to the field of philanthropy itself and serve to question some of the dominant philanthropic practices and assumptions, and, ultimately, help us reflect on "who is benefiting (and who is not) and how" from these as an initial step in advocating for a paradigmatic renewal (or some might say a return to an older paradigm) in philanthropy.

ACKNOWLEDGMENT

I am grateful to Alan Feinstein for his review, editing, and comments to an earlier version of this article.

REFERENCES

ADB (Asian Development Bank). 2015. "Overview of the Greater Mekong Subregion." http://www.adb.org/countries/gms/overview.

Asiart Archive. 2007. "Perspectives: The Mekong Art and Culture Project." [Online] Available from: http://www.aaa.org.hk/Diaaalogue/Details/38.

Beals, Ralph L. 2009. *Politics of Social Research*. New Brunswick, NJ: Transaction Publishers.

Becker, William H. 2013. "Innovative Partners: The Rockefeller Foundation and Thailand." Rockefeller Foundation Centennial Series. https://assets.rockefeller foundation.org/app/uploads/20131001203515/Innovative-Partners.pdf.

Bill and Melinda Gates Foundation. 2013. "Grand Challenges in Global Health." http://gcgh.grandchallenges.org/GrantOpportunities/Pages/default.aspx.

CIBA Foundation. 1975. *The Future of Philanthropic Foundations*. Ciba Foundation symposium 30. Amsterdam: Associated Scientific Publishers.

Connolly, Paul. 2011a. "The Best of the Humanistic and Technocratic: Why the Most Effective Work in Philanthropy Requires a Balance." *The Foundation Review* 3 (1): 120–36. http://www.tccgrp.com/pdfs/Connolly_The_Best.pdf.

———. 2011b. "Grant Makers Must Lead with Their Hearts as Well as Their Heads." *The Chronicle of Philanthropy*, July 24. http://philanthropy.com/article/Why-Grant-Makers-Must-Lead/128340/.

Elliot, Larry, and Ed Pilkington. 2015. "New Oxfam report says half of global wealth held by the 1%." *The Guardian*, January 19. http://www.theguardian.com/business/2015/jan/19/global-wealth-oxfam-inequality-davos-economic-summit-switzerland.

Feinstein, Alan. 2012. "International Philanthropy in Southeast Asia: Case Studies from Indonesia and the Philippines." In *Understanding Confluences and Contestations, Continuities and Changes: Towards Transforming Society and Empowering People; The Work of 2009/2010 API Fellows*. Bangkok: API. http://www.api-fellowships.org/body/international_ws_proceedings/09/P3-Alan.pdf.

Hickel, Jason. 2015. "The Death of International Development." *Red Pepper*, February. http://www.redpepper.org.uk/essay-the-death-of-international-development/.

IDRC (International Development Research Centre). 2015. "Pre-announcement: New CIFSRF Call for Proposal in 2015." http://www.idrc.ca/EN/Documents/CIFSRF-2015-PRE-CALL-ANNOUNCEMENT.pdf.

Jagpal, Niki, and Kevin Laskowski. 2000. *Real Results: Why Strategic Philanthropy is Social Justice Philanthropy*. Washington, DC: National Committee for Responsive Philanthropy. http://www.ncrp.org/files/publications/Real_Results_Why_Strategic_Philanthropy_is_Social_Justice_Philanthropy.pdf.

Mingsarn Kaosa-ard and John Dore, eds. 2003. *Social Challenges in the Mekong Region*. Chiang Mai: Chiang Mai University.

MMN (Mekong Migration Network). 2015. Website. http://www.mekongmigration.org.

Packard Foundation, David and Lucile. 2015. "Population and Reproductive Health." http://www.packard.org/what-we-fund/population-reproductive-health/.

PETA (Philippine Educational Theater Association). 2015. "The PETA-Mekong Partnership Project." http://petatheater.com/peta-mekong-partnership-program/.

Pratt, Brian, John Hailey, Michela Gallo, Rebecca Shadwick, and Rachel Hayman. 2012. "Understanding Private Donors in International Development." INTRAC Policy Briefing Paper 31. http://www.intrac.org/data/files/resources/747/Briefing-Paper-31-Understanding-private-donors-in-international-development.pdf.

Renz, Loren, and Josefina Samson-Atienza. 1997. "International Grantmaking: Patterns and Priorities." Unpublished paper. The Foundation Center. http://www.tgci.com/sites/default/files/pdf/International%20Grantmaking%20Patterns%20and%20Priorities_0.pdf.

RCSD (Regional Center for Social Science and Sustainable Development, Chiang Mai University). 2015. "Research Fellowship Program." http://rcsd.soc.cmu.ac.th/v2012/index.php?sfile=smallresearch.

Rockefeller Foundation. 2008. "Review of Legacy Grants: Cross-Border Health." Unpublished report.

Rodney, Anna M., and Peter Hill. 2014. "Achieving Equity within Universal Health Coverage: A Narrative Review of Progress and Resources for Measuring Success." *International Journal for Equity in Health* 13 (72). http://www.equityhealthj.com/content/13/1/72.

Santos, Soliman M., Jr. 2012. "Constructively Engaging Non-State Armed Groups in Asia." In *Understanding Confluences and Contestations, Continuities and Changes: Towards Transforming Society and Empowering People; The Work of 2009/2010 API Fellows.* Bangkok: API. http://www.api-fellowships.org/body/international_ws_proceedings/year9.pdf.

Sciortino, Rosalia, et al. 2006. "Labor Migration in the Greater Mekong Sub-region." Unpublished Report. Bangkok Regional Office, Rockefeller Foundation.

———. 2013. "Reminiscences on a Grantee-Grantor Relationship" Originally posted in SALT (e-magazine from the National Volunteer and Philanthropy Centre). http://www.salt.org.sg/2314/reminiscences-on-a-grantee-grantor-relationship/ (site discontinued).

Simms, Andrew, and Stephen Reid. 2013. "The private sector is superior: Time to move on from this old dogma." *The Guardian*, April 25. http://www.theguardian.com/commentisfree/2013/apr/25/private-sector-superiority-mythbuster.

SEA-CHULA (Southeast Asian Studies Program, Chulalongkorn University). 2014. "Research Monographs." http://www.seachula.grad.chula.ac.th/web/research_monographs.php.

Thompson, Andres. 2007. "Hard Lessons for Economic Development." *Alliance Magazine*, June 1. http://www.alliancemagazine.org/feature/hard-lessons-for-economic-development/.

Toyota Foundation. 2015. "International Grant Program." https://www.toyotafound.or.jp/english/program/asian_neighbors.html.

USAID (United States Agency for International Development). 2015. "Lower Mekong Initiative (LMI)." http://www.usaid.gov/asia-regional/lower-mekong-initiative-lmi.

WHO-SEARO (World Health Organization-Southeast Asia Regional Office). 2015. "History of the WHO South-East Asia Region." http://www.searo.who.int/about/history/en/.

Scholarship, Expertise, and the Regional Politics of Heritage

Oscar Salemink

INTRODUCTION

After the 2008 inscription of the Khmer Preah Vihear temple on the UNESCO World Heritage list, Thailand disputed that the temple—located right on the border between Thailand and Cambodia—was fully Cambodian. The People's Alliance for Democracy, which was said to have connections with the Democrat Party and the Thai military, mounted a campaign to claim Phra Wihan (as the temple is known in Thai) for Thailand. This event was just the latest in a series of standoffs over the site and the contested border. During the nineteenth century, Cambodia was dominated by its two more powerful neighbors, Siam and Vietnam, until it became a French protectorate in 1867. A series of border conflicts between Siam and France resulted in a Franco-Siamese agreement which forced Siam to give up some predominantly Khmer territories that are now part of Cambodia. The border demarcation was done by French engineers

Parts of this chapter have been presented at the ten-year Implementation of the UNESCO Convention for the Safeguarding of Intangible Cultural Heritage: Experiences, Lessons And Future Directions, Hoi An, June 22–23, 2013; at the 2nd International Conference on Vietnamese and Taiwanese Studies, Tainan, May 18–20, 2013; at the Fourth International Conference on Vietnamese Studies: Vietnam on the Road to Integration and Sustainable Development, Hanoi, November 26–28, 2012; and at the International Conference on Economic and Social Changes and Preservation of the Gong Culture in Vietnam and the Southeast Asian Region, Pleiku City, Vietnam, November 9–11, 2009. I thank the commentators at these conferences and especially Prof. Michael Herzfeld for their valuable comments on earlier versions; all mistakes, however, remain my responsibility.

who generally followed the Damrek mountains watershed when drawing the border, except at the precise site of the Preah Vihear temple, which is on the Thai side of the watershed but which the engineers added to Cambodia. During World War II, Thailand—the new name for Siam—took the lost territories back from the French, but after the war the Thai had to give these up again. The Thai government, however, never abandoned its claim to Phra Wihan, which became an issue in the late 1950s. Cambodia brought the case before the International Court of Justice (ICJ), which in 1962 ruled largely in favor of Cambodia. Thailand reluctantly evacuated the temple, which played a role again in the 1980s and '90s when the Khmer Rouge waged a guerrilla war against the Vietnam-backed Hun Sen regime and took possession of the temple with Thai military support (Keyes 1993). Then the World Heritage inscription in 2008 led to a serious conflict between the two countries.

These various events surrounding the temple involved a diverse array of intellectuals and cultural experts. The most fateful would be the 1930 visit by Prince Damrong, a leading political and intellectual figure in Siam, to the temple, where he was greeted by the French Resident and the archaeologist Henri Parmentier under a French flag. The nonprotest by Prince Damrong was later interpreted by the ICJ in its 1962 decision as acquiescence to the status quo, and it became the main argument for allocating the temple to Cambodia (Cuasay 1998). On the Thai side this fed into a narrative of national humiliation about the loss of territories to surrounding states as a result of imperialist intervention (see Strate 2013). This countered a Cambodian narrative of national reawakening against attempts by these two neighboring powers to incorporate parts of Cambodia into their respective territories. These narratives were, and are, sustained by intellectuals who combine historical and archaeological expertise, which they use for the heritage work and for claiming the temple for their country on legal or historical grounds. The most obvious example is the 2009 debate "Who owns the Preah Vihear temple?" in the *Journal of East Asian International Law* between Monticha Pakdeekong ("A Thai Position") and Bora Touch ("A Cambodian Position"). But these "national" narratives are subtly reinscribed by international scholars working from one linguistic base. While Cuasay (1998) and Hinton (2006) focus on the Cambodian side of things, Croissant and Chambers (2011) and Shane Strate (2013) highlight the Thai side of the equation. A working paper of the EU-funded SEATIDE research program contains a part written by Volker Grabowsky about the Thai perception and by Sok Udom Deth about the Cambodian side (Grabowsky 2014). On the other hand, the renowned Thai historian Charnvit Kasetsiri, along with Cambodian diplomat Pou Sothirak and international relations scholar Pavin Chachavalpongpun (2013), pleads for a denationalization of the site by both sides, but to little avail so far.

Especially if the heritage in question is inscribed by UNESCO as World Heritage or Intangible Cultural Heritage, or if such UNESCO recognition is aspired to, the arena for heritage work and heritage contestations is definitely international. But within that international arena, the main responsibilities for the heritage in question fall to the sovereign state that is both a member of UNESCO as part of the UN system and a signatory to the various international heritage conventions. In other words, heritage work inevitably brings in the state as holder of territorial sovereignty in the national space where the heritage site, object, or practice is located. And as the conflict between Cambodia and Thailand over Preah Vihear/Phra Wihan shows, states always refer to the nations they stand for, as states are the containers and territories the spaces in the "national order of things" (see Malkki 1992). Heritage, then, may be deemed of global significance (as brought out in "world heritage") or seen as embodying culturally or historically unique values within nations, but the heritage is claimed by the state on behalf of the nation—Thai, Khmer, Việt, and so on. One example is the northern Khmer heritage in Isan, Thailand, which has been analyzed at length by Alexandra Denes (2012a, 2012b, 2015) as a Thai state appropriation of Khmer culture. Another example is the Mỹ Sơn World Heritage Site in what is now Vietnam but which is what remains of a sprawling temple complex of Bhadresvara—dedicated to Shiva—in a former Cham polity located in what is now the Vietnamese province of Quảng Nam. In the wake of the Việt conquest of the coast of Central Vietnam, the Cham population was much reduced, and today scattered Cham communities—many of them Muslim—can be found in Ninh Thuận and Bình Thuận Provinces east of Ho Chi Minh City, in the Mekong Delta, in Cambodia, Malaysia, and on Hainan island, as well as in France and the US. The Mỹ Sơn site is claimed and managed by the Vietnamese state on behalf of the Vietnamese nation, and not of the Vietnamese or transnational Cham community, which does not seem to be much focused on the site as *their* heritage.

In this chapter I would like to focus on one peculiarly localized instance of UNESCO heritage—namely, the Intangible Cultural Heritage of the "Space of Gong Music in the Central Highlands of Vietnam." Intangible cultural heritage is usually performative ritualized practice, and so is the UNESCO-recognized intangible cultural heritage of gong music in Vietnam. As performative ritual, gong music has a variety of different meanings and functions, primarily for the ritual community (see Baumann 1992) in a limited ritual setup (see Augé 1999)—especially if such rituals are not mediated. If labeled "heritage," however, the performance requires recognition by other people outside the own ritual community and hence requires an outside spectatorship and constituency in an extended, usually mass-mediated, ritual setup, thus superseding localized concerns. In this paper I focus on the role of scholars and experts in the heritagization of culture, and on the cross-border, regional setting of gong music as intangible cultural heritage, thus addressing a particular relation between scholarship and power that exceeds local confines.

CULTURAL POLITICS OF INTANGIBLE CULTURAL HERITAGE IN VIETNAM

In the 1990s a new subdivision for intangible cultural heritage was established at UNESCO's Paris headquarters, largely funded by Japan and staffed by Japanese officials (see Aikawa 2004; Ms. Noriko Aikawa was the director of the Intangible Cultural Heritage section of UNESCO during those years). At the time, the (linguistic-anthropological) notion of intangible cultural heritage constituted an experimental departure from the established (historical-archaeological) practice of heritage conservation focusing on material sites and objects. The concept of culture long dominant within UNESCO was very much in line with the Lévi-Straussian concept of culture as more or less bounded entities that could be pluralized as "cultures."[1] These days most anthropologists and cultural scholars worldwide see "culture" not as a bounded collection of "things" connected up with a clearly delineated ethnic group but as an ever-changing process with fuzzy boundaries. In his critique of the UNESCO concept of culture, Thomas Hylland Eriksen (2001; see also Arizpe 1998) traces a Lévi-Straussian influence on the notion of cultures (plural) as isolated islands by the UNESCO commission, which tends to link "culture" to "indigeneity." Eriksen emphasizes the problematic tension between universal concepts of individual rights and communitarian notions of rights implied in culture as necessarily collective, localized, and hence exclusive. This tension can also be seen in the history of cultural claims and rights in Vietnam's Central Highlands—the designated arena for gong culture—as I argued in 2006.

The 2003 UNESCO Convention for the Safeguarding of Intangible Cultural Heritage defines intangible cultural heritage as "the practices, representations, expressions, knowledge, skills—as well as the instruments, objects, artifacts and cultural spaces associated therewith—that communities, groups and, in some cases, individuals recognize as part of their cultural heritage."[2] UNESCO introduced

1. Claude Lévi-Strauss (1908–2009) was a very influential French anthropologist whose work on cultural diversity formed the philosophical basis for much subsequent "urgent" or "salvage" anthropology which aimed to record and if possible, save "cultures" before these would become "extinct" (i.e., change), a practice for which the concept of intangible cultural heritage was intended to give legitimacy.

2. Article 2 of the 2003 convention begins as follows:

1. The "intangible cultural heritage" means the practices, representations, expressions, knowledge, skills—as well as the instruments, objects, artefacts and cultural spaces associated therewith—that communities, groups and, in some cases, individuals recognize as part of their cultural heritage. This intangible cultural heritage, transmitted from generation to generation, is constantly recreated by communities and groups in response to their environment, their interaction with nature and their history, and provides them with a sense of identity and continuity, thus promoting respect for cultural diversity and human creativity. For the purposes of this Convention, consideration will be given solely to such intangible cultural heritage as is compatible with existing international human rights instruments, as well as with the requirements of mutual respect among communities, groups and individuals, and of sustainable development.

the term "intangible cultural heritage" (ICH) in Vietnam already in 1994, when it sponsored two back-to-back "expert meetings" in Vietnam on the intangible cultural heritage of ethnic minorities and of the culture of the former imperial city of Huế. I was invited to participate in the International Expert Meeting for the Safeguarding and Promotion of the Intangible Cultural Heritage of Minority Groups in Viet Nam (Hanoi, March 1994), and became the rapporteur for the meeting and editor of the resulting volume (Salemink 2001), thus acting myself as a "cultural expert."[3] The interest in ICH in Vietnam caught on after the official UNESCO recognition of five world heritage sites—the three historical sites of Huế, Hội An, and the Mỹ Sơn temple complex, and the two natural sites of Hạ Long Bay and Phong Nha cave—resulted in a phenomenal boost in tourist visits and in national pride.[4] In 2003 and 2005, respectively, *nhã nhạc* court music from Hue and the "space of gong culture" (*không gian văn hóa cồng chiêng*) of ethnic minorities of Vietnam's Central Highlands were proclaimed Masterpieces of the Oral and Intangible Heritage of Humanity; in 2008 both were transferred to the new ICH List of Intangible Cultural Heritage in Need of Urgent Safeguarding. In 2007, Vietnam nominated *quan họ* as well as *ca trù* singing for UNESCO

---

2. The "intangible cultural heritage", as defined in paragraph 1 above, is manifested inter alia in the following domains: (a) oral traditions and expressions, including language as a vehicle of the intangible cultural heritage; (b) performing arts; (c) social practices, rituals and festive events; (d) knowledge and practices concerning nature and the universe; (e) traditional craftsmanship.

(http://www.unesco.org/culture/ich/index.php?pg=00006)

3. Subsequently, I was involved in cultural heritage work as editor of a UNESCO volume on Vietnam's minorities; as grantmaker on behalf of the Ford Foundation, as participant in international workshops on the gong cultural space intangible heritage in Pleiku in 2009 and on the Hung kings in Phú Thọ in 2011, and as advisor for the UNESCO-sponsored research project "Safeguarding intangible cultural heritage and development in Vietnam," carried out by Prof. Lê Hồng Lý, Dr. Nguyễn Thị Hiền, Dr. Đào Thế Đức, and Dr. Hoàng Cầm under the auspices of Prof. Nguyễn Chí Bền of the Vietnam Institute of Culture and Arts Studies in 2012.

4. In 2010 the Imperial Citadel of Thăng Long was added to the list, as was the Hồ Dynasty Citadel in 2011. In 2014 the Tràng An karst landscape was inscribed as a mixed cultural and natural heritage site.

recognition,[5] and in May 2009, both forms of musical heritage were officially recognized by UNESCO.[6] In addition, in 2010 the Gióng festival of Phù Đổng and Sóc temples was inscribed, followed in 2011 by *xoan* singing in Phú Thọ and in 2012 by the worship of Hùng kings in Phú Thọ. Finally, in 2013, a southern Vietnamese tradition, *Đờn ca tài tử* music was inscribed, and in 2014 a Central Vietnamese tradition, *Ví* and *Giặm* singing was added.

In contrast with the fuzzy concept of culture, many sites, objects, and practices labeled as heritage are more or less clearly delineated, making their management and protection possible, at least in theory. Both cultural and natural heritage sites have geographic boundaries which spatially mark off the heritage site from the outside world, and within which the work of time is supposed to be slowed down against the accelerating pace of change through conservation. Borrowing from Thomas Hylland Eriksen's concept of the world as "overheating" (see Eriksen n.d.), one could imagine its spatiotemporal disjuncture with heritage in terms of "freezing" of the latter, as if in an attempted denial of coevalness (Fabian 1983). This meshes well with Michael Herzfeld's metaphor of the pedestal for tradition, which from a different angle—upside down—can become a tethering post which holds artisans and other custodians of tradition back (Herzfeld 2004). In a recent critique of the "fundamentally Cartesian distinction between tangible and intangible culture," Michael Herzfeld (2015, 43) asserts that it is the very separation of the material and immaterial which relegates what passes as ICH "to a pedestal of glorious irrelevance to the modern world."

For the ICH program, UNESCO marries the concept of culture to that of heritage, thus focusing it on a particular cultural or artistic practice that is locally and temporally specific. Within Vietnam many examples of ICH are fairly circumscribed cultural or artistic traditions,

5. For *quan họ* singing, I refer to Le Ngoc Chan (2002 and n.d.) and Meeker's *Sounding out Heritage* (2013). For *ca trù* I refer to the work of Barley Norton (1996, 2005, and http://www.roehampton.ac.uk/catru/) as well as Nhung Tuyet Tran (2013).

6. See http://www.unesco.org/culture/ich/index.php?RL=00183 and http://www.unesco.org/culture/ich/index.php?USL=00309.

like the "refined court music" *nhã nhạc* from the old imperial capital Huế; the alternate singing style *quan họ* between two men and two women from different villages, from the northern provinces of Bắc Ninh and Bắc Giang; and the "bluesy" chamber music featuring a highly individualist singing style, *ca trù* (see Salemink 2013a). More specific than the fuzzy notion of culture itself, cultural heritage can arguably be seen as more inviting to cultural interventions from outside as the arena for intervention is cordoned off more neatly. Cultural policies can target particular practices and practitioners of the heritage without having to take the much wider culture or cultural context into account. But for the intangible cultural heritage of gong music in Tây Nguyên, the concept of "heritage" was wedded to both "culture" and "space," thus making the arena of safeguarding and intervention much more fuzzy again, even when localizing this culture within specific geographic—national and provincial—borders.

But "space" may have different meanings than "cultural space" alone. For starters, "space" has a clear geographic connotation, as it circumscribes the places where the cultural practices are supposed to take place. This spatial circumscription refers to the Tây Nguyên region, currently made up of the five provinces of Kontum, Gialai, Đắk Lắk, Đắk Nông, and Lâm Đồng. In that sense, it is also a political space, denoting the five administrative units now making up the Tây Nguyên region—as the Central Highlands are known in Vietnam. It leaves out the upland districts in surrounding coastal provinces where ethnic minorities live with similar gong musical practices, and it leaves out regions in Cambodia and Laos with ethnic groups that are similar or even the same, living across the Vietnamese border. The political character of the "space of gong culture" is also brought out by the fact that Tây Nguyên is an integral part of Vietnam's national territory, with the Vietnamese government filing the dossier for UNESCO recognition and ultimately responsible for safeguarding this heritage.

But "space" refers also to the ecological, economic, and social space that forms both the context and the subtext for gong culture, along with myriad other cultural practices. As a subtext and context for the cultural space of gong culture, the ecological, economic, political, and social spaces are changing extremely fast. Việt migration into the

Central Highlands has forever altered the demographic composition of the region. The forest that once encompassed the swidden fields has retreated and made way for endless fields of coffee gardens, rubber plantations, and other cash crops. Remaining natural forest has been converted to production forest or is protected. Villages have been resettled and changed their character. Along with the landscape, the ethnoscape, and ideoscape, to paraphrase Arjun Appadurai (1996), the "religioscape" (see Turner 2006) of the Central Highlands has changed profoundly as well, with Highlanders converting massively to Christianity over the past twenty years, which can be interpreted as a conversion to modernity, as in many conversion movements in Asia and around the world (Hefner 1993; Van der Veer 1996; Salemink 2009). The Central Highlands are no longer a "remote area" but are a hotspot of globalization, integrated into national and international market networks and subject to global cultural flows. There is no way to reverse that situation, nor would that be desirable. The "space of gong culture" refers to this changing landscape of Tây Nguyên, as one Paris-based UNESCO officer pointed out to me.[7] Rather than bounded, both the "space" and "culture" of gong culture are reminders of the changing "scapes" (technoscape, financescape, ideoscape, ethnoscape, mediascape) which contextualize and influence our lifeworlds, to paraphrase Arjun Appadurai (1996).

Intentionally or inadvertently, this label opens up entire highlander lifeworlds to external inspection, intervention, and management, as it is no longer limited to the specific cultural or ritual practice deemed under threat. The subjects of that inspection, intervention, and management are specific outside agents—cultural experts, state officials, and tourist entrepreneurs—who articulate what Laurajane Smith calls "authorized heritage discourse" in her comprehensive treatise *Uses of Heritage* (2006), which is predicated on

the idea of heritage not so much as a "thing", but as a cultural and social process, which engages with acts of remembering that work to create ways to understand and engage with the present.... Indeed, the work

7. Frank Proschan, personal communication, 2008.

starts from the premise that all heritage is intangible. In stressing the intangibility of heritage, however, I am not dismissing the tangible or pre-discursive, but simply depriviging and denaturalizing it as the self-evident form and essence of heritage. While places, sites, objects and localities may exist as identifiable sites of heritage ... these places are not inherently valuable, nor do they carry a freight of innate meaning. (Smith 2006, 2–3)

In her book she identifies an "authorized heritage discourse ... that privileges expert values and knowledge about the past and its material manifestations, and dominates and regulates professional heritage practices" vis-à-vis popular and community heritage discourses and practices (Ibid., 5).

In heritage policy and practice this "authorized heritage discourse" privileging expert knowledge is deeply imbricated with the state, which ultimately authorizes and defines what is considered heritage— especially *national* heritage (see Herzfeld 1997, 2010, 2014a). Whereas world heritage sites and intangible cultural heritage are recognized by UNESCO, it is important to keep in mind that although in its heritage conventions UNESCO formally allows NGOs to nominate sites, objects, or practices, it remains an intergovernmental organization which will only accept a nomination if it is supported by the government of the country where this heritage is located. That state must assume special responsibilities regarding the management, the conservation or preservation, and the protection or safeguarding of the heritage. In order to do that, the state must make the heritage "its" state property, to be investigated, managed, and showcased by its experts and its officials. In this way, the heritage and the communities living close to (i.e., in the "buffer zone") or embodying that heritage ("culture carriers") are turned into sites of intervention and discipline by the state. At the same time, the heritage becomes a source of national pride and an icon of the nation in the international arena; hence it becomes exclusive "national property" (see Salemink 2013a). In the next section I will zoom in on an instance of this in which cultural experts double as community activists.

EXPERT ACTIVISTS

The privileging of expert values and knowledge in the field of heritage often works to facilitate intervention for the sake of conservation and management of the heritage site, object, or practice. Some experts, however, used their expertise to champion the diverse causes pursued by people—communities, groups, artisans, individuals—living with, or embodying, cultural heritage. Laurajane Smith's (2006) work with indigenous and working-class communities in Australia and Britain, respectively, is a case in point. But one prominent anthropologist who has worked consistently on people living with heritage—in Greece, Rome, and Bangkok—is Michael Herzfeld, Professor of Anthropology at Harvard and contributor to this volume. After his earlier work on cultural intimacy and nationalism in Greece (1997), he moved on to record the combined effects of heritagization and gentrification in Rome, which he summed up as eviction (2009). His work in Rome and especially in the Pom Mahakan neighborhood in Bangkok turned Herzfeld into a scholar-activist, as he supported specific groups of residents in their resistance against eviction by turning an anthropological lens toward the discursive and political practices of experts, bureaucrats, and investors, and by supporting residents with their articulation of a counterhierarchical heritagization narrative contesting the "global hierarchy of value" (Byrne 2011, 147; see also Herzfeld 2004 and 2006, 2009, 2010, 2013, 2014b). For Herzfeld, the use of cultural or anthropological expertise for policy and political purposes is part of his scholarship; in his provocative article "Engagement, Gentrification, and the Neoliberal Hijacking of History" in *Current Anthropology*, he makes the distinction between "applied anthropology"—for the benefit of policy or project formulation and implementation—and "engaged anthropology"—siding with the groups and communities that resist the negative consequences of such policies (Herzfeld 2010, S265; see also Eriksen 2006).

The distinction that Herzfeld sketches between applied and engaged anthropology often blurs in connection with heritage, for a variety of reasons. One reason given by Herzfeld for the Pom Mahakan residents is that most of its 300 inhabitants seek to demonstrate their skills as guardians of the historic site. Indeed, they have already demonstrated an extraordinary ability both to conserve the site and to manage their own affairs. They have maintained their living space as a clean, tranquil oasis that contrasts dramatically with the noise and pollution outside. (Herzfeld 2013)

In other words, the Pom Mahakan residents claim that they can manage and conserve the area better than the Bangkok Metropolitan Authority, thus seemingly buying into the heritage label and the heritagization discourse. In another article, Herzfeld's questions the chances of success, since the

residents can talk about the advantages to the Thai economy of making the site more interesting for tourists by treating it as an outdoor museum of Thai traditions and lifestyles. But such appeals to national tradition, once again, trap them into using the same discourse as the authorities; and it is a tussle that they cannot win. The best they can hope for at present is a stand-off. (Herzfeld 2014b, 297)

I hasten to emphasize that this rendering of events, attitudes, and motivations in Pom Mahakan is based on incomplete ethnographic information, which will soon be remedied by Herzfeld's new book.[8]

But another, implicit reason exhibited by anthropologists and other cultural experts when confronting eviction and other fallout of heritagization is that anthropologists usually do not oppose the label of heritage in their oft-stated critique of "the noise and pollution outside"—meaning the overheating, neoliberal globalization which appropriates built environments and cultural lifeworlds alike. As mentioned above, the label of heritage seeks to freeze life in separate spatiotemporal pockets, carved out of an overheating world, like the chaos of Bangkok. But the distinction between applied and engaged

8. Next year the University of Chicago Press will publish Michael Herzfeld's new book, *Siege of the Spirits: Community and Polity in Bangkok*, about the Pom Mahakan community; unfortunately, I cannot cite that book at the point of writing.

anthropology is not always so neat—and certainly not in a country like Vietnam where open opposition is political suicide. This does not mean that voicing opposition is impossible, but that it has to be done from within a framework of acceptance of that political system—not unlike Herzfeld's Pom Mahakan residents who play along with the heritage rhetoric and practice while resisting eviction.

These paradoxes inherent in heritage validation policies and policy practices, were brought out very clearly in a recent report on cultural heritage in Vietnam, commissioned by UNESCO in Hanoi (Lê Hồng Lý et al. 2012), and recently included in a Harvard Yenching–funded book published in Hanoi (Lê Hồng Lý and Nguyễn Thị Phương Châm 2014). The research was commissioned in order to take stock of the results realized by the Vietnamese government in its considerable efforts toward safeguarding and promoting cultural heritage in Vietnam. In particular, the objectives were to identify obstacles to safeguarding, to identify good practices in Vietnam and internationally, and to start a policy dialogue with relevant government agencies about the balance between safeguarding heritage and development. Under the auspices of Prof. Nguyễn Chí Bền, former director of the Vietnam Institute of Culture and Arts Studies, under the Ministry of Culture, an excellent research team was assembled consisting of some of Vietnam's best culture researchers.[9] The team was guided by a specialist from the UNESCO office in Hanoi,[10] and advised by a team of senior scholars.[11] Four research sites were identified: (1) Phú Thọ

9. Of the team, Đào Thế Đức and Hoàng Cầm hold PhDs in anthropology from the University of Washington; Nguyễn Thị Hiền holds a PhD in folklore studies from Indiana, and Lê Hồng Lý has published internationally—as has Dr. Nguyễn Thị Phương Châm, who coedited the resulting volume. The team was assisted by Ms. Nguyễn Thị Hồng Nhung.

10. The team was guided by Dr. Dương Bích Hạnh, who works at the UNESCO office in Hanoi and holds a PhD in anthropology from the University of Washington.

11. I served on this team along with three eminent Vietnamese scholars. Nguyễn Văn Huy is the former founding director of the celebrated Vietnam Museum of Ethnology and recipient of the John D. Rockefeller 3rd Award of the Asian Cultural Council. Dr. Lê Thị Minh Lý is former head of the Heritage Department of Vietnam's Ministry of Culture. Mr. Trần Kỳ Phương is a well-respected scholar of Chăm history and archaeology in Vietnam and beyond who publishes internationally.

(home of the Hùng king temples, rituals, and festival); (2) Hà Nội (Phù Đổng and đền Sóc, home to the Gióng festival); (3) Khánh Hòa (the Poh Nagar tower in Nha Trang); and (4) Lâm Đồng (home to the Lạch/Lat ethnic group and its gong cultural practices). These four case studies were expected to complement each other nicely in terms of geographic location (north-central-south, lowlands-highlands, rural-urban); ethnic constituency (Việt and minority—Chăm and Lạch); mix of "tangible" and "intangible" aspects of the heritage (although the emphasis was clearly on intangible heritage), degree of official recognition of the heritage, state intervention, and tourism development and commercialization.

This excellent report, which praises the efforts of government agencies at various levels as well as of communities toward the safeguarding and promotion of Vietnam's heritage, draws attention to a number of developments that tend to have the effect of disenfranchizing the very people who are—to use the UNESCO term—the "culture carriers."[12] The authors draw attention to the policy of "selective preservation," which singles out specific cultural elements as either good—worthy of preservation—or bad—to be abandoned (see Salemink 1997). If culture is understood as an integral whole, discouraging or forbidding certain constitutive elements as "backward," "wasteful," or "superstitious" risks undermining the cultural integrity of the practice. It draws attention to certain aspects of invention or innovation of tradition (sáng tạo truyền thống), which makes practices more "fanciful" and tends to instrumentalize the cultural practice for ulterior purposes. This is related to the tendency to turn the cultural practice—which usually had ritual and religious aspects—into a theater performance (sân khấu hóa). Although most rituals have performative and even theatrical aspects—for

12. I do not like the term "culture carrier" or "culture bearer" for a number of reasons. First, the term "culture carrier" reifies culture as a bounded thing that can be carried. This conception of culture prevalent in UNESCO documents has been criticized especially by anthropologists like Thomas Hylland Eriksen (2001). Second, the notion that one "carries" one's culture metaphorically transforms culture into a burden, where it could better be seen as a repertoire and a resource. And third, it risks reducing people—as agentive subjects—to vessels filled with a particular cultural content.

Vietnam, think of *nhã nhạc, quan họ*, or *lên đồng*—the tendency for "theatricalization" is directed at a different audience than the limited ritual constituency. Usually aimed at outside—often tourist—audiences, theatricalization necessarily decontextualizes the ritual performance from the community and recontextualizes it in a larger setting. With reference to the saying "*bỏ cũ, xây mới*" (abandon the old, build new), local authorities often wish to abandon or demolish old buildings and objects in favor of new—larger, more beautiful—ones and embellish existing practices, which they hope would be more "suitable" for such outside tourist audiences.

But the report shows that the ritual community and the environment change as well. Urbanization, industrialization, and modernization make agrarian-based cultural practices harder to organize or to participate in for the (former) village population. The process of secularization makes participation a choice rather than a ritual obligation and effectively creates a disincentive for younger people to learn the skills and invest their efforts and resources into maintaining the heritage practice. After all, ritual requires investment of time, labor, and resources and hence competes with other purposes and needs; if the ritual is no longer seen as necessary, it may become a burden. In some cases, like among the Lạch, religious change makes it more difficult for people to perform the (ritual) music and dance that they associate with the abandoned religious tradition, now deemed pagan. Urbanization and urban planning around heritage sites profoundly change the rural environment and ritual atmosphere of the heritage practice and its community. Oftentimes, this is related to tourism development that seeks to capitalize on the popularity of the heritage site or practice and benefit from it. Whereas tourism may be important to generate benefits that could sustain the cultural heritage practice, it often has the effect of completely changing the ritual and cultural landscape; moreover, the benefits are not always reinvested in the heritage practice or shared with the heritage community. For these reasons, the report recommended that as matters of principle, the cultural diversity and cultural integrity of the heritage practices should be guaranteed through a "hands-off" policy. Regarding the role of state agencies, the report privileges the participation of the community and the sharing of (economic) benefits with the community, while noting that the state should prioritize cultural value in its management rather than economic or other interests. Regarding education and training, the report proposes training for state cadres and programs to educate young people within communities about the value and the importance of their heritage.

What the authors obviously sought to achieve was to call more attention to the legitimate interests of the communities living close to, or embodying (in the case of ICH) the heritage. It did not dispute the rationale for heritage protection, nor did it criticize the general gist of heritage policy in Vietnam—let alone dispute the legitimacy of its government. Instead, it looked at circumstantial, global processes like urbanization, industrialization, and modernization and their effects on the communities that in the past sustained the heritage and that in the present are expected to do the same. It also drew attention to unintended and unwanted effects of "too much" interference by the local and national governments and by market forces. In order to capture these unintended consequences of heritage policies, the report uses the term *di sản hóa* (heritagization) explained as "the possibility to result in the erosion of rights (to manage, organize, create, receive benefits) with reference to the cultural heritage of the owning community" (Lê Hồng Lý et al. 2012, 13, see also p. 21), referring to my intervention during a meeting on February 24, 2012. When I used the term *di sản hóa* during that meeting it was a neologism in Vietnamese, and I used it in order to refer to the risk inherent in heritage recognition and management—namely, that it may disenfranchise local communities and turn their cultural objects and practices into sites of outside—state, NGO, expert—intervention with sometimes undesired results. The report in fact gives a few examples of how the label of heritage resulted in accelerated change of cultural sites and practices, in contrast with the stated aims of the Vietnamese government and UNESCO alike. In this way, the report confirms other ethnographic reports about the "vacating" effect of heritagization on communities that are "pushed out" of the heritage site or its "buffer zone" in places as far apart as Rethemnos (Herzfeld 2004, 19), Phnom Rung (Denes 2012a), and Hội An (Avieli 2015).

Heritagization is an increasingly common, if ill-defined, analytical concept in heritage studies, cultural studies, history, and anthropology, emerging in the critical tradition of heritage studies, as exemplified by such scholars as David Lowenthal (1996), Laurajane Smith (2006), Melanie Smith (2009), Sharon MacDonald (2013), and Rodney Harrison (2013). The term "heritagization" itself was introduced in 1987 by Robert Hewison in his book *The Heritage Industry: Britain in a Climate of Decline* (1987), in which he refers to the heritagization of certain sites. This spatial definition of heritagization—the idea that places could become labeled and managed as heritage sites—caught on among a wide range of scholars—too many to mention here. A different meaning of heritagization was suggested by Kevin Walsh (1992) in his *The Representation of the Past: Museums and Heritage in the Postmodern World*, in which he spoke not only of a transformation of certain spaces (in terms of aestheticization) but of the past as well (as *ahistoric* aestheticization) that has only a "few local associations or affiliations" (Melanie Smith 2009, 162). Still referring to heritagization in spatial terms, Walsh also included temporal ("past"), representational ("aesthetics"), and constituency ("community") dimensions in his discussion. It was Regina Bendix (2009) who applied the term to human practices rather than sites and objects. Although refraining from a strict definition, Bendix offered the most comprehensive treatment of heritagization up to then, based on the intuitive notion that it refers to the elevation of particular objects (art, monuments, landscapes, memorial sites) and practices (performances, music, rituals, and related cultural practices and memories) to the status of heritage as something to be consciously preserved for present and future generations.

However, heritagization is still a fairly new concept with reference to the Vietnamese situation. Kirsten Endres (2012, 182) used the term in her recent book on spirit mediumship *(lên đồng)* when she described how both scholars and spirit mediums attempted to gain official acceptance for the practice by labeling it "heritage" rather than "religion"—or worse, "superstition." The alternating and sometimes contradicting trends of secularization, religious suppression, and heritage validation were a well-known pattern in post-independence

Vietnam, as Edyta Roszko (2012) shows in her study of the decrees on religion and heritage in the *Công báo* ("Official Gazette of Vietnam") from 1953 onward. For both Endres and Roszko, heritage validation of religious sites and practices works as the political validation of such sites practices amidst Vietnam's past and present secularist policies. This alternation is especially evident with the northern *lên đồng* tradition of spirit mediumship in Vietnam, as mediums and practitioners, clients and laypeople, and sympathetic scholars seek recognition for the practice. While some scholars campaign for official recognition as intangible cultural *heritage*, some mediums would instead like to see the Bureau of Religious Affairs give official recognition to their practices as valid *religious* activities, which in the Vietnamese context of Leninist governmentality would necessarily result in a liturgical homogenization and organizational hierarchization of the ritual community and practice (see Endres 2012; Norton 2009; Thaveeporn 2003; Salemink 2015a). Both paths toward official state recognition refer to the same set of spirit-possession practices but invoke diametrically opposed perceptions, different types of disciplinary expertise, and very different state politics, predicated on the "modern" distinction between the religious and the secular.

The point to note here is the peculiar type of scholarly activism at play here, both among the authors of the UNESCO report—on behalf of "heritage communities"—and the scholars campaigning for state recognition of spirit mediumship as a legitimate practice as either heritage or religion. The activism of my Vietnamese colleagues and friends can only work to the extent that it is disguised as expertise—or if the applied and engaged anthropology fuse into one. This can take the form of engagement within an applied research project, as was clear from the UNESCO report. Alternatively, it can take the form of loyal dissent over particular issues—for example, campaigning within the boundaries of politically acceptable discourse, without questioning the ultimate correctness of the political direction and the legitimacy of the regime. I have worked both approaches in Vietnam. I have tried the first approach of seeking to expand the boundaries of accepted discourse and practice through projects as a grantmaker for the Ford Foundation—something that brought me in close contact and collaboration with Achan Chayan

Vaddhanaphuti, who operated under similar premises as a teacher and coach. For the second approach of campaigning I let my Vietnamese friends and colleagues take the lead and decide for me when my input was desired (see Salemink 2013b, 2015b). In both cases, the activism was not confrontational or oppositional, as one might expect in more open societies, like some Western countries.

THE SPACE OF GONG CULTURE AS VIETNAMESE HERITAGE

There are two things that none of these various Vietnamese-style scholar-activists questioned, however. One unassailable axiom was that the various sites, objects, and practices constitute cultural heritage and should be managed and conserved as such; and the other axiom concerns the essentially Vietnamese character of the heritage—even, for instance, when the Mỹ Sơn temple complex and the Poh Nagar tower in Nha Trang are legacies of the historical Chăm presence in what is now Vietnam. This brings us back to Michael Herzfeld's reflections on heritage as the property of the nation (see above) and to Richard Handler's (1986) observation that the quest for cultural authenticity is a corollary of modern nationalism. In this section, I shall discuss both axioms with reference to the space of gong culture as ICH against the backdrop of recent historical developments in the Central Highlands—some of which have been mentioned briefly above. The UNESCO report confirms my own research findings (Salemink 2003, 2004, 2006) that the basis for the community-centered ritual life which UNESCO calls "gong culture" is disappearing fast in the contemporary milieu of wide-ranging ecological, economic, religious, and subjective transformations. In an economy that puts a premium on competitive individual—or at least household—performance, the community solidarity that underpinned agricultural ritual is perennially under threat. With livelihoods less and less based on the subsistence swidden agriculture of "eating the forest" (see Condominas [1957] 1982), the cosmological environment as the context for ritual action ceases to have meaning, and the agricultural cycle changes with the new cash crops introduced. Many people lack the resources to invest in ritual, making them feel permanently in debt vis-à-vis their deities and hence at risk of hazard. In this situation, many highlanders opt for a new, more individualist and scripturalist religion with completely different liturgical ritual: Christianity. With the conversion to Christianity, the performance of gong music during life-cycle rituals is no longer self-evident and is sometimes even actively condemned as "pagan" by followers of the new religion. The cultural transmission of knowledge of ritual and gong music skills to younger generations is becoming difficult in this context.

While Christian highlanders condemn their "pagan" past, the Vietnamese regime condemns highlander Christianity. In January 2001 and April 2004, many highlanders demonstrated in some of the major towns in the Central Highlands, like Pleiku and Buôn Ma Thuột, as well as in some of the more remote districts like Chu Xe in Gialai Province. Their demands concerned freedom of religion and land rights but were overseas articulated by the anticommunist diaspora organization the Montagnard Foundation as a call for "Dega" autonomy—Dega being a new, politicized ethnonym for the indigenous groups of Vietnam's Central Highlands. This putative association with Dega diaspora politics triggered a strong repression of highlander political and religious articulations. Some of the frequently reported political responses were attempts by security personnel to force people to recant their Christian confession and to perform specific versions of "pagan," non-Christian rituals—indeed the very rituals that in the times of high socialism were branded backward, superstitious, unhygienic, and wasteful. I have discussed the dynamics of rights claims, protests, and repression elsewhere (see Salemink 2006); here I would like to focus on Vietnam's official response in terms of cultural politics. Just one month after the first protest in 2001, Vietnam's government gave the largest grant for social-science research in its history—namely, the equivalent of one million US dollars for researching, collecting, recording, translating, analyzing, and publishing the long epics of the Central Highlands. The project was managed and carried out by the Institute of Folk Culture Studies of the Vietnam Academy of Social Sciences, which published well over sixty volumes of epics over the years. The dossier for the UNESCO inscription of the space of gong culture was prepared in

2004, right after the second protest, during Easter 2004. Just like the forced recantations of Christianity, the sudden conservationist cultural policies were predicated on religious and ritual practices that highlanders had abandoned or were abandoning.

In other words, what was called (intangible) cultural heritage in the 2000s were religious concepts and cultural and ritual practices that had been condemned and suppressed by successive political regimes as backward and superstitious and that had been rendered practically unsustainable by the disruptive ecological, economic, demographic, political, and cultural transformations in the Central Highlands. Given the deep politicization of both Christian conversion and official cultural politics in Tây Nguyên, the label of heritage for largely abandoned cultural practices creates much tension within communities and between communities and state agencies. This is one of the dilemmas facing the gong practice among the Lạch group in Lâm Đồng, as noted by Lê Hồng Lý et al. (2012) in the UNESCO report "Safeguarding and Promoting Cultural Heritage against the Backdrop of Modernization." Many Christians refused to play the gong or even to possess a gong set, seeing it as an instrument of the devil. The report found that in places where an accommodation could be reached between Christian liturgy and gong music, the official predicate of "heritage" bestowed by the state or by UNESCO incited local actors or even national agencies to make investments or "improvements" that are in contradiction with the idea of heritage preservation, that disenfranchise local communities who used to be in control of the cultural practice now dubbed heritage, and that privilege outside actors or interests (tourism, economics, politics, etc.) who conceive of intangible cultural heritage as a spectacle.[13]

This brings us to Guy Debord's (1994) analysis titled *Society of the Spectacle*. In the case of Intangible Cultural Heritage, people themselves become a spectacle, just like the celebrities analyzed by

13. In the late 1990s the former director of the Huế Monuments Conservation Centre, Mr. Thái Công Nguyên, showed me how he shortened the *nhã nhạc* court music scores, which in their original form were too long and hence "boring" to watch by tourists. He conceived of that as an improvement. (I could give many examples of such improvements.)

187

Debord and by Rosemary Coombe (1998); but where celebrities become individual brands, Central highlanders become collectively branded through the validation and certification processes undertaken or overseen by UNESCO. In the case of gong culture, it is specific ritual labor which acquires meaning within the setting of a restricted ritual community—and perhaps a slightly wider but *vernacular* ritual constituency—and which becomes a spectacle validated by outside experts and consumed by outside audiences of officials and tourists. As a spectacle—but not a ritual—such ICH becomes "spectacular" in the sense that aesthetic and performative aspects are privileged over substantive signification as ritual. This "spectacularization" of the practice is predicated on external notions of "improvement" that seek to make the performance shorter, louder, and wilder—oftentimes in a context of artistic competition.

Examples of the latter I witnessed at the International Conference on Economic and Social Changes and Preservation of the Gong Culture in Vietnam and the Southeast Asian Region, which was held in Pleiku in November 2009 and took place in the context of an international gong-music festival organized by Vietnam's Ministry of Culture, Sports, and Tourism to celebrate the UNESCO inscription of the space of gong culture one year earlier. The opening ceremony was a grandiose, loud, and mass-mediated performance choreographed by vice-minister and people's artist Lê Tiến Thọ, in which a swirling mass of hundreds of dancers, musicians, and drummers, as well as some elephants, performed a mockery of the usually quiet ritual gong music for an audience of officials and guests, local people, and—via television—the nation. But an opening ceremony is often a grandiose event, certainly in Vietnam, and hence not necessarily representative of—in this case—gong music itself. But the festival itself had the format of a competitive music meeting, in which more or less professional gong troupes from different ethnic groups, provinces, and even countries performed in a competitive atmosphere, inducing the troupes to perform in ever more spectacular fashion—often adding drums to the performance as well. In such a context, gong music becomes professionalized, meaning that it is entirely taken out of the ritual context of the village community and performed by semiprofessional artistic troupes performing for outside audiences. As I noted in my paper to the conference, what was missing in this movement of cultural decontextualization from the ritual community and recontextualization in a tourist context was any attempt to recontextualize gong music in a different ritual context— namely, of church liturgy.[14] Highlander Christians and Vietnamese state officials seemed suspicious enough of each other to prevent that from happening—with some Catholic Bahnar groups as the proverbial exception.

This can be interpreted as an instance of possessive cultural nationalism (see Handler 1985, 1991; Coombe 1998) in the sense that a particular cultural object—in this case practice—is seen as the property not of an individual (e.g., an author or artist) but of a collective. Whereas UNESCO seeks to ascribe ownership of ICH to specific cultural groups, in actuality the cultural practices that go under the label of heritage become the property of the state, which assumes the responsibility to protect, preserve, and manage the heritage. In this case the heritagization of gong culture amounts to a process of large-scale cultural dispossession. This happens first of all because of the wholesale ecological, economic, demographic, cultural, and cosmological transformation of the Tây Nguyên landscape, which works as a classic movement of enclosure in Karl Marx's sense of the term. Second, the state performs a mockery of highlander gong culture in which highlanders have no say and from which they are largely absent. Third, to the extent that highlanders do perform themselves, they are turned into a spectacle devoid of ritual meaning, to the point that they are dispossessed of the product of their ritual labor. And fourth, highlanders are practically prevented from reintroducing gong music into their new liturgical rites and thus from recontextualizing it into their own ritual communities. The state is not directly implicated in the loss (sale, theft) of cultural objects like gong sets, which is another

14. I made this observation in my conference paper "Where is the Space for Vietnam's Gong Culture? Economic and Social Challenges for the Space of Gong Culture, and Opportunities for Protection," presented at the International Conference on Economic and Social Changes and Preservation of the Gong Culture in Vietnam and the Southeast Asian Region, Pleiku City, Vietnam, November 9–11, 2009.

impediment for the continuation of gong culture as ritual practice in the villages. [15]

In this section I argued that the heritagization of "gong culture" marks another step in the disenfranchisement of highlanders with regard to their own culture, after having been dispossessed of their "cultural space." The official UNESCO label of ICH at once incorporates highlander cultures into Vietnamese national space while excluding highlanders from ownership over their culture, which is appropriated by the state (see Salemink 2013a). By the same token, other examples of similar ritual gong music in the region, both in Vietnam and in Laos, Cambodia, and beyond, are not recognized as heritage and hence are not valued as equally unique and authentic to merit the label of world heritage. While the main protagonist in this is the Vietnamese state—especially the Ministry of Culture and the various provincial authorities—the process of UNESCO inscription can only happen with the active collaboration of scholars and cultural experts, most pointedly within the above-mentioned Vietnam Institute of Culture and Arts Studies under the Ministry of Culture. In that sense, the UNESCO report authored by critical scholars as well as my own work can only be regarded as rearguard actions.

CONCLUSION

Beginning with a brief discussion of the involvement of experts and scholars in the most explosive heritage dispute in the region—that of Preah Vihear/Phra Wihan—I explored the role of experts and scholars as applied or engaged researchers with reference to UNESCO-inscribed Intangible Cultural Heritage in Vietnam. I zoomed in on the space of gong culture in Vietnam's Central Highland provinces, which I described in terms of incorporation (into the nation-state), of spectacularization (i.e., the reduction of ritual practice to a spectacle for outsiders), and of dispossession and disenfranchisement (of the cultural space as well as of the ritual practice). I broached the question of what modalities there are for scholars who choose to engage with

15. See Van Dat, "Sacred Gong Culture in Need of Spiritual Revival," *Việt Nam News*, September 23, 2009.

the state—as initiator and guarantor of heritage—and with local heritage communities, alternatively as applied researchers, cultural experts, or activists. In Vietnam, many scholars develop a critical stance, but their room for maneuver is limited. As an oppositional or confrontational style would backfire, they often choose to work within the system by voicing critical insights in applied research—a style that I adopted as well in my own work. Summarily comparing that with the more confrontational style adopted by Michael Herzfeld in protesting an eventual Pom Mahakan eviction, I found that also in that case both the local community and the supportive anthropologist articulate their opposition not in terms of opposing heritagization but of alternative—and better—heritage management and conservation. In other words, styles may vary but they seem to operate within specific discursive boundaries, which may take the form of "playing along" or of pushing the discursive envelope.

Returning to the situation in Vietnam's Central Highlands, which in my analysis is rather bleak for the indigenous highlanders themselves, the highly politicized tensions in that region seem to force scholars to accept the boundaries of political and scientific discourse, condemning those of us who are willing to take up more activist positions to fight rearguard actions. The acceptance and eventual reinscription of an authorized heritage discourse, however, would cast highlanders as traditional, with the dual effect of placing them on the pedestal of heritage while simultaneously tying them to the tethering post of "unmodernity" and backwardness. Only time will tell to what extent a critical scholarship that unpacks and critiques dominant or hegemonic concepts and practices which place heritage communities in temporal straightjackets might be effective in political practice in Vietnam.

REFERENCES

Aikawa, Noriko. 2004. "An Historical Overview of the Preparation of the UNESCO International Convention for the Safeguarding of the Intangible Cultural Heritage." *Museum International* 56 (1–2): 137–49.

Appadurai, Arjun. 1996. *Modernity at Large: Cultural Dimensions of Globalization.* Minneapolis: University of Minnesota Press.

Arizpe, Lourdes. 1998. "Letters: UN Cultured." *Anthropology Today* 14 (3): 24.

Augé, Marc. 1999. *An Anthropology for Contemporaneous Worlds*. Stanford, CA: Stanford University Press.

Avieli, Nir. 2015. The Rise and Fall (?) of Hội An, a UNESCO World Heritage Site in Vietnam. *Sojourn* 30 (1): 35–71.

Baumann, Gerd. 1992. "Ritual Implicates 'Others': Rereading Durkheim in a Plural Society." In *Understanding Rituals*, edited by Daniel de Coppet, 97–116. London: Routledge.

Bendix, Regina. 2009. "Heritage between Economy and Politics: An Assessment from the Perspective of Cultural Anthropology." In *Intangible Heritage*, edited by Laurajane Smith and Natsuko Akagawa, 253–69. London: Routledge.

Bora Touch. 2009. "Who Owns the Preah Vihear Temple? A Cambodian Position." *Journal of East Asian International Law* 2 (1): 205–27.

Byrne, Denis. 2011. "Archaeological Heritage and Cultural Intimacy: An Interview with Michael Herzfeld." *Journal of Social Archaeology* 11 (2): 144–57.

Charnvit Kasetsiri, Pou Sothirak, and Pavin Chachavalpongpun. 2013. *Preah Vihear: A Guide to the Thai-Cambodian Conflict and Its Solutions*. Bangkok: White Lotus.

Condominas, Georges. (1957) 1982. *Nous Avons Mangé le Forêt de la Pierre-Génie Gôo (Hii saa Brii Mau-Yaang Gôo): Chronique de Sar Luk, village Mnong Gar (tribu proto-indochinoise, des Hauts-Plateaux du Vietnam central)*. Paris: Flammarion. Based on the 1974 edition published by Mercure.

Coombe, Rosemary. 1998. *The Cultural Life of Intellectual Properties: Authorship, Appropriation, and the Law*. Durham: Duke University Press.

Croissant, Aurel, and Paul Chambers. 2011. "A Contested Site of Memory: The Preah Vihear Temple." In *Cultures and Globalization: Heritage, Memory and Identity*, edited by Helmut Anheier and Yudhishthir Raj Isar, 148–56. London: Sage.

Cuasay, Peter. 1998. "Borders on the Fantastic: Mimesis, Violence, and Landscape at the Temple of Preah Vihear." *Modern Asian Studies* 32 (4): 849–90.

Debord, Guy. 1994. *The Society of the Spectacle*. Translated by Donald Nicholson-Smith. New York: Zone Books. Originally published in French in 1967. http://www.antiworld.se/project/references/texts/The_Society%20_Of%20_The%20_Spectacle.pdf.

Denes, Alexandra. 2012a. "Mapping Living Heritage at the Phnom Rung Historical Park: Identifying and Safeguarding the Local Meanings of a National Heritage Site." *Journal of the Siam Society* 100:183–215.

———. 2012b. "The Revitalisation of Khmer Ethnic Identity in Thailand: Empowerment or Confinement?" In *Routledge Handbook of Heritage in Asia*, edited by Patrick Daly and Tim Winter, 168–81. London: Routledge.

———. 2015. "Folklorizing Northern Khmer Identity in Thailand: Intangible Cultural Heritage and the Production of 'Good Culture.'" *Sojourn* 30 (1): 1–34.

Endres, Kirsten. 2012. *Performing the Divine: Mediums, Markets and Modernity in Urban Vietnam*. Copenhagen: NIAS Press.

Eriksen, Thomas Hylland. 2001. "Between Universalism and Relativism: A Critique of the UNESCO Concepts of Culture." In *Culture and Rights: Anthropological*

Perspectives, edited by Jane K. Cowan, Marie-Bénédicte Dembour, and Richard A.Wilson, 133–47. Cambridge: Cambridge University Press.

————. 2006. *Engaging Anthropology: The Case for a Public Presence.* Oxford: Berg.

————. n.d. "An Overheated World: A Short Introduction to Overheating." http://www.sv.uio.no/sai/english/research/projects/overheating/.

Fabian, Johannes. 1983. *Time and the Other: How Anthropology Makes Its Object.* New York: Columbia University Press.

Grabowsky, Volker. 2015. "Heritage and Nationalism in the Preah Vihear Dispute." With a response by Sok Udom Deth, "Voices from Cambodia. Discourses on the Preah Vihear Conflict." SEATIDE Online Paper 3. http://www.seatide.eu/?content=activitiesandresults&group=3.

Handler, Richard. 1985. "On Having a Culture: Nationalism and the Preservation of Quebec's Patrimoine." In *Objects and Others: Essays on Museums and Material Culture*, edited by George W. Stocking, 192–217. Madison: University of Wisconsin Press.

————. 1986. "Authenticity." *Anthropology Today* 2 (1): 2–4.

————. 1991. "Who Owns the Past? History, Cultural Property, and the Logic of Possessive Individualism." In *The Politics of Culture*, edited by Brett Williams, 63–74. Washington, DC: Smithsonian Institution.

Hefner, Robert W. 1993. *Conversion to Christianity: Historical and Anthropological Perspectives on a Great Transformation.* Berkeley: University of California Press.

Herzfeld, Michael. 1997. *Cultural Intimacy: Social Poetics in the Nation-State.* New York: Routledge.

————. 2004. *The Body Impolitic: Artisans and Artifice in the Global Hierarchy of Value.* Chicago: University of Chicago Press.

————. 2006. "Spatial Cleansing: Monumental Vacuity and the Idea of the West." *Journal of Material Culture* 11 (1–2): 127–49.

————. 2009. *Evicted from Eternity: The Restructuring of Modern Rome.* Chicago: University of Chicago Press.

————. 2010. "Engagement, Gentrification, and the Neoliberal Hijacking of History." *Current Anthropology* 51, supplement 2:S259–67.

————. 2013. "Pom Mahakan Eviction Would Be a Calamitous Loss." *Bangkok Post*, September 27.

————. 2014a. "Heritage and Corruption: The Two Faces of the Nation-State." *International Journal of Heritage Studies* 21 (6): 531–44.

————. 2014b. "Cultural Rhetoric and Social Practice in the Search for Social Justice in Thailand: A Case History from Bangkok." *South East Asia Research* 22 (3): 285–301.

————. 2015. "Intangible Delicacies: Production and Embarrassment in International Settings." *Ethnologies* 36 (1–2): 41–57.

Hewison, R. 1987. *The Heritage Industry: Britain in a Climate of Decline.* London: Methuen.

Hinton, Alexander. 2006. "Khmerness and the Thai 'Other': Violence, Discourse and Symbolism in the 2003 Anti-Thai Riots in Cambodia." *Journal of Southeast Asian Studies* 37 (3): 445–68.

Keyes, Charles. 1993. "The Case of the Purloined Lintel: The Politics of a Khmer Shrine as a Thai National Treasure." In *National Identity and its Defenders: Thailand, 1939-1989*, edited by Craig J. Reynolds, 261–91. Chiang Mai: Silkworm Books.

Lê Hồng Lý, Đào Thế Đức, Nguyễn Thị Hiền, Hoàng Cầm and Nguyễn Chí Bền. 2012. "Safeguarding and promoting cultural heritage against the backdrop of modernization: Case studies in beliefs and worship with reference to the Hùng kings (Phú Thọ), the Gióng festival (Hanoi), the Tower of Lady Poh Nagar (Khánh Hòa) and the gong culture of the Lạch people (Lâm Đồng)" [in Vietnamese]. Unpublished report, UNESCO, Hanoi.

Lê Hồng Lý and Nguyễn Thị Phương Châm, eds. 2014. *Di sản văn hóa trong xã hội Việt Nam đương đại / Cultural Heritage in Vietnam Contemporary Society* [inVietnamese]. Hà Nội: NXB Tri Thức.

Le Ngoc Chan. 2002. "Quan Ho Singing in North Vietnam: A Yearning for Resolution." PhD diss., University of California, Berkeley.

———. n.d. "Quan Ho Singing in Ritual-Festivals in Bắc Ninh Region (Vietnam)." Australia Asia Foundation. http://sonicgallery.org/2014/01/14/quan-ho-singing-in-bac-ninh-region-vietnam/.

Lowenthal, David. 1998. *The Heritage Crusade and the Spoils of History*. Cambridge: Cambridge University Press.

MacDonald, Sharon. 2013. *Memorylands: Heritage and Identity in Europe Today*. London: Routledge.

Malkki, Liisa. 1992. "National Geographic: The Rooting of Peoples and the Territorialization of National Identity among Scholars and Refugees." *Cultural Anthropology* 7 (1): 24–44.

Meeker, Lauren. 2013. *Sounding Out Heritage: Cultural Politics and the Social Practice of Quan Ho Folk Song in Northern Vietnam*. Honolulu: University of Hawai'i Press.

Monticha Pakdeekong. 2009. "Who Owns the Preah Vihear Temple? A Thai Position." *Journal of East Asian International Law* 2 (1): 229–37.

Norton, Barley. 1996. "Ca Tru: A Vietnamese Chamber Music Genre." *Nhac Viet: The Journal of Vietnamese Music* 5 (special issue): 1–103.

———. 2005. "Singing the Past: Vietnamese Ca Tru, Memory and Mode." *Asian Music* 36 (2): 27–56.

———. 2009. *Songs for the Spirits: Music and Mediums in Modern Vietnam*. Champaign, IL: University of Illinois Press.

Roszko, Edyta. 2012. "From Spiritual Homes to National Shrines: Religious Traditions and Nation-Building in Vietnam." *East Asia* 29:25–41.

Salemink, Oscar, ed. 2001. *Diversité culturelle au Viet Nam: Enjeux multiples, approches plurielles*. Paris: Éditions UNESCO (Mémoire des peuples).

———. 2003. *The Ethnography of Vietnam's Central Highlanders: A Historical Contextualization, 1850–1990*. London: RoutledgeCurzon; Honolulu: University of Hawai'i Press.

———. 2004. "Development Cooperation as Quasi-religious Conversion." In *The*

Development of Religion, the Religion of Development, edited by Oscar Salemink, Anton van Harskamp, and Ananta Kumar Giri, 121–30. Delft: Eburon.

———. 2006. "Changing Rights and Wrongs: The Transnational Construction of Indigenous and Human Rights among Vietnam's Central Highlanders." *Focaal: Journal of Global and Historical Anthropology* 47:32–47.

———. 2009. "Is Protestant Conversion a Form of Protest? Urban and Upland Protestants in Southeast Asia." In *Christianity and the State in Asia: Complicity and Conflict*, edited by Julius Bautista and Francis Khek Gee Lim, 36–58. London: Routledge.

———. 2013a. "Appropriating Culture: The Politics of Intangible Cultural Heritage in Vietnam." In *Property and Power: State, Society, and Market in Vietnam*, edited by Hue-Tam Ho Tai and Mark Sidel, 158–80. New York: Routledge.

———. 2013b. "Between Engagement and Abuse: Reflections on the 'Field' of Anthropology and the Power of Ethnography." In *Red Stamps and Gold Stars: Fieldwork Dilemmas in Upland Socialist Asia*, edited by Sarah Turner, 241–59. Vancouver: UBC Press; Copenhagen: NIAS Press.

———. 2015a. "Spirit Worship and Possession in Vietnam and Beyond." In *Routledge Handbook of Religions in Asia*, edited by Bryan S. Turner and Oscar Salemink, 231–46. London: Routledge.

———. 2015b. "Securing Access." In *SSRC Handbook of Research Management*, edited by Robert Dingwall and Mary McDonnell. London: Sage.

Smith, Laurajane. 2006. *Uses of Heritage*. London: Routledge.

Smith, Melanie. 2009. *Issues in Cultural Tourism Studies*. Oxon: Routledge.

Strate, Shane. 2013. "A Pile of Stones? Preah Vihear as a Thai Symbol of National Humiliation." *South East Asia Research* 21 (1): 41–68.

Thaveeporn Vasavakul. 2003. "From Fence-Breaking to Networking: Interests, Popular Organizations and Policy Influences in Post-Socialist Vietnam." In *Getting Organized in Vietnam: Moving in and around the Socialist State*, edited by Benedict Kerkvliet, Russell Heng, and David Koh, 25–61. Singapore: ISEAS.

Tran, Nhung Tuyet. 2013. "The Commodification of Village Songs and Dances in Seventeenth- and Eighteenth-Century Vietnam." In *Property and Power: State, Society and Market in Vietnam*, edited by Hue-Tam Ho Tai and Mark Sidel, 141–57, New York: Routledge.

Turner, Bryan S. 2006. "Religion and Politics: Nationalism, Globalisation and Empire." *Asian Journal of Social Sciences* 34 (2): 209–24.

Van der Veer, Peter, ed. 1996. *Conversion to Modernities: The Globalization of Christianity*. London: Routledge.

Walsh, Kevin. 1992. *The Representation of the Past: Museums and Heritage in the Postmodern World*. London: Routledge.

The Rise and Fall of UNODC's Alternative Development Program

Ronald D. Renard

Achan Chayan Vaddhanaphuti's involvement in social issues has extended beyond Thailand for years prior to the establishment of the Regional Center for Social Science and Sustainable Development. No later than 1995, when I was working with UNDP's Highland Peoples Programme, Achan Chayan participated in training in Ratanakiri in Cambodia. At the end of the mission, instead of returning home, he stayed on in order to find social scientists at the Royal University of Phnom Penh with whom he could plan future research and cooperation. On trips to Vientiane and elsewhere, he did the same with scholars at the new university at Dong Dok.

Achan Chayan had been working with highland peoples in a proactive way since he returned to Chiang Mai University in 1984 with his doctorate from Stanford University.[1] Among the first organizations he worked with was the Mountain Culture and Development Education Foundation, which was established in 1984 by Dr. Leo Alting von Geusau, a Dutch social scientist who had conducted considerable research on the Akha. Out of this, the Inter-Mountain Peoples Education and Culture in Thailand Association (IMPECT) emerged. The objectives of this multiethnic group (later run by hill people) were to give minorities equal access to modern education, citizenship, and integration into the national economy. This was to

---

1. Achan Chayan is nonetheless human. When he came back from Stanford, the fact that his course of studies just might have tested him was evidenced in his once handsome black hair that had become all white (and no less handsome).

grow into a major NGO in northern Thailand with political clout and links to like-minded agencies around the world. Achan Chayan has played a key role in the activist agenda of IMPECT and similar agencies in the North—so much so that he was once (along with several other Chiang Mai University social scientists) burned in effigy by displeased Thai lowlanders from Chiang Mai who thought these scholars were too actively and unfairly siding with hill people.

Achan Chayan also worked with international organizations as a consultant. Besides UNDP, he also was a consultant and advisor for highland alternative development projects in northern Thailand. The principal UN agency involved in this work changed names and organizational definition a couple of times but is now the United Nations Office on Drugs and Crime (UNODC). Later on, in the 1990s and 2000s, Achan Chayan focused more on work with ethnic minorities in Thailand as well as on developing social science capacity at Chiang Mai University in cooperation with academic institutions in neighboring countries. While not forgetting the issues involving minorities in neighboring countries, he devoted more of his time to setting up and developing the Regional Center for Social Science and Sustainable Development, which was established in 1998. With this base, he would deal with minority issues in the entire region, starting from the academic level. The remainder of this chapter deals with the activities of UNODC and its predecessors in the mainland Southeast Asia region.

UNODC

UNODC (like its predecessor agencies) belongs to the UN Secretariat, the organization that carries out the day-to-day work of the UN rather than implementing projects, which is done by the so-called specialized agencies such as the United Nations Development Programme (UNDP). Among UNODC's primary duties is measuring how member nations adhere to the UN conventions on drug control. In fact, it was the Convention on Psychotropic Substances (1971) that created the United Nations Fund for Drug Abuse Control (UNFDAC), one main task of which was to control the manufacture and trafficking of illegal drugs.

Under the mandate of this new agency, UNFDAC officials decided to try something new and implement projects. This began in Thailand (where opium had been outlawed in 1958) in 1971 (much to the displeasure of UNDP staff in the country who thought their organization should be in charge). The first project was to find replacement cash crops for the opium poppy. This approach was already being pioneered by the Royal Projects Bureau, itself just established in 1969. The Royal Project had selected a site on Doi Suthep near a poppy-growing Hmong village, not far from the newly established royal palace and just west of the city of Chiang Mai, to serve as an experimental station. UNFDAC and the Royal Project worked closely together, even sharing the same project manager, Prince Bhisatej Rajani.[2]

The project's main objective was to identify cash crops that could replace opium poppy. This was considered the key to eliminating poppy cultivation. Much less attention was given to treating the opium users in the growing communities. This was because of the mistaken belief that replacing opium was more of an economic problem, while users could be rehabilitated relatively easily through short courses in lowland detoxification centers, such as at hospitals. It was found, however, that when detoxified addicts returned to the hills where they met old friends who were still smoking opium, over 90 percent relapsed. Many hill people underwent detoxification more than once, only to relapse each time. Project staff realized that so long as there was a large number of opium users in the hills, eliminating poppy would be difficult. Furthermore, since opium users tend to grow less productive than nonusers, introducing new crops and other activities

2. Richard Mann, an American Baptist agricultural missionary fluent in Karen who was recruited to join the staff of the first highland projects and then remained heavily involved in subsequent projects until about 1994, noted that making the decision was facilitated by the ready availability of donor money. As a part of President Richard Nixon's "war on drugs," he sent Egil (Bud) Krogh, White House deputy for domestic affairs. Under heavy White House pressure to put a halt to the increased use of drugs, particularly heroin, in the United States, Krogh had committed funds for a crop replacement project modeled on what the Royal Project was already doing (Interview with Richard Mann, 1999).

would always be challenged by villagers unable to participate fully. From this time on, for a period of some two decades, treating opium addicts in the poppy-cultivating areas was refined in Thailand and, subsequently, in Laos to the point where it became highly efficient.

Although this was very much a learning experience for all concerned, UNFDAC, followed by UNODC, went on to implement more crop replacement projects throughout northern Thailand. The focus expanded to a range of alternative development activities, including livestock, infrastructure, and education, and at a level beyond what the organization's headquarters was designed to handle. This design mismatch manifests itself in UNODC having insufficient budgetary resources for project implementation, which necessitated it seeking funds from donors. In Thailand during the 1970s and 1980s, this was no obstacle as it was the only country in the Mekong region where such work could be carried out. Thailand had a surfeit of donors in many fields, not just in alternative development. Since the agency gained administrative overhead from all its projects, however, these funds served to justify implementation of other projects.

By the 1980s, there were a dozen UN and bilateral highland development projects operating in northern Thailand, all with a purpose related to replacing opium poppy cultivation. At the same time, these projects almost always treated the growers and their non-growing neighbors with more respect than they had been accustomed to receive from official agencies. Although these projects have been maligned for forcing change on the hill people and for not being sufficiently sensitive to their needs, this was the first time in Thai history that lowland-based development projects reached out to the hill people in a positive way. Police General Chavalit Yodmani, who was secretary-general of the Office of Narcotics Control Board, recalls the early days when the project staff had virtually no experience in the cultures of the hill people and merely hoped to gain their acceptance: "We just wanted them not to hate us" (Interview with Chavalit Yodmani, 2004). Achan Chayan participated officially as a consultant and unofficially as a behind-the-scenes advisor in many of these projects.

In 1979, the United Nations International Drug Control Programme (UNDCP) was established as an amalgamation of three bodies: (1)

the Division on Narcotic Drugs; (2) the International Narcotics Control Board, a quasi-judicial control and regulatory body that monitored implementation of the UN drug control conventions with the Commission on Narcotic Drugs, the central policymaking body on drug-related measures; and (3) the United Nations Fund for Drug Abuse Control (UNFDAC). The last was mainly a fundraising body but also implemented alternative development projects in exceptional situations. The many projects in Thailand were all considered exceptional cases. In 2002, UNDCP merged with the Centre for International Crime Prevention, a policymaking and information exchange body, to become the United Nations Office on Drugs and Crime. Most of UNODC, including the corporate structure, was, as with UNDCP and UNFDAC, devoted to policymaking, information exchange, and normative tasks, but not to project implementation.

Even before the end of thirty years of work in the northern hills, during which time the Thai government also provided significant infrastructure inputs (e.g., schools, roads, clinics, etc.), poppy production had declined to the point where Thailand had become a net importer of opium. Hill people had become more integrated into the Thai sociopolitical system and had increased access to educational, health, and other services. At the same time, lowlanders were moving into the hills to settle, practice agriculture, build resorts, and make other use of the natural resources there. The Thai government was enacting new regulations that established national parks, forest reserves, and a watershed classification system, all of which restricted the ability of indigenous peoples to survive, remain in their ancestral villages, and carry out their traditional way of life. The hill peoples' position was further challenged by the fact that relatively few of them had Thai citizenship or formalized rights to the land on which they lived and subsisted.[3]

---

3. Obtaining Thai citizenship for anyone not born in the country to Thai parents is generally difficult. The lack of citizenship of many hill people was noted as a challenge by UN project staff in the early-1970s since it threatened the ability of farmers to have land rights over crop replacement plots. Although some projects, such as the Thai/UN Doi Yao–Pha Mon Highland Development Project that operated in Nan Province in 1990–94, made an overt effort in close cooperation with

This increased contact between lowlanders and highlanders (almost all of whom were not "ethnic Thai") created tensions and confrontations. NGOs and newly established hill peoples' groups grew more active in calling for the rights of highlanders to live and work in Thailand. Achan Chayan played an important role in supporting these activities both academically and proactively. As time went by, young people from the hills began entering universities in Thailand.[4] Now there are NGOs and INGOs run by hill people, several of whom have earned doctorates, while other hill people are teaching in Thai institutions of higher education.

These events within Thailand coincided with changes in the Mekong region. Following the lead of China, Vietnam and Laos adopted market economies. In Cambodia, after two decades of strife, peace was finally being achieved. In Myanmar, although armed rebellions were raging, a certain amount of stability was growing as some ceasefire agreements were concluded that raised hopes among some that conditions were improving. For the first time in decades, movement between the hill areas of the Mekong was becoming possible, and UNDCP took advantages of these changes. As the major UN highland projects in Thailand came to an end by 1995, a regional office of the United Nations International Drug Control Programme was set up in Bangkok comprising the six Mekong-region countries (including Yunnan of China). From then on, the United Nations work in alternative development began to move to neighboring countries such as Laos, Myanmar, and Vietnam. By now, UNDCP implemented what it called a balanced approach. This included alternative development, much-expanded from crop replacement, law enforcement (which had to come from the government and was not evenly provided), and drug treatment.

UNDCP was, along with the GTZ-funded[5] Thai-German Highland Development Programme, one of very few agencies carrying out

---

the local government departments and local officials to issue citizenship to qualified individuals, these achieved only moderate success.

4. As of 1976, there seems to have been only one hill person (who identified as such) who had graduated from a Thai university. Now, there are hundreds.

5. GTZ stands for Gesellschaft für Technische Zusammenarbeit (Society for International Cooperation, Germany).

development in which treating drug users was an integral part. Partly based on its initial efforts in Thailand where there was high relapse, UNDCP recognized that reducing addiction was essential to development.[6] Both agencies supported drug treatment, increasingly at the community level in Laos, the next country where alternative development was carried out. UNDCP went on to run alternative development projects in poppy-growing regions in Laos, Myanmar, and Vietnam. In general, these projects followed the approach pioneered in Thailand. Project documents used in Thailand were adapted to the local situation and improved upon in general for use in the other countries. Some staff from the Thai projects took up work in the new initiatives, carrying knowledge of best practices and an awareness of local people, such as Hmong, Mien, Lahu, and Akha, many of whom were living in the new project areas.

Among the lessons learned in the projects in Laos was that opium poppy cultivation is usually a poverty indicator. Surveys in Laos and later in the Wa Region of Myanmar found that despite the cash income the farmers receive, many also get addicted to the substance for a variety of reasons but often as an outgrowth of using opium for its powerful medicinal properties. Once addicted, farmers tend to work less energetically and less productively, resulting in lower income. More recently, this was shown in Nang Kham Nyo Oo's (2011) study of Pa-O villages in Hopong, Southern Shan State, where villagers were changing from making cheroots (homemade cigars) to growing poppy. This situation changes, though, when the price of opium increases. A subsequent study of poppy cultivation among Pa-O in Southern Shan State shows that if the price of opium increases substantially, the income derived from poppy growers rises to where it usually is not a poverty indicator, notwithstanding the other detrimental factors caused by drugs (Moe Htun 2014).

---

6. In this regard, however, General Chavalit Yodmani suggested flexibility was useful. He told government officials in Laos that they should avoid eliminating opium completely because there were sure to be some older users who could not stop, and these older individuals should be given some leeway. However, he did advise the Lao that use among younger villagers had to be stopped.

A MAN FROM THE BUSH

Already working with highland projects in northern Thailand was a fellow from Brisbane named Trevor Gibson. He came to work initially with the Thai-Australian Highland Agricultural Project in 1972 (Hickey and Wright 1975, 75–76). Although he barely knows who Achan Chayan is, he has been motivated by the same desire to help the hill people. He has done this through over forty years of work in highland projects throughout the region, including Vietnam, Laos, Thailand, Myanmar, and Bhutan. To further his effectiveness, he obtained a doctorate in soil science because of the vital importance soil has to agricultural development. As a recent graduate in livestock management, he first began working in alternative development with the Department of Public Welfare (as a "pasture agronomist") to investigate, from 1972–75, whether the fallow fields in the hills could be turned into productive grasslands for ruminant livestock. While some of the first people working in the hills thought this might solve environmental and economic problems at the same time, Gibson, along with Thai staff working with him, concluded that "there was not going to be any simple way in which large areas of *Imperata* could be converted into productive nutritious pasture" (Hickey and Wright 1975, 77).

In all his work in the hills, he manifested a bottom-up approach, beginning by studying the local economy and then identifying possible economic solutions. He rarely stayed in project staff housing, preferring to live with villagers in their houses or, at least, in communal structures in a village. Although he endeavored to follow the directives in project documents, he has diverged from it when he thought it would be advantageous to the local people.[7] This did not always work

---

7. Alas, he is human also. In 2006, he took a group of staff to survey a proposed irrigation canal site that he suspected was unwise to build. He was correct in that the canal was projected to traverse a steep slope on which maintenance would have been very difficult. He was more than correct in that it took so long to walk the route that darkness overtook them, and he slipped and then fell about 10–15 meters down the slope, thoroughly banging himself up. The group helped him to a shelter on the way to their destination village. Because he was walking barefoot, he got a bacterial infection. He also got malaria. When he was given a powerful cocktail of medicines,

to his personal benefit. Once while working in the north of Laos, the project document called for a gradual reduction in opium poppy production. However, during the life of the project, the Lao government decided to expedite the time frame and to eliminate poppy growing in the next couple of years. Gibson protested so persistently that his visa to work in Laos on that job was not renewed and he had to seek employment elsewhere.

In his decades of experience, he has amassed a comprehensive knowledge of highland farming systems, the natural environment, and the different groups there and how they all interact. From this he is able to make astute judgments on what approach a development project ought to take in a given place and time. One anecdote from the Lahu village of Baw Kwee in the Mong Pawk area of the Wa Region shows how he can make effective inputs. In 2006, we visited a place where he had introduced a demonstration plot for forage crops (generally legumes). They were grown in order to give pigs something more nutritious than the banana stalks the villagers normally gave them but which do little more than fill up their stomachs. On arriving he saw a bed of the crops growing profusely—so much so that he asked if the project workers had given the forage crops to the pigs. "Oh they don't eat that," said one of them. At that point, Trevor grabbed a handful of tips off one bush and put it before a pig, which immediately ate it all up. There was astonishment all around, with one of the workers managing to murmur, "They ate it."

In 2003, he was recruited for a position in the UNDCP Wa Project in Myanmar. The Wa are an important minority group that had effected an unsigned (but still in force) ceasefire with Khin Nyunt on May 18, 1989, when he was Secretary 1 and one of the most powerful people in the country. According to this agreement, the Wa agreed to remain within the Union of Myanmar forever. Khin Nyunt said that

he developed chemically-induced hepatitis. Although he insists that it was necessary to take that jaunt, when his daughter visited him in Chiang Mai where he went for medical treatment, she said she thought he would die (and that would have devastated more than just the project). He survived and came back to good health. It should be noted that here his style diverges from that of Achan Chayan, who has not been known for taking extreme physical risks.

in return the Wa would have considerable autonomy in what the government recognized as Special Region 2.[8] This has included the maintaining of an army some twenty thousand troops strong, close ties with China, and the use of Chinese telecommunications facilities as well the common currency being the renminbi (yuan). Until 2005, the Wa Authority allowed poppy cultivation and was the largest producer of opium in the country.

UNDCP work in Myanmar had come to a halt following the uprisings and violent suppression of protests in 1988 surrounding the last weeks of Ne Win's government. Within two years, however, UNDCP, motivated by its mandate to support the control of poppy production throughout the world, and concerned over widespread poppy cultivation in Myanmar, which at the time was the highest in the world, resumed discussions with the new leadership. In May 1991, UNDCP executive director Giorgio Giacomelli went to Beijing in the lead-up to finalizing a memorandum of understanding that all six Mekong countries, including Myanmar, signed by the end of 1992. In the action plan that was drawn up, there were several cross-border projects involving Myanmar, Thailand, and China. Giacomelli went to Myanmar in May of the following year, visiting Lashio, Kengtung, and Tachilek in addition to Yangon. Chinese, Lao, and Thai officials also participated in the mission, as did the regional center director, William Beachner.

Soon after that, UNDCP started some small projects in the northern Wa areas. The first was in Silu District of Special Region 4, to the east of the Wa Special Region No. 2.[9] Scheduled to begin in July 1993 with a proposed budget of about four million US dollars, it actually got underway in January 1994, although it was underfunded.

---

8. Special regions were areas controlled by groups that had formerly been in rebellion against the Myanmar government, as shown in the map in this chapter. The first was in Kokang, to the north of the Wa.

9. The leaders of Special Region 4, along with the Wa and Kokang, had together with the Communist Party of Burma been fighting the government from about 1970 until 1989, when all three agreed to ceasefires with the government. The region includes three main ethnic groups: Tai Lu, Akha, and Tai Loi (Blang, a Mon-Khmer group). The top leadership is Chinese.

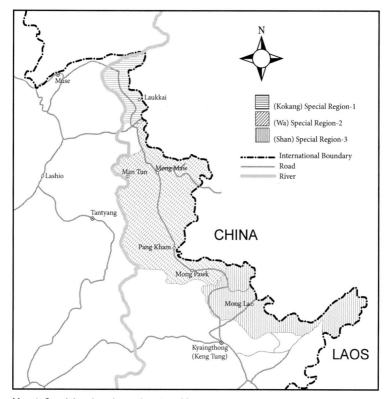

Map 1. Special regions in northeastern Myanmar

Another project was set up in Kokang and based in Laukkai, the capital of Kokang. The third project was for the north of the Wa, based in Nam Tit. The latter two were to last about six months, and each received about two hundred thousand dollars in funding. These two projects served UNDCP more as feasibility studies to assess working conditions in the region as well as to decide on what kinds of activities would be most beneficial.

THE WA AUTHORITY

A Wa saying tells that their people live in *ciet sheung piet meung kao hwe sip loi*, which means "seven countries, eight cities, nine canyons, and ten mountains." The tallest mountain, at 2,706 meters, is Mong Lin, in the far northern township of Nam Tit in Wa Special Region 2. Two other important mountains in the region are the sacred Wa peak of Kong Loi Mu near Mong Mau, with an elevation of 2,584 meters, and Aw Law, east of Mong Pawk Town on the China border, at a height of 2,465 meters, which the Lahu there revere. The valleys range from 800 to 1,200 meters in elevation.

These countries, cities, canyons, and mountains cover the area traditionally considered the Wa Region. This is partly in Northern Shan State, as well as partly in the Wa autonomous counties of Cangyuan, Gengma, Lancang, Monglien, and Ximeng across the border in China. The Wa have dominated this region for at least a thousand years, and probably considerably longer. The present Wa capital is Pang Kham Special Township (formerly called Pang Sang),[10] and the Nam Hka River, which runs through Pang Kham and flows westward into the Salween, traditionally marks the southern extent of what might be called the Wa heartland. This is the land that the Wa, at least in Myanmar, refer to as Meung Pa-raog, "the Pa-raog Country." Lying east of the Salween, the main part of the Wa Region comprises three mountain ranges running in parallel mostly from north to south for about 70–80 kilometers each. Between the two western ranges is Kong Loi Mu, the peak symbolizing the Wa Region. The western range forms the eastern bank of the Salween gorge. To the east, the range goes south from Ai Chung (east of Mong Mau) through Ying Pan and Nam Kham Wu to just before Pang Kham.

Within the northern Wa Region, the area to the east typically is composed of fine-grained soft sedimentary rock (mudstone and siltstone with some minor metamorphosis to phylite). Except for the few pockets of limestone hills throughout the region, such as around the cities of Long Tan and Pang Kham, cultivators must deal with infertile soils as they seek to make a living. At the edge of the monsoon climate, rainfall in most years is barely enough to support rice

10. The Shan who lived here named the place Pang Sang, meaning "Field of [a certain kind of] Bamboo." However, *sang* means "destruction" in Chinese. Wa leaders, preferring a more favorable-sounding name, officially renamed the place Pang Kham (Field of Gold; *kham* also means health in Chinese) in 1995.

agriculture. The hills are steep and the valleys narrow. The Wa have adapted to living in hillside settlements, practicing a hunting-and-gathering way of life supplemented with swidden rice and other crops. After the Chinese leadership of the Communist Party of Burma left the Wa Region in 1989, the Wa Army took over all the old communist bases. As the only unified region-wide organization in the area, the army also took charge of all administration. As soon as possible, it established the United Wa State Party (UWSP) as its quasi-civilian arm through which the Wa Authority operated. The Wa Authority was able to overcome topographical obstacles and shortcomings in training to establish an administrative system, generate revenue, and maintain twenty thousand armed troops. At the top, the central officials managed affairs in a top-down way that controlled all aspects of life in the Wa Region. Local people had few rights and little representation in decision making.

Although the UWSP was comprised mainly of untrained individuals with little managerial or technical expertise, they were able, with the help of Chinese experts, to establish an administration and plan for the development of the region, something they had never done before. The UWSP held its first central committee meeting in November 1989, at which an economic development plan was adopted. The plan stressed infrastructure such as roads, schools, health clinics, and irrigation schemes. The planners also wished to encourage economic development. Over the next two decades, the Wa Region would develop in an unprecedented fashion. This plan comprised three five-year sections, from 1990 to 2005. Included in the plan was the goal of eliminating poppy cultivation by 2005.

Before this goal could be accomplished, poppy cultivation in the Wa Region surged during the 1990s. After years of fighting, Wa farmers were impoverished and lacking in medicine and other possessions. Poppy growing, which had been severely impeded by the unrest, was resumed because opium provided cash as well as medicine. Despite rules seeking to contain cultivation, including establishment of local opium control committees, the Wa Authority lacked the means to enforce them, especially in rural areas beyond the reach of the few roads in the region. Because of the farmgate price for opium of one hundred dollars per kilogram in 2002 in Mong Pawk (Joint Assessment Team 2003), which was about 50 percent lower than the national average, and the fact that the average grower only produced about one kilogram per year, this lump sum of cash constituted a significant share of the rural family's income. Soon the Wa Region was full of opium. By Chairman Bao's estimate, poppy cultivation soared to approximately seventy thousand hectares (Interview with Chairman Bao, 2003). If the average yield is estimated at ten kilograms per hectare (as UNODC surveys found was the case in the Wa Region in 2002–4), this would constitute seven metric tons, or around two kilograms per person in the early 1990s. This served as the main cash crop and source of income for most of the Wa people.

In February 1993, some Wa leaders approached the UN staff working in the Silu Project to request urgent development assistance as a part of their plan to stop growing poppy by 2005. UNDCP referred the matter to the government, which was dissatisfied with the Wa for approaching UNDCP first. Nonetheless, after discussion, Hotao was decided on by all sides as an appropriate site to start a project with UNDCP in the Wa Region. It was located in the south and adjacent to Mong Yang, which was under government control. Road access to Kengtung and the rest of Myanmar was possible for most of the year. In addition, there was an all-weather road to the Chinese border seven miles to the east. Furthermore, Hotao had ample ethnic diversity, with an estimated sixteen different groups. And in this area of 372 villages and approximately fifty thousand people, over 6 percent (3,100 individuals), were said to be growing poppy or using opium.

It was at this point that a long process of formulating a project approach agreeable to UNDCP, the Wa Authority, and the Myanmar government began. The Wa leaders told the others that they could manage the development by themselves. They informed the UNDCP and the government that instead of money they would prefer to receive experts in development projects, by which they meant mining and similar macro-level undertakings. Their idea of development was shaped by what they knew from China and included large infrastructure projects as well as commercial development. In exchange, the Wa leaders promised to shut down heroin refineries in Hotao and in Pang

Kham (seat of the Wa Authority). This they did by the end of the year (as verified to the author by Wa Project staff).

Out of these pilot projects, the much larger Wa Project was designed. The project document was designed collaboratively by staff at the UNDCP regional center at Bangkok and in the Myanmar country office. For the Myanmar government, officials from the Central Committee for Drug Abuse Control and also the Ministry for Progress of Border Areas and National Races and Development Affairs provided inputs. The result was a document promoting community development at the grassroots level using such techniques as participatory rural appraisals that were similar to practices promoted in many places in the world. The project document also included a sizeable infrastructure component and was externally satisfactory and consistent with previous alternative development projects in Thailand so that it passed the approval process in Vienna. The United States, through the State Department's Narcotics Affairs Section, agreed to be a donor, later to be followed by Japan.

However, although they were consulted to some degree, Wa leaders were not fully involved in the process. Travel restrictions, the remoteness of the Wa Region, political sensitivities, still-bitter memories of years of fighting, language obstacles, and Wa unfamiliarity with the process for formulating UN project documents impeded opportunities for exchange. Furthermore, the project designers were not able to travel extensively in the Wa Region to learn about the situation and to discuss plans with Wa leaders.

LEARNING EXPERIENCES

A serious misunderstanding challenged the viability of the Wa Project. During the first year of the project, in 1997–98, the Wa Authority had unilaterally hired a Chinese contractor to build a road from Mong Hpen to Mong Pawk. The Wa Authority, seeing that this was a planned project activity with an allocated budget, went ahead and had the work done without officially notifying the project. Since the project was only notified after the work was done, UN regulations did not allow the project to pay for it. With this serious breach in understanding between the Wa Authority and UNDCP, the project manager, an

Australian named John Dalton, wanted to do something to get the project moving ahead and in the good graces of the Wa Authority. Among the remaining infrastructure activities budgeted for the project was the electrification of Mong Pawk town at a cost of about six hundred thousand dollars. Deciding that proactive steps were more important than waiting for official approval from UNDCP headquarters in Vienna, Dalton went ahead and approved the six hundred thousand dollars to pay for the power lines from Pang Kham to Mong Pawk. Despite the fact that this step was very much appreciated by the Wa leaders, Dalton was summarily removed from his job by authorities in Vienna.[11]

After a transitional period lasting several years, during which the Wa Authority came to understand the approach of the project, and with the date for the opium ban of 2005 nearing, UNDCP (reorganized and given the new name of UNODC) worked out plans to expand operations to the entire Wa Region in order to assist the Wa Authority in introducing alternatives to opium poppy as well as to coordinate more effectively with the central leaders in Pang Kham, which up to this point had not been within the project area. It was here that Trevor Gibson played the key role in adapting the project document to meet the needs of the local farmers who faced severe problems when their main source of cash income was abruptly removed.

The divergent understandings of how the Wa Project should be implemented led to another serious incident in an Akha village named Ha Dah, located near Hotao. This village was selected for a community-based drug treatment camp because 19 percent of the villagers were using opium (which affected at least half the households). The mean household annual income was sixty-three dollars, and the mean per capita income was about fifteen dollars. All the villagers were illiterate and twenty-six out of twenty-nine households had a rice deficit. Opium addiction had been identified as a poverty indicator in the village. The project, led by Khun Lu, convinced the Wa leaders to allow a

11. For years afterward (and maybe even still now), a billboard showing John Dalton alongside Wa leaders greeted people crossing the bridge into Pang Kham from China.

community-based treatment camp to be held in the village. The project staff, however, was sufficiently aware of the implications of starting community-based drug treatment in the Wa Region, where all treatment before had been institution-based (or enforced "cold turkey"). Insufficient attention was also paid to the fact that one participant in the treatment camp was a Wa battalion commander not on good terms with some of the other Wa Army leaders.

When (rather noisy) group activities were being carried out, the attention of the Wa military at a nearby base was aroused. Some officers suspected that a plot was being hatched, particularly because of the presence of the battalion commander. Soldiers from the base raided the camp and detained all the patients and UNODC staff. The Wa battalion commander was executed while Khun Lu's staff were released the next day. Community-based treatment and most direct work in the village was forbidden. Activities were scaled back significantly.

A MAN FROM THE HILLS WHO LOVED HIS PEOPLE

When Trevor Gibson arrived in the Wa Region, he met Khun Lu, a Wa leader of the princely line of the Hu family of Lincang, located in the Wa area of southern Yunnan, just across from Myanmar's Wa Region. When asked about his childhood, Khun Lu explained, "At the age of eleven, I was running around naked in the village" (Interview with Khun Lu, 2006). Besides learning several Wa dialects as he grew up, he also became acquainted with Chinese. His village-based life changed forever in 1955 when his father, who had traveled out of the Wa Region and had decided that formal education would be useful for his children, sent Khun Lu to the Kutkai Convent School in Lashio, where he was given the name Desmond (and also learned Burmese and English). From there he went to St. Joseph's School in Maymyo and Rangoon University, where from 1966 to 1970 he completed a course of studies in mining engineering. He worked as a government engineer from 1970 to 1976 in such places as the jade mines of Hpakant and the ruby mines at Mogok. From there he went to the Thai border and, in ways that he never told us, linked up with General Lao Lee in the city of Chiang Mai until 1982, when the building in which he was staying was blown up by political opponents.[12]

At some point after that he established (or reestablished) contact with another Wa prince, Maha San, who had founded the non-Communist Wa National Organisation on the border with Thailand in 1976. His language skills resulted in him serving as a liaison officer with the Karen National Union in the 1980s. In 1993, Khun Lu left the border to join the Wa Authority as education minister, among other roles. He was among those who were supporting the proposed opium ban for the Wa. At the same time, his previous connection with Maha San and his splinter group, considered enemies of the Wa Authority, resulted in his having a rocky relationship with some other Wa leaders. Nonetheless, in 2001, after the UNDCP Wa Project was beginning to expand its operations, Khun Lu was appointed the Wa Authority liaison with the project. That came to an end in 2002 when he disappeared, fleeing north to a house he owned in government-controlled Hopong after the Ha Da incident, at which he was one of the staff running the camp. When the situation settled down, he returned in about 2004 to work as the Wa Authority liaison with the UNODC project and later as the station manager in the northern Wa town of Mong Mau. Khun Lu bought into the approach of the Wa Project and sought to use his contacts and experience in extending the benefits the project could bring to the people of the Wa Region.[13]

By 2005, UNODC had established sufficiently good relations with the Wa Authority to allow it to extend its activities to both Wein Kao and Mong Mau Districts, opening offices in each place. This was an

12. Khun Lu said he was saved because he fortuitously had gone to the toilet. This of course caused some of General Lee's associates to blame Khun Lu as part of the plot to kill the general and led to his move out of Chiang Mai.

13. Khun Lu also is human. In early 2006, representatives of the UK's Department for International Development and the European Union visited the Wa Region. So proud was Khun Lu of all the accomplishments that he stood in front of a briefing in Gawng Bee Village, near Mong Mau, dominating the discussion and answering for all the Wa villagers there. At last one of the donors took me aside and asked me to keep Khun Lu away so they could talk directly to the people since they wanted direct feedback.

essential factor in the rapid increase of new agencies working in the Wa Region, where before only UNODC had been present. Without the years of preparatory work and the give-and-take inherent in this emerging relationship, there could have been no such rapid increase. Without this, the international support for the Wa opium ban would have been much less effective.

The project, however, adapted its approach to the conditions of the Wa Region. Recognizing the absence of legal protection for land holdings, Trevor Gibson, Khun Lu, and Jeremy Milsom designed a new approach, which Gibson described as follows:

> Most market oriented AD interventions are not likely to greatly benefit the poor, ex-poppy growers. This is fundamentally because the Wa Authorities ... do not seem to believe in, and/or do not practice in the field, the principles of self-help, self-sustainable, village participatory development.[14]
>
> On several occasions, the project has been told [by authorities] that it is ineffective as it only promotes small-scale development at the village level. ... The Wa Authority always refer to the success of such large, Government-controlled activities in China which obviously do greatly benefit the local villagers. The difference between China and the Wa is that it was the Chinese Government that supported these initiatives [with] . . . human and financial resources. . . . The Wa Authority does not have such capabilities.

However, Gibson goes on to note that after years of UNODC presence and trust-building with the Wa Authority, interventions on a different scale have taken place. UNODC has gained significant ground in terms of dialogue and collaboration—something that was very difficult in the Wa Project before then. From a time when some community-level work was rejected outright, it later became possible to do some grassroots work with villagers (especially through initiatives coordinated by Khun Lu). In doing this, though, UNODC worked with the leaders assigned by the Wa Authority, whom it sought to convince

---

14. Such as embodied in the UNODC project document.

of the value of this type of work. No longer did the Wa Project try to impose its process for selecting leaders on the Wa Authority.

One popular initiative was the promotion of household-level rice production in irrigated (rather than rainfed) paddy fields. Since the rice produced was for home consumption, this responded directly to the need of the villagers for more food to eat after the opium ban went into effect and the Wa villagers would be unable to purchase much if any rice.[15] There were no market requirements or permissions to obtain (like there would be if a cash crop were being cultivated). Since there were no crop sales, this was essentially a noncash operation and less likely to put villagers in a position where authorities could take advantage of them. And since the Wa Authority had ceased collecting the rice tax after the opium ban of 2005, all the rice produced by the farmers could be utilized by them. The rice promoted was China-203, an open-pollinated variety for which farmers can retain their own seed for propagation the next year. Since China-203 also resulted (in field tests in the Wa Region) in at least a 30 percent increase in yields, most villages at elevations of less than 1,500 meters, where it yields well (including those with which the project had not worked directly), adopted it for their own use. In some areas, the project introduced a second cropping system of "summer rice" (so called because it is grown during the dry time of year, comparable to summers in Europe) for sowing in January and harvesting in about May. The training was given in the field directly to farmers in "hands-on" situations.

In many cases, this paddy development was carried out together with the building of small-scale irrigation schemes. This included the construction of small masonry and gabion weirs, flumes, and other structures. Sometimes when rock blasting was required, the project was able to get the Wa Authority to contribute this part of the work, which was needed because of UN rules against handling explosives in such activities. The project trained the villagers in masonry, water

15. This approach had been considered when the first projects were being started in Thailand. However, the Hmong, who were the largest poppy cultivators at the time there, much preferred that alternative cash crops could be identified and developed that they could then sell. After buying the rice they needed, they appreciated having extra cash on hand to buy other items.

management, and group organization so that they understood all aspects of small-scale irrigation system management and could carry on operating the schemes without any outside support.

Another popular and sustainable innovation was village clean-water supply systems. Although some of this work had been carried out since the start of the project, dozens of such schemes were completed after 2005 throughout the project area. Often these schemes brought water from 5–9 kilometers away through uneven terrain. Once completed, these setups provided clean water in villages that reduced diarrhea and, thus, child mortality. These schemes also reduced the amount of work women had to do since fetching water was almost always considered women's work in the Wa Region. Cleanliness was enhanced and the waterpoints in the village provided places for socializing, washing clothes, and—for children—playing in the water. Villagers were trained in group organization as well as system maintenance in order that the schemes could be operated independently after the end of project support. In one month, September 2006, the Wa Project completed 121 kilometers of feeder roads that connected isolated villages with the region's main transportation routes, 30 kilometers of main roads, thirty hectares of rice fields, and dozens of fish ponds.

A new project medical officer, Dr. Sai Seng Tip, reworked the UNODC approach on detoxification in ways the Wa Authority approved and which also yielded better results. To replace the institutional approach, which made patients feel uncomfortable and contributed to relapse, he introduced a halfway system. The centers were built by villagers, under project staff direction, from bamboo, and placed just outside of Nam Kham Wu and Wein Kao towns—close enough to satisfy the Wa but sufficiently rural to make the patients feel at home and relax. While the detoxification procedure followed the previous UNODC protocol, with marvelous insight Dr. Sai Seng Tip added vocational training in carpentry, veterinary health, and other fields to the treatment course. When the ex-users completed this training, they returned to their villages proud of their new skills, able to make money, and much less likely to resume drug use. For the next twelve months, Dr. Sai Seng Tip also sent teams to follow up with those who had completed the treatment. By itself, these measures would have reduced relapse significantly. However, when combined with two external factors—the rising cost of opium as well as the harsh punishments the Wa exact on continued users—relapse one year after treatment declined to less than 5 percent—among the lowest in the world and raising skepticism even among Dr. Sai Seng Tip's friends.

CONCLUSION: THE DEMISE OF UNODC'S ALTERNATIVE DEVELOPMENT PROGRAM

The approach outlined above was introduced in the Wa Region where poppy cultivation was all but eliminated in a 2005 ban by the Wa Authority that was 99 percent effective. In the Wa Authority, however, the situation was complicated by midlevel officials and influential families more interested in their own income than the welfare of the farmers. Nevertheless, in a project lasting from 1997 to 2008, a focus was placed on rice production, introducing high-yield open-pollinated varieties that grew well in the region. Small-scale irrigation projects and clean drinking water systems were also built. A modified community-based drug treatment and vocational training program was introduced with a success rate of about 90 percent for patients one year after the treatment. The purpose of the project was to make the farmers more self-reliant and resistant to demands by more affluent and influential people in the region. This was the biggest and longest-running development project carried out in Myanmar, and it brought about significant change under difficult and sometimes severe conditions.

Despite the project's successes, UNODC as an agency is moving to a focus on law enforcement and criminal justice. Alternative development is not promoted even in Afghanistan, the site of the world's largest poppy cultivation and where techniques pioneered by UNODC could be useful in areas where poverty is the key factor leading to poppy cultivation. Even by 2005, UNODC's role in Myanmar began to be reduced when the United States government, operating on probably false accusations against the Wa, stopped funding the project. The agencies in Myanmar that have taken over the development work among ex–poppy growers lack the ability to treat drug use as successfully as UNODC (and some have no such program at all). UNODC's shrinking influence and the lack of treatment capacity by other agencies (and less effective law enforcement outside the Wa Region) are major contributing factors to the resurgence of poppy cultivation in the country.

Despite UNODC's success in reducing poppy cultivation in Southeast Asia and the progress in this regard made through the balanced approach of law enforcement, alternative development, and demand reduction in the Lao PDR, UNODC is now following a counterintuitive path away from the positively evaluated projects in the Lao PDR where there was continued donor support. This is obvious in Afghanistan where, out of a portfolio of well over twenty million dollars and a dozen projects, there was only one that deals with alternative development—the "I87" project, called "Strengthening Provincial Capacity for Drug Control." Even here, however, only one of the four objectives directly supported alternative development. This was to help the Afghanistan Ministry of Counter Narcotics initiate high-impact alternative livelihood activities in cooperation with other agencies that actually implemented the work.

Both Trevor Gibson and I were part of an evaluation of eight projects in Afghanistan in the fields of Law Enforcement, Criminal Justice, and Alternative Livelihoods in 2012–13. In the final report (of which I was the lead author as the team leader), we along with two other authors strongly encouraged UNODC to adjust its internal structure in order to support more project implementation and to do more alternative development. The report passed through the UNODC system and was posted on its website. As far as we can see, some adjustments have been made to issues such as procurement but not to the promotion of alternative development.

Thus it was that the institutional imperative of UNODC and its heightened focus on crime overtook the accomplishments it and its predecessors had achieved in alternative development. The alternative-development program of UNODC runs counter to the organization's basic rationale. All project implementation involves operating under counterintuitive rules dictated by headquarters in Vienna. Among other things, this keeps the amount of cash on hand very low and forces the agency to follow tedious procurement regulations. At one point a donor offered the UNODC office in Afghanistan twenty million dollars to support different activities. However, due to procedural difficulties the office had to close down the project because the international staff in Afghanistan did not think that the office would be able to make use of that much money in a timely manner while being subject to UNODC regulations.

REFERENCES

Hickey, Gerald C., and Jesse Wright. 1978. "The Hill People of Northern Thailand: Social and Economic Development." USAID report, Bangkok.

Joint Kokang-Wa Humanitarian Needs Assessment Team. 2003. "Finally Replacing Opium in Kokang and Wa Special Regions." Report submitted to the UNODC Myanmar Country Office, Yangon.

Moe Htun, Khun. 2014. "Negotiation of Opium Cultivation among Rural Uplanders in Southern State, Myanmar." Master's thesis, Chiang Mai University.

Nyo Oo, Nang Kham. 2011. "Factors Influencing Changes from Cheroot Production to Poppy Production in Special Region Six, Myanmar." Master's thesis, Chiang Mai University.

Renard, Ronald D. 2013. "The Wa Authority and Good Governance 1989–2007." *Journal of Burma Studies* 17 (1): 141–80.

Sai Lone, Ca. 2002. "The Emergence of United Wa State Army (UWSA)." Report to the UNDCP Wa Project.

UNODC. 2013. "Independent Project Cluster Evaluation of the Drug Demand Reduction Projects in Afghanistan." Submitted to the Independent Evaluation Unit, UNODC, Vienna. http://www.unodc.org/documents/evaluation/ Independent_Project_Evaluations/2013/AFG_H09_H87_G68_Cluster_ Evaluation_Final_Report_22JUL2013.pdf

INTERVIEWS

Bao Yu Xiang. 2003, 2006–7 (multiple occasions). Pang Kham, Wa Region.

Chavalit Yodmani. 2004. Bangkok.

Khun Lu Maha. 2006–7 (multiple occasions). Wa Region.

Richard Mann. 1984–2000 (multiple occasions). Chiang Mai.

Meeting Educational Needs in Marginal Areas of the State: Reflections on Research in Myanmar

Mandy Sadan

I first met Achan Chayan in 2007, when I had the opportunity to spend some time as a visiting fellow at the Regional Center for Social Sciences and Sustainable Development (RCSD). As is well known, Chiang Mai has a large migrant population from Myanmar, and in recent years a flourishing Kachin community had also developed there (Seng Maw Lahpai 2007). The RCSD was a perfect base for furthering some of my research on the cultural politics of ethnic identities in Myanmar, especially exploring how those issues were influenced by cross-border interactions. Achan Chayan had developed the center as an integrated but relatively autonomous base within Chiang Mai University in order to facilitate academic and community connections and to encourage a positive research-activist environment in which diverse interests could be explored. The center felt very much a part of Chiang Mai, bringing in locally based artists, activists, and others to participate in academic engagement around issues that, although ostensibly distant from the city, were nevertheless relevant to it as a highly diverse urban area. This facet of RCSD is the element that has had most resonance for me in thinking about higher education in marginalized areas of Myanmar. This chapter, therefore, will describe how a process of research-activism was conducted in Myanmar before the current reforms were introduced. I will then consider how an institution such as RCSD could in many ways act as a model for local, autonomous research institutions in such settings, but that current educational reforms in Myanmar still have a long way to go before such developments can take place.

DEVELOPING A RESEARCH-ACTIVIST COLLABORATION IN MYANMAR IN THE 1990S

I first went to Myanmar in 1996 when I was a master's student at SOAS, University of London. I had left my studies early to take up a post at the British Council in Yangon. As I have written elsewhere (Sadan 2000, 2007), I had brought with me a photocopied selection of a couple of hundred or so historical photographs taken in Burma in the 1920s, about which there was at that time little information. These photographs were being curated by what was then called the Green Centre for Non-Western Art at Brighton Pavilion and Museum in the UK. The museum had acquired them, along with a significant collection of textiles, from the army officer Colonel James H. Green (other objects collected by the colonel were placed in the Pitt Rivers Museum in Oxford) (Dell 2000). There was a mutual interest in the research being carried out for both myself and the museum curators at that time, as well as, so it was to turn out, a group of local Kachin activist-researchers who were deeply interested in working on the material in collaboration with us. This was, of course, a highly sensitive political decision on the part of all of us, given that external collaborations were not allowed unless mediated by government control. Publicly funded institutions in the UK such as the Brighton Museum had to be circumspect about the anti-engagement agenda of the dominant Burmese opposition movement in Myanmar and in exile at that time. Yet the museum had an obligation to develop knowledge about their collections, and under a new South African–born keeper, Elizabeth Dell, who had experienced the educational boycott of South African academics who had nonetheless opposed the apartheid regime, a willingness to explore alternative avenues for direct community engagement was initiated. Donors and their families desire to see their collections "live" and so there was some concern about seeing development in this direction. The slight opening up of borders and the conclusion of a number of ceasefires in regions controlled by ethnonationalist armed groups now made the prospect for this more likely than in previous years and of course had also provided the opening for my own extended stay in the country. However, developing new research connections for foreign institutions such as the museum, especially one embedded in local governance and supported by public funds, was still a sensitive political issue, and there were great risks for all involved—not least the Kachin researchers who initiated and pushed for the collaboration.

A great deal has already been written about the development of this research in Myanmar and should not, therefore, be repeated here. The essential element was that it soon became clear that the photographs of which I had copies were almost entirely connected with the visits of Colonel James H. Green to the Kachin Hills region of Burma and other parts of so-called Unadministered Territory. He went there several times as part of the recruitment drive to enlist "Kachin"[1] soldiers to the Indian Army as part of the Burma Rifles (Enriquez 1924). The concentration in my own work that has emerged around the Kachin, therefore, was almost entirely accidental and was to a large extent determined by a hasty selection of images to take with me.

I soon came into contact with Kachin students through my job at the British Council. They drew me into a very different world in the suburbs of Yangon from what I encountered with my Burmese Buddhist students. This was a world of church attendance, of easier friendship-building between young Kachin men and women who all knew their respective relationships to each other through the expansive Kachin Jinghpaw kinship system.[2] It was a world in which people moved easily between Burmese and various minority languages. Indeed, fluency in a language little-heard in urban Yangon seemed also to constitute a "secret language" at times, preventing conversations being understood

1. Though "Kachin" is a widely recognized term, it is not used internally by the groups labeled as such; the group referred to as Kachin includes a wide range of subgroups, and the term "Kachin" relates to a complicated range of ethnopolitical issues. In this case, although all the soldiers were called Kachin, which often meant Jinghpaw (see note 2), they came from a wide range of groups and many of them would not have referred to themselves as Kachin in any other context. Though I do sometimes use the term as a generalization in this chapter, I nonetheless caution the reader against the essentialization of ethnic identities that can arise from using such blanket terms.

2. Jinghpaw is the largest subgroup of the Kachin, and the kinship system has over many generations been mapped onto a range of other subgroups to help integration. See Sadan (2013) for a detailed discussion of these processes historically.

by native Burmese speakers in tea shops and elsewhere when it was deemed necessary. Many of these young people were university students who were being forced at high speed through the dysfunctional higher education system. It was primarily a world that felt very different to the dominant Burmese Buddhist environment of the country's then capital. Kachin people in the capital created an alternative space that was to a large extent beyond the purview of the rest of the city's population. It felt closed, comforting, and above all highly welcoming to someone from "outside" who dared to express an interest in it. These Kachin students were also highly active in the cultural and literary organizations of the Yangon University student body, as well as those groups at the Myanmar Institute of Theology (MIT) at Insein. Insein is another suburb at the outskirts of Yangon and MIT is in an important educational outlier for many non-Buddhist, largely non-Burman groups of young people. I took the photographs from the Green Collection to MIT at the invitation of the students, it being prohibited for foreigners to enter Yangon University. We met outside in a small group in order not to arouse too much attention. There was excitement, curiosity, and some confusion as the students pored over these images from a world about which they had heard but had not directly experienced.

From these initial contacts we were eventually introduced to a small group of relatively elderly cultural researchers calling themselves the Yup Uplift Committee. They had been passed copies of copies of the images and were quick to express a keen interest in the photographs. They stated early on that they would like to be provided with access to all of them as the images were critically important historical documentation of their communities, given the sense of cultural loss that had prevailed through so many decades of conflict and that the photographs were unavailable elsewhere. It was they who suggested that the images could form part of a "museum in a computer." The use of this phrase in 1996 was striking. Myanmar had only recently opened up its borders to new forms of cross-border trade, and there had been a noticeable increase in access to some hardware items in the urban centers of Yangon and Mandalay. Individual computer ownership without official permission was still illegal, but there had been a proliferation of ad hoc education centers where people could go to take courses in basic computing skills. This was important for many young people given that the closure of the universities was so frequent during these years, but it was also clearly a new and exciting opportunity for many. The local impact of access to IT hardware and software was soon evident in many areas of city life despite the strict censorship and ostensibly tight controls on accessing computer equipment. The internet was starting to expand exponentially outside Myanmar, and the country was not entirely cut off from those developments, despite its still-prevalent sense of restriction and relative isolation. The notion, therefore, that one could conceptualize a "museum in a computer" in urban Myanmar in 1996 showed how far and how deep at least a basic awareness of the possibilities of digital cultures had spread.

The more remarkable thing about this statement was perhaps that it came from the mouths of some relatively elderly Kachin gentlemen. The Yup Uplift Committee had been founded collaboratively by a group of elders connected with the Kachin Baptist Church. They were led by Pungga Ja Li, who had previously been a pastor but now concentrated his efforts on overseeing attempts to make archival recordings of local spirit practices. In the predominantly Christian cultural environment of Kachin ethnonationalism, these rituals were a rarely performed, socially contentious, and highly esoteric set of practices in contemporary Kachin society. Ja Li's own expertise also lay in his extensive knowledge of Kachin languages, and he had a particular interest in translating the archaic ritual language of these practices into a colloquial Jinghpaw idiom, which is the language that tends to act as a lingua franca of the Kachin group. This was seen as a vital part of the effort to strengthen knowledge of local languages, especially among young Kachin people, after so many decades of war, which had only been brought to an end with the signing of a ceasefire two years previously.

The concern with these rituals and the languages in which they were performed was influenced by perceptions of threat arising from the dominant use of Burmese in daily communication, partly as a result of exclusion of minority languages from the national educational system. Again, a great deal has already been written about this process and the longer-term research that developed out of these connections, and so the focus here shall be on the local context of the education system in the Kachin region that made this research so important to this group of Kachin researchers at this time.[3] Many of the concerns and difficulties that led to this work of cultural "salvage" are still prevalent, despite the political developments that have taken place in certain areas of political life in Myanmar in recent years. These concerns and difficulties also help to explain why research and activism are almost impossible to separate for Kachin researchers who engage with their own histories and cultural practices in a contemporary setting in which those feelings of threat and vulnerability still prevail.

THE SIGNIFICANCE OF "CULTURAL PRESERVATION" IN A KACHIN CONTEXT BEFORE THE CEASEFIRE OF 1994

The activities that the Yup Uplift Committee undertook were completed principally in the four years before the ceasefire agreement between the Kachin Independence Army (KIA) and the Myanmar government in 1994. The access that ethnomilitary elites had had to audio and visual recording technologies had expanded quite dramatically in the 1980s, enabling the recording work to take place. The elites of many armed groups were able to communicate more directly with state officials in Thailand in particular during this time, and many were able to gain access to cameras and recording equipment from their networks in Thailand as a result (Sadan 2014). The minute photographic or video documentation of every detail of their activities is a marked characteristic of many of Myanmar's nonnational armed groups from this period.[4] Many of them eagerly seized the propaganda and political possibilities of these technologies. The Shan leader Khun Sa, leader of the Mong Tai Army, was a particularly active exponent of a more obsessive desire to make a visual record of every official action in his domain. But the KIA, too, has accumulated over the years relatively large amounts of visual material—especially video—of

3. See http://mandysadan.weebly.com for details of this material.
4. See http://www.esrc.ac.uk/my-esrc/grants/RES-000-22-2668/read.

itself and its activities, including both of armed actions and of the more prosaic aspects of daily life in a militarized world.

The opportunities for people who had connections with these networks to acquire audio and visual recording equipment, therefore, expanded throughout the 1980s, and by 1990 it was relatively easy to bring them across the border through established networks. Access to equipment such as this enabled the work of making an audio and visual archival resource of what were considered to be extremely vulnerable and "endangered" cultural practices to take place during the latter years of preceasefire conflict. The Yup Uplift Committee was provided with financial support for purchase of the equipment and other logistics of research by the owner of the JadeLand company, Yup Zau Hkawng. As the committee had its origins in the Kachin Baptist church hierarchy, the project also had a degree of protection in KIA-controlled areas by the institutional connections in the ethnonationalist movement between the Kachin Baptist Church and the Kachin Independence Organization (KIO). Local young people interested in the project of cultural preservation, many of whom were students at the local theological college, were tasked with photographing various rituals and performances. They made shaky video recordings of dances, of offerings, and of local communities brought together for this purpose. Some had the duty of sitting patiently for hour after hour holding a microphone to the mouth of an elderly *dumsa*, or local spirit practitioner, as he chanted the language of spirit rituals, sometimes incoherently because of his opium-addled state. These performances had barely been heard in these years of conflict and were by the early 1990s even more rarely understood by those who listened than had been the case in the past.

This research activity, however, was potentially highly sensitive politically if government officials got wind of it and thought that it was part of an ethnonationalist agenda. In other places, one could anticipate that such vital work of cultural documentation should have been undertaken and overseen from within a research center in the local- or state-level higher education system. Yet there had long been a prohibition on any research activities that might be deemed expressive of ethnonationalist intent or that challenged the dominant narrative of the Burmese Buddhist–centric nation. Research activities that might be deemed of Kachin historical significance were specifically prohibited because the teaching of an autonomous sense of Kachin history independent of the national narrative was not permitted in the state education system at any level. Likewise, any work that might be considered of anthropological significance had to be approved by an official committee from the respective government-controlled educational institutions. Any anthropological research project had to be vetted and its findings censored to ensure that it did not contravene the prevailing narratives of the nation, its social and cultural origins, and military-government discourses on its ethnic composition.

Beyond the national- and state-level education systems, autonomous religious institutions such as the Kachin Theological College at Nawng Nang in Myitkyina were able to circumvent some of these constraints. Religious freedom had always ostensibly been provided for in the national constitutions of Myanmar, and religious establishments were always, therefore, capable of asserting a degree of autonomy in the development of their own educational programs; but clearly they could not transgress certain boundaries in asserting this autonomy. Yet the research undertaken by the Yup Uplift Committee was also potentially problematic within the ethnonationalist Kachin movement itself, and, inevitably, these local educational institutions applied some of their own constraints on research freedom. Research activities into the spirit practices of autochthonous spirit cults, for example, could only be tolerated primarily as a form of salvage ethnography within the Christian mission–inspired educational institutions. However in the context of the Christian missions, the process of salvage might also lead to the extinction of the ritual being documented, and indeed, this was considered a desirable outcome by many. Recognizing the distinctive cultural importance of such practices could not outweigh the greater need of converting those practitioners to the correct path of Christian faith. This created a thin line between cultural preservation and cultural "destruction," which in its most literal form might even take the form of symbolic burning of all vestiges of the rites as a marker that they would not take place again (Tegenfeldt 1974).

This was the local heritage of documenting these practices that the Yup Uplift Committee had to be very conscious of in its own research and recording activities. Even for internal dissemination in the wider Kachin community, such research could not appear to be doing anything other than recording a "dying" tradition. In particular, it could not be seen to be promoting an agenda to restore or rejuvenate these practices, as that might in turn undermine the ethnonationalist symbol of a commonly held Christian belief system among the Kachin of Myanmar as an important part of the struggle against Burmese hegemonic control. However, within the political context in which they conducted their research, it was also clear that it would be impossible to disengage this research from an activist agenda.

This was a balancing act that could easily tip toward arousing the suspicions both of the state authorities and of nonstate authorities, leading to pressure from both sides to desist from the research. Just prior to our meeting in 1996, the balancing act had slipped quite markedly in one particular direction. The local military intelligence network in and around Myitkyina started to become suspicious of Pungga Ja Li, who had by this point left the Baptist Church and was working as a nonaffiliated researcher. Seeing the capacity of his recording activities to be part of a potentially ethnonationalist-inspired project, the loosely collated archive of recordings had been investigated, with a real threat that the materials would be destroyed. This was the immediate context in which the "museum in a computer" was being requested: the extreme vulnerability of these by-now very disordered and rapidly disintegrating film-based materials had been made all too apparent in this investigation. The "museum in a computer" reflected this sense of vulnerability and the need to provide secure spaces away from scrutiny while also holding in reserve the possibility of relocating these materials some day to a public setting where they might inspire young people with a clearer sense of their cultural distinctiveness.

The request for a "museum in a computer," therefore, came not just from a sense of the possibilities of public engagement and other museological concerns that may often act as drivers for digital humanities in a Western context. Rather, in 1996, it was felt this would best help these materials to be tucked away and kept safe until such time as a social space might be found in the heart of Myitkyina for them to be put on public view in a controlled way. The addition of the historical photographs from the Green Collection would provide historical reference points and context. In the meantime, the committee would work on the documentation digitally, smoothing out the rough edges of the recordings they had made, selecting those they thought were a good fit for the discourse they hoped to massage carefully into a new public consciousness of the value of tradition in a society that was deemed cautious if not downright hostile to these practices through lack of contemporary knowledge about them. When we met the committee, they hoped to undertake a project of standardization and selection for later public consumption, and the historical photographs of the Green Collection would also be mapped against these concerns with appropriate explanations and captions added for a local audience. This was an intellectual agenda born out of decades of conflict. It reflected experience of a national education system that similarly sought to control, to censor, and to limit unwelcome intellectual agendas. For us to expect that the aspirations of these local researchers should have been any different would have been to expect too much from people raised in the strongly nationalist environment of the Kachin Baptist Church and its educational framework in a society feeling itself oppressed and vulnerable to a hostile state.

With the support of the James Henry Green Charitable Trust as well as the Open Society Institute, we worked together on digitizing to a reasonable standard the documentation of the Yup Uplift Committee, using the Green Collection images as useful starting points for developing further research questions (Dell 2000). This also included documenting and archiving some new materials as well as the committee's fast-fading photographs, painfully fragile video tape, and scratchy, tangled, and sticky audio tapes of these rarely seen and more-rarely performed ritual activities. There was a shared hope that one day the "museum in a computer" might be placed in a public space, setting the Brighton Museum's historical photographic collections on a new trajectory with some of its so-called source communities.

Yet the underlying problem was that the years of conflict had not enabled a secular space for research to emerge. This was necessary if the research was ever to be placed within a context that was not seen as controlled by the dominant nexus of nationalism centered upon the Baptist Church and the civil branch of the nationalist movement, the Kachin Independence Organisation (KIO). While the KIO and the Baptist Church are undoubtedly the main sociopolitical actors in the Kachin region, and their combined activities have to a large extent defined the central nationalist agenda of the Kachin region with the government, there are of course a multitude of other interest groups within the complex and large Kachin umbrella. Furthermore, within the Kachin region there are of course many communities other than the Kachin, and these communities may also see these cultural artifacts as a part of a more collective history. Yet all of these notions are largely hypothetical in a highly volatile and socially fragmented environment emerging from decades of armed conflict. However, for as long as there was no autonomous space where these materials could be housed for further research, they would always be bound into the nationalist activist-research arc of the KIO and the Baptist Church. These cultural practices were, by all accounts, deeply significant as intangible cultural heritage, and the records of them were vital as documents of a society that had changed dramatically and of local practices that were rapidly disappearing. However, without a proper secular research space subject to transparent academic governance and a clear framework of ethical review processes and procedures, it was very difficult to find a physical setting—a library, a college, a training center, a university, a museum—in which these historical photographic materials could be housed in readiness for public engagement.

Fundamentally, the limits of what was possible to do in relation to collaborative research relationship building had been made clear in this process of looking for an end location for the materials that had been recorded and the research that had been conducted. The chronic failing of educational systems and structures both nationally and locally meant that we would, inevitably, shortly strike a brick wall around issues of public access until such time as political developments made further development of this part of the research possible for all parties. What was needed, in essence, was an autonomous center of higher education in Myitkyina similar in some respects to RCSD: a center that was locally embedded and which facilitated local and other researchers in carrying out independent scholarly inquiry, sympathetic toward and engaging with the activist supported by academic research, rather than disengaged from it. What follows, therefore, is a brief overview of some of those early attempts to circumnavigate the limitations placed on the development of a research space of this kind which, on the one hand, could operate with autonomy from government interference and which, on the other, could facilitate research from and influenced by a variety of social, cultural, and religious perspectives.

THE SEARCH FOR A PUBLIC SPACE FOR KACHIN CULTURAL RESEARCH IN THE EARLY CEASEFIRE PERIOD

I was able to meet Pungga Ja Li and his wider network because of the ceasefire that had been signed in 1994. By the time I arrived in Yangon in 1996, and over the next three years while I lived there, there had already been a rapid, early exploration of the possibilities that this ceasefire would offer for a Kachin cultural presence rooted more firmly in what were understood by Kachin people to be "Kachin spaces." These included the repossession of the historical *manau* ground that had been used during the colonial period and had since fallen progressively under the control of local state authorities. The *manau* dance was a major ritual of many Kachin groups and had in recent years become a symbol of the Kachin ethnic umbrella (Sadan 2013; Farrelly 2013). It had since the colonial period acquired an official setting in the heart of the Kachin State capital, Myitkyina, in a special site dedicated to its performance. However, the issue of land ownership in the heart of Myitkyina had been ongoing since the 1950s, and with the ceasefire, the issue reasserted itself in relation to the ground where public, non-government-controlled *manau* dances could be performed; this *manau* ground had become a symbolic feature of Kachin space and ownership of territory. Following 1994, it became possible for more autonomous *manau* performances to take place, whereas in recent years they had been held almost entirely under the auspices of the Kachin State government in Myitkyina's heartland. The ceasefire provided an opportunity for the reclamation of this cultural space to be envisaged, and again, Yup Zau Hkawng, the wealthy jade businessman, was the most prominent local figure to publicly put money behind the project of possessing the site wholesale by pressing ahead with the building of large concrete posts and a related *manau* "house." Building the house would resonate with the traditional practice of the *manau* as being a ritual held under the auspices of a local chief, while the dance would be aligned with the main posts of the house.

It was immediately mooted that the digital archive of the Green Collection of images might find a home in this setting, and this was one possibility that we looked toward over the next three years. There were a number of related issues in a project of this kind. One was to find a space where such material might be accessible to all. In this, as noted, there was some divergence in how this might be interpreted or experienced; for many of the local researchers, this might bring with it a degree of vulnerability or loss of control of the discourse around the materials, which reflected the political environment in which they worked and had grown up. Another concern related to the technical infrastructure of accessibility. This included the need for stable electricity supplies in a place where such infrastructure simply did not exist in public areas, even in the heart of the Kachin State capital. Related to this was the even more important requirement of having human resources capacity: the elderly members of the committee needed the support of technically able young people who could maintain the materials and help update them with new research. The reality of such digital projects on a daily basis is perhaps their generally high levels of tedium. Scanning images and inputting information to databases is both time consuming and somewhat unrewarding as a full-time activity; a genuine interest in the materials would be required to carry out such work over months or even years. People with this range of interests and having technical capabilities would in any society be few and far between, as those who have recruited technicians to work on large digital projects elsewhere will recognize; the same was true in Kachin society at this time. While many young people with technical skills expressed an interest in these images and recordings, that interest could wane after a relatively short period when more pressing concerns reentered their lives. There were, however, a few notable and remarkable young people who had a passion for cultural research. Few in number, they were critical for the long-term viability of enabling local public engagement with these materials. They naturally started to gravitate towards Pungga Ja Li as his requirements for technical support became clear.

Over the next few years we also took advantage of the new desktop publishing possibilities to develop a text from the ritual language materials, with the intention that it could be used as a primer for cultural and linguistic knowledge in the wider society (Pungga Ja Li 1999). Again, however, exactly where it might be used was not certain at the outset. The book circumnavigated some of the heavier constraints of the censorship board by being presented as a book on religion and family history, not "Kachin history." This classification had a dramatically lower threshold. As the book was in Jinghpaw, all that was required was that a thirty-page summary of the book's contents be provided along with the payment of a "charge." This was one area in which it was actually an advantage to be part of a minority language community; the censor board seemed awfully inadequate in its capacity to assert textual control over publications that were not written in Burmese.

By the time my direct involvement in the project had to end in 1999, there had been no resolution to the problem of finding a secular base in which these materials could be housed for research. Despite the ongoing ceasefire, there were barriers that came in this situation, and the fact that real political progress was yet to be seen either nationally or locally was reflected in the limits of this cultural documentation project. There was some success in having the textbook that had been developed integrated into a course on Kachin philosophy at Mandalay University. In that institution there were a couple of faculty of Kachin origin, and they were keen to provide opportunities for teaching beyond the narrow rubric of Burmese Buddhism and nationalism, while being very alert to the limits imposed upon them. However, this book was clearly defined as a text on "traditional"—read "primitive"—practice, and could not in any sense be presented or construed as a medium to teach about Kachin history. There were also academics of

Kachin origin in Myitkyina University who were passionate about the history, languages, and cultures of their own communities and who made it their personal preoccupation to research these issues in their own time. They greatly appreciated having access to these materials via the Yup Uplift Committee. Yet their engagements, which could have been so productive *within* Myitkyina University and could have helped to carve out a secular space for discussion and research, had to take place *outside* the university as they were not permitted to occur within it.

The transfer of this material to a digital medium had also succeeded in bringing in a small group of passionate, talented, and committed young people who vowed to continue the research and documentation until such a space could be found. A year or two later, some of these highly motivated young people decided to use the textbook we had published together to set up the Advanced Jinghpaw Language Summer School. This was highly successful and introduced these rare recordings to a new audience of educated and pre-university- and university-level young Kachin people who otherwise would have had no immediate understanding of these fast-disappearing ritual practices. This experience, inspired by using the materials we had created, encouraged these young researchers to take this educational model further to address wider limitations within the national education system that they perceived were affecting young Kachin people. They established a boarding house and provided an intensive training program for high school students from poorer rural areas who it was felt were not passing their high school matriculation examinations because of discrimination within the national education system toward ethnic minorities and these minorities' own poverty trap. This proved a step too far for the authorities, however, who insisted that the boarding house be closed.

The result was that these innovative young people were then, through fear of persecution for their activism, forced into the borderworld headquarters of the KIA at Laiza. In this setting, their cultural interests became ever more refracted through the lens of cultural threat and vulnerability as the political situation deteriorated in the years leading to the collapse of the ceasefire in 2011. These young people were those with whom I had discussed many times the prospects and possibilities of developing local cultural research institutions where cultural and historical research could take place— or at the very least a space beyond the church and beyond state control. It is the sad reality of this situation that instead of enriching their local communities with their cultural and historical research they are now based in Laiza, at the heart of the ethnomilitary project, employing their expertise and technical capacity to develop support for the KIA among youth groups inside and outside the country. If finding a suitable secular base, a publically accessible space, had been a key driver for all of us in our collaborative research, this remains to this day elusive.

Yet, given the progress that many observers see in the political landscape in present-day Myanmar, it is worth considering in more detail what the implications of this ongoing limitation of a local research space in Myitkyina might be. It still affects the capacity of any foreign researcher wanting to develop meaningful, collaborative research within the region; it also affects local researchers who would like to develop collaborative research projects and to explore the boundaries of their intellectual ambitions with greater freedom, constrained by neither political nor religious concerns; it is a matter, therefore, to which more consideration needs to be given and is not subsidiary to other national developments in peace and reconciliation. In this respect, the research that we undertook and the lack of a suitable space for its further development through public engagement even today needs to be considered in relation to the much broader subject of higher education policy in Myanmar as part of the current political transition. All the people with whom I had worked were activist academics who were doing their best to develop cultural research in a postconflict setting, but the postconflict setting itself was too unstable to facilitate their goals in developing autonomous research and educational establishments of the kind that were sorely needed.

THE RELATIONSHIP BETWEEN EDUCATION AND ETHNIC CONFLICT IN MYANMAR

As already indicated, the experience of the national education system at a general level is deeply embedded in the perception of discrimination against and marginalization of many non-Burman communities. The research-activism of the Kachin people engaged in this work was also a direct response to the educational limitations that had been placed upon them by a system that did not allow autonomous research or inquiry into "nonapproved" subjects. Educational autonomy was, however, a vital part of the Kachin ethnonationalist movement, long predating the emergence of the KIO or KIA. A leveling of the educational playing field was explicitly requested when Kachin delegates went to see the governor in the 1920s (citing educational inequalities as a main reason why they needed to be given autonomy— they would forever be playing a game of catch-up that could never be won). Delegates explained the experience of educational inequality at the Frontier Areas Commission of Enquiry in 1947. They expected educational development to be a foundation stone for the economic development of the region when independence came in 1948, and without it the new state they hoped for would wither and die. Access to good, equitable, community-embedded education has been a constant, unchanging refrain.[5] Yet this demand originally had little to do with own-language education. Kachin elites certainly did not want their local languages to be actively discriminated against, but the demand for educational development was based upon good-quality education in Burmese and English for economic improvement. Over time, and with the experience of conflict becoming normalized, this perception has changed, but it was not originally expressed in this way.

Historically, the higher education experience had an important role to play in the development of many ethnonationalist elites. Concentrating on the rural populations as the main ethnic constituency—a consequence partly of stereotyping and assumptions about their lack of social development—ignores the fact that most movements of resistance did not emerge ideologically through these constituencies. While ordinary people from rural areas were drawn into armed ethnonationalist movements as soldiers, both willingly and unwillingly, the leadership and the early networks of armed movements were often formed through the general and higher education systems of Burma

5. For a fuller discussion of all these issues see Sadan (2013).

in the 1950s and 1960s. The Burmese higher education system was a formative social experience for many of those who mobilized and organized the first armed opposition movements. In this respect, Burmese nationalists and Kachin ethnonationalists have a more common history than they might realize. For example, the group of seven young Kachin nationalists who went on to help found the KIO/KIA emerged through Rangoon (Yangon) University. This experience, often framed negatively, refined their sense of nationalism, just as it did for many Burmese nationalists, communist revolutionaries, and others.

Today, too, as noted, the educated, urbanized, technologically savvy young men and women who mobilize support for the KIA and organize relief provision for internally displaced persons along the border are also products of the general Burmese education system and its higher education institutions. They speak and write Burmese fluently, understand Burmese politics, and know fully what is going on and can analyze it critically. More reflection needs to be given to their experience of this system and why it should contribute to this outcome. Presently there seems to be a lack of awareness in the minds of policymakers of all political persuasions in Myanmar that while the higher education system needs to be improved, simply improving without addressing issues of societal discrimination merely reinforces negative experiences; historically these experiences have been used to justify the existence of armed opposition movements based around arguments of social and educational inequity. The research-activism of my young Kachin colleagues was undoubtedly a direct intervention against this injustice within the educational system that they had also experienced directly while studying in Yangon and elsewhere.

In relation to higher education provision in Kachin State and its relationship to current problems, we can see how this is a conjoined problem that ran through every aspect of the research that was undertaken collaboratively with the Yup Uplift Committee in the mid-to-late 1990s and continues to this day. In many ways it would make perfect sense for all of our research to be embedded in the local university at Myitkyina. Yet sadly, it is true that many of the bright, energetic young men and women who were so involved in this earlier cultural research and who are currently so active in the political affairs of Kachin State avoided and continue to avoid Myitkyina University. In recent years, since the ceasefire of 1994, many parents have actively discouraged their children from enrolling at that institution because the perception is that they are more likely to come out of the place with a serious heroin addiction than a worthwhile degree. This is incredibly sad in an environment where the call for educational access has been central to the social demands of the ethnonationalist movement since the early 1900s.

For these reasons, young Kachin people are often discouraged from attending Myitkyina University because they feel it is complicit in a state-defined conspiracy to undermine their intellectual and physical well-being.[6] The failure of Myanmar's higher education system in Myitkyina has resulted in many young people opting to attend the theological colleges instead, because these do genuinely aspire to create future leaders among their students and give them a social vocation that maps well with communalism as a dominant feature of Kachin ethnonationalism. These institutions place social leadership at the heart of their educational ethos. This was very clearly seen in the activities of the young people who came to support the Yup Uplift Committee and who then independently went on to develop their own educational development programs locally. All these young people had connections with the theological college in Myitkyina rather than the local university. At the very least, higher education policy needs to take the social and educational role of these theological institutions into account when considering models of local development rather than disregard them, as they have invariably provided the educational model upon which many ethnic-minority communities base their notions of good practice and aspiration.

Myanmar's higher education system, therefore, has been implicated in the production of armed ethnonationalist movements in quite complex ways that have changed over time, yet this issue is only peripherally in view in current debates. Here then, perhaps, is an opportunity. By paying attention to bringing key local institutions like Myitkyina University up to standard in tandem with the reinvigoration

---

6. For a detailed discussion of many of these issues, see Sadan (forthcoming).

of that of Yangon, not leaving them simply to catch up when they can, educational policymakers might demonstrate sincerity in a much longed for, tangible way. The rather blinkered view that only the universities of Yangon and Mandalay are crucial should be questioned more than it has been. It is in this respect, too, that institutions such as RCSD, which developed under Achan Chayan's careful mentoring and guidance, may provide a valuable model. RCSD is embedded within an institution but it has a relatively autonomous capacity for developing degree programs and other activities. It is oriented toward being locally relevant in the sense that it engages actively with the social issues that are visible in relation to the local communities of Chiang Mai and its environs, making connections outward into local activist groups and NGOs, providing them with a space in which they can engage in activities that feed into academic analysis. Yet the center is also alive to the regional setting and works comparatively to encourage researchers from within the region to work together and form networks. My own encounter with RCSD was through its other function of providing a base from which foreign researchers can work and develop understandings about issues of concern in the center. Perhaps this is a model that is worth aspiring toward when thinking about the development of a strong higher education system in Myanmar beyond the two universities of Yangon and Mandalay. The development of such an institution in Myitkyina would have provided the base from which the research projects that were so carefully honed could have been allowed to flourish and to develop further. The fact that there is still no clearly viable space capable of transcending social and political divisions in the Kachin region demonstrates that the political transformations of the country are still yet to reach one of its most important peripheries.

CONCLUSION

The resumption of armed conflict in Kachin State in June 2011 has been treated in some quarters rather as an inconvenience along the path to political progress. However, the progress of the research outlined in this chapter and the endemic barriers to its further development in a secular, autonomous setting subject to proper procedures of review and scrutiny suggest that the barriers to social and educational change in Myanmar are both deep and broad. Rather than being an impediment to progress, the difficulties following the collapse of the 1994 ceasefire suggest rather that many of these social and cultural issues have simply not been dealt with in the current concerns with political transition at the center. Kachin State is facing many challenges environmentally and socially, and substantive solutions to these problems will require far deeper levels of understanding about local societies and communities than we presently have; it will require policy-oriented academic research to assist this process of recovery from conflict. Such research should not be mediated solely or even mainly through Yangon and Mandalay Universities. It should have a base in local institutions that are connected to the communities within which they sit in meaningful ways. How wonderful it might be if we could envisage a local, autonomous research center such as that of RCSD as part of a newly invigorated Myitkyina University where outside researchers could come to develop their projects with local support and learn local languages, and where local researchers could gain access to a wider range of funding through the connections they build outward, with all parties focused on better understanding the many complex societies and cultures that inhabit the polyethnic and polyreligious suburbs and rural areas around the city. How great it would be for this kind of locally embedded institution to become a local center that could support public engagement with the historical and contemporary documentation of the many rarely performed, almost disappeared rituals such as the ones that have been described in this chapter. To realize this would require a very different vision of priorities within the national higher education system than that which currently prevails.

REFERENCES

Dell, Elizabeth, ed. 2000. *Burma: Frontier Photographs 1918–1935*. London: Merrell Publishers.

Enriquez, Colin Metcalfe. 1924. *Races of Burma*. Calcutta: Central Publication Branch, Government of India.

Farrelly, Nicholas. 2013. "Nodes of Control in a South(east) Asian Borderland." In

Borderland Lives in Northern South Asia, edited by David N. Gellner. Durham, NC: Duke University Press.

Lahpai, Seng Maw. 2007. "Politics of Identity and Articulations of Belonging: A Transnational Kachin Community in Northern Thailand." Master's thesis, Chiang Mai University.

Pungga, Ja Li, with Chyahkyi Brang. 1999. *Shanhpyi Laika: Lanyi*. Yangon: A Z Offset.

————. 2000. "The Kachin Photographs in the J.H. Green Collection: A Contemporary Context." In *Burma Frontier Photographs: 1918–1935*, edited by E. Dell, 51–65. London: Merrell Publishers.

Sadan, Mandy. 2007. "Historical Photography in Kachin State: An Update on the James Green Collection of Photographs." *South Asia: The Journal of the South Asia Studies Association of Australia* (Special issue): 457–77.

————. 2013. *Being and Becoming Kachin: Histories Beyond the State in the Borderworlds of Burma*. British Academy Postdoctoral Monographs. Oxford: Oxford University Press.

————. 2014. "The Historical Visual Economy of Photography in Burma." *Bijdragen tot de taal-, land- en volkenkunde* [Journal of the humanities and social sciences of Southeast Asia] 170 (2–3): 281–312.

————, ed. Forthcoming. *War and Peace in the Borderlands of Burma: The Kachin Ceasefire 1994–2011*. Copenhagen: NIAS Press.

Tegenfeldt, Herman G. 1974. *A Century of Growth: The Kachin Baptist Church of Burma*. South Pasadena, CA: William Carey Library.

Afterword
Modest Reflections on Extraordinary Virtue: Chayan Vaddhanaphuti and the Ethics of Engaged Scholarship

Michael Herzfeld

It is a great honor to be asked to write a few words at the conclusion of this important testament to Chayan Vaddhanaphuti's untiring efforts on the engagement of social-science scholarship with the needs and problems of the most marginalized populations of mainland Southeast Asia.[1] I trust it will not be an abuse of that honor to say that, while I thoroughly endorse the ethnographic and historical specificity that lends all these essays a tough, empirical, and skepticism-resistant core, my own intervention may perhaps add something of value if I partially explore how this regional focus speaks to the ethical charge of the social sciences in general—and social and cultural anthropology in particular—in the current global context.

My personal context for phrasing these comments in this way is straightforward. I first encountered Achan Chayan when I was more or less beginning my own research in Thailand, having hitherto been focused entirely on southern European societies. I have elsewhere discussed the forces that both led me from Europe to Asia and persuaded me to transition from an arid scholasticism to something that might actually be useful to the people to whom I owed all my knowledge of their lives (Herzfeld 2012). So subtle was Achan Chayan's influence on my thinking that I did not make the connection until I read these essays, and came to a much fuller insight of how my first

---

1. I am deeply indebted to Oscar Salemink for this opportunity to pay my personal respects to Achan Chayan, as well as for his good editorial care and efficiency.

lecture visit to Chiang Mai University had already generated a curiosity about the work of Chayan and his colleagues Anan Ganjanapan and Pinkaew Laungaramsri, among others, and to an appreciation that their research was genuinely engaged with the political, ecological, and social realities of discrimination and exclusion—topics that, in a more formal sense, had been at the center of my own intellectual adventures in anthropology more or less from the start.

Over the years that followed, our contacts, although infrequent, have always been marked by Achan Chayan's characteristic gentleness and generosity toward someone who, after all, could have just as easily been rejected as a clumsy and ignorant interloper in a complex regional field. Most recently, in a workshop and summer school on craft practices in Asia held at Chiang Mai University and initiated by International Institute for Asian Studies director Philippe Peycam, I had a breathtaking view of Chayan's leadership skills, organizational efficiency, and deeply seasoned understanding of the critical dimensions and practical local implications of the current fascination with the idea of heritage—an aspect of his work that does not loom large in the present collection, but that has similarly been inspired by his concern to empower local actors and to create a space for their critical examination of the process we call "culture."

Recent years have seen the emergence of an approach identifiable as "engaged anthropology" (see Eriksen 2005; Low and Merry 2010); I have found it useful, moreover, to contrast this approach to the more institutional framework that is usually called "applied anthropology" (Herzfeld 2010). Engaged anthropology cannot start from a specific humanitarian goal; it must begin with a critical and grounded engagement with a particular research problem and may indeed entail criticism of the theoretical and methodological approaches that begin instead with the goal of a particular intervention. The discourse of human rights, for example, deserves a hard look, not because we should reject its original ethical commitments, but because, as empirical scholars, we must recognize that the most well-meaning talk can all too easily be co-opted by less well-intentioned power brokers (Cowan, Dembour, and Wilson 2001). Even a commitment to local empowerment does not guarantee ideological innocence; as Rosalia

Sciortino delicately points out in this volume, such ventures as microfinance have often ended up being a source of both oppression and scandal.

Chayan's answer to this dilemma is a deep and passionate pragmatism. Not only do his approaches to specific social problems all emerge from a careful investigation of the particular and the local, but he neither turns his nose up at the administrative complexities that successful interventions often entail (as so many academic have done) nor offers top-down generalities that ignore local sentiment, knowledge, or experience. Moreover, his willingness to talk to even the most repressive governments and their representatives has shifted the moral burden onto the shoulders least inclined to accept it. He has achieved some success in that direction, but the current neoliberal context, with its marketization of social issues, is a formidable obstacle. The local has become unfashionable; area studies centers are threatened with extinction in universities the world over; the universities are themselves becoming increasingly mechanistic in their understanding of what constitutes true knowledge; and it is only the determined work of scholar-activists like Chayan that can stem the tide until the world again comes to its senses—if it ever does.

Chayan may not have been the first anthropologist to posit an engaged approach as an alternative to the more crass versions of applied work. Thomas Hylland Eriksen (2015, 198) has recently shown how Fredrik Barth not only was an advocate of the discipline's engagement in the world of social issues but also was always arguing for the importance of anthropology for critically examining the social problems of his own country, Norway, as well as of far-distant places and societies. There is a further similarity, in that, like Barth (Eriksen 2015, 196), Chayan is a prophet with honor in his own country, deeply respected and indeed loved among those who work in Thailand and its neighbors. As was the case with Barth for many years as well, his work arguably does not yet have the international recognition that it deserves. Barth, however, always aimed to contribute to the theoretical expansion of anthropology in ways that are not directly favored by the very nature and circumstances of Chayan's day-to-day involvement. Regionally, to be sure, much like another scholar-activist, the Pakistani architect-planner Arif Hasan, Chayan has been very successful at crossing national boundaries. By bringing these three names together here, I am aiming at what is something of an engaged operation in itself: to argue that, just as we should (and as Chayan does) recognize the theoretical and conceptual capacities of the people we study (a more difficult acknowledgment than the increasingly hackneyed bows toward the conventionalized category of "local knowledge"), we should also acknowledge that the practical nature of engagement sometimes occludes the theoretical innovations that are contained in what its practitioners actually do.

Chayan's critique of development, nicely summarized in his interview with Celia Lowe (2004), is an example of a theoretical position that has been articulated by others in different ways but for related ends (notably Escobar 2012; Ferguson 1990; Gupta 1998). Indeed, Chayan mentions Escobar, perhaps in the process understating his own contribution to this important critique. The language of progress and development—so nicely (and in true colonial style) exemplified by the designation of Ratchadamnoen, the first main road in Bangkok, as "the king's progress" but also as the "Champs-Elysées of Asia"—has arguably been not only a barrier to real progress in the emancipation of poor and marginal populations but also a means whereby foreign powers have maintained their control over Thailand. The obsessive regulation of borders has meant that populations practicing transhumance and swidden agriculture have been the object of a great deal of suspicion; as Thongchai (1994) has shown, mapping borders was from the start a mainstay of what I have called the cryptocolonial polity that is Thailand today (Herzfeld 2002). Part of the well-documented official hostility to Chayan's contribution springs, I suspect, from some measure of awareness that his championing of ethnic minorities raises awkward questions about the ways in which the borders, established in part to protect the interests of neighboring colonial powers, have also, and increasingly, served the interests of members of the internal elite.

If one wishes to make a difference, these are realities with which one must come to terms, and the difficult question is how to do so without compromising on matters of principle. Chayan, in his interview with Lowe, is very polite but also admirably forthright (and sadly accurate) in saying that the bureaucrats do not learn from the people. But bureaucrats are themselves social actors with cultural interests that partly intersect and even overlap with those of the people whose lives they seek to control. What Chayan's operation perhaps could not afford to do—although among his colleagues Pinkaew Laungaramsri is now moving into this intellectual territory—is to tackle the question, one that is no less ethnographic than any foray into a tribal society, of what stops the bureaucrats from learning from the people. In my work on Pom Mahakan, I gradually realized that Thai bureaucrats were themselves caught in a structure of fear. This is not to exonerate them of the charge of obstructionism. But some Thai bureaucrats are clearly compassionate and willing, within certain limits, to risk the ire of their superiors in order to help the poor and the marginal. All of them must recognize the power that can turn that ire into punitive consequences, especially where personal interests are at stake.

Chayan's soft-spoken observation recognizes this pragmatic reality—there is no point, he implies, in antagonizing everyone—but it also pinpoints a key difficulty. Since anthropology is typecast as the study of exotic groups, it will always be easy for conservative forces to mock the idea that its practitioners should also study the powerful forces that produce inequality and exploitation. In a sense, to be sure, bureaucratic responses are already part of the ethnographic record produced by Chayan and his associates, but the bureaucrats themselves remain shadows in the darkness of their own fear—a fear embodied by the bullying autocrats who charge Chayan with disloyalty. Oscar Salemink, then, notes in his introductory remarks that activism's limits are defined by the official ideology; to fight the state, one must also, to some extent, buy into its terms of reference.

At the level of public rhetoric, this is undeniably true. Nevertheless, an examination of the use—as opposed to the referential content—of such rhetoric warrants, I suggest, a more optimistic view; were that not so, Chayan's struggle would have little meaning. He himself pays clearly sincere homage to conceptions of Thainess also endorsed by the official state. Like many of the disenfranchised, however, he is able, through a gently phrased and respectful embrace of the prevalent value system, to suggest with great delicacy but undeniable moral force that those in power often betray precisely the value system they claim to be defending. As my friends in the Pom Mahakan community have also both discovered and demonstrated, one can adopt the moral symbolism of the state in order to show how its own functionaries have failed to be good people.

The Pom Mahakan residents, of course, could lay historical claim to Thai ethnic identity, and this, coupled with a stupendous mastery of the prevalent rhetoric, has reinforced the challenge they pose to the bureaucrats' assertions of devotion to the ideals of Thainess. For minority persons the task is much harder, the path more steeply uphill. Yet their exclusion from the mainstream is in no sense a necessary condition of minority status. The generosity preached and practiced by the Pom Mahakan leaders, who sent volunteers to help the tsunami-stricken Muslim communities in the South, again suggests by contrast that the bureaucratic elite's Thainess is sorely deficient. Their president, in one address to the entire community, was quick to evoke that transcendent community of suffering. Poor communities in Thailand, regardless of their political affiliations, today realize that they share the experience of exclusion from resources to which citizenship ought—logically, legally, and ethically—to entitle them. And the exclusion of some from citizenship itself satisfies only the bureaucratic logic of a state still operating on cryptocolonial and Cold War principles; although it clearly does not itself guarantee access to those precious resources, citizenship's enlargement to include all long-established populations should be considered as the first step in eradicating the discrimination that most obviously, but by no means exclusively, stalks those who have been denied the at least nominal protection it promises.

Some minorities have evidently internalized a sense of the "inferiority" of their forms of knowledge. This is a tragedy of inequality. By the same token, however, we must beware of the thoughtless adulation of "local knowledge" that is sometimes encountered in elite Thai discourse. When it is inconvenient to the bureaucratic state, local forms of knowledge are often not recognized as knowledge at all, but are treated, with an ignorance that fully expresses the bitter irony of official attitudes toward the reality of local experience, as evidence of its absence; for example, swidden agriculture is treated as necessarily damaging to the environment, in an approach that seems motivated by the politics of ethnic assimilation rather than by serious ethnographic research (see Keyes, this volume). When such knowledge appears as actual resistance to central power, as in the northern meditation practices described by Shigeharu Tanabe, it provokes deep suspicion on the part of authorities who, unable to control it, do not accord it the folkloric status that places other traditions under the state's paternalistic hand (see Denes 2015).

It is hard for anthropologists to persuade others that local knowledge is an economic and social asset rather than an exotic ornament for official self-congratulation. Few non-anthropologists have been willing—as, for example, Katherine Bowie was in the mat-weaving enterprise she describes here—to shake conventional social and political wisdom by empowering the poor from within rather than through top-down management and trickle-down economics. The task becomes even harder when the top-down structure is international, as both Ronald Renard's and Sciortino's essays demonstrate here; their accounts show how procedural decisions can become increasingly divorced from local realities so that knowledgeable actors experience a corresponding loss in their ability to induce changes in the attitudes of national officials.

One corollary of the elite's condescending and highly selective adoption of local knowledge is the refusal of citizenship to non-Thai highland minorities, a destructive policy that Olivier Evrard (chapter 2 in this volume), following the lead of Chayan and Pinkaew among others, correctly associates with the politics of Cold War frontier control. That exclusionary pattern is one of the diagnostic traits of cryptocolonialism, a condition in which the rejection of minorities ironically reflects and reproduces, as it does in Greece and other similarly circumscribed nation-states, the comparative lack of independence on the part of the nation-state. As Charles Keyes's eloquent description reminds us, Chayan's protest tactics provoked nationalistic ire because they exposed internal injustice—the nation's embarrassingly dirty laundry—to the eyes of those colonial powers who still effectively controlled Thailand's international status and were thus in a position to visit punitive action upon its perpetrators.

The strength of Chayan's perspective is precisely that it does not dichotomize the world into bureaucratic devils and angelic minorities. On the contrary, majority populations can be "minoritized" through poverty or political repression, or, as in Salemink's account, territorial dispossession in the name of conserving a "heritage" deemed too important to be left to the local communities' protection; the authorities try to generate a self-fulfilling prophecy whereby resistance translates into uncouthness, but gifted local leaders do sometimes manage to turn the tables on clumsy bureaucrats. Moreover, as Christopher Joll demonstrates here, uncivility is not a prerogative of either state officials or minority leaderships, and it certainly does not inhere in one or another religious or ethnic tradition. Joll's article sounds a larger warning in a world in which Islamophobia is rapidly acquiring the dangerous—because unreflective—status of common sense, a status that the state's passive tolerance of public stereotypes continually reinforces, creating and feeding off "knowledge" (as in the phrase "this is what everyone knows") that actually amounts to systemic ignorance.

Nor is civility necessarily associated with the law. As Italians, for example, know very well, civility is often associated with defying a state that is weak, distrusted, and chaotic; the civil does not necessarily map the civic (see Herzfeld 2009, 79–84). Chayan's stance, while respectful of institutions, does not entail automatically assuming their civility; the onus of proof is on them, not on those they are supposed to serve but so rarely and inadequately do serve.

The essays collected here make good on Achan Chayan's gentle challenge to official obtuseness. They remind us that social blindness, while not the exclusive domain of officialdom, feeds on the bureaucracy's well-known reluctance to innovate; is amplified by international organizations that would prefer to work with states than with genuinely knowledgeable locals; and reproduces inequalities that uphold no one's interests except those of a currently ascendant and expanding elite. It would be easy for scholars to refuse engagement with those inequalities with the ready-made excuse of powerlessness; states and international agencies wield far greater power, at least in the popular imagination, than any academic group. Nevertheless, a few strong souls remain undaunted by the challenge, and they reinforce their engaged scholarship with administrative skill and political diplomacy, neither of which is allowed to taint the ethical commitments that underlie their work.

Achan Chayan's remarkable achievement in institutionalizing the means of rectifying administrative and political blindness, and in bringing the populations of neighboring countries into the resulting field of vision (an urgent necessity that Mandy Sadan's essay especially illustrates), offers hope for a better future—not only for the poor and the marginalized people of northern Thailand but for the country as a whole and for its neighbors. This is engaged anthropology of the highest order, for its efforts toward bettering the life conditions of those whom powerful interests have passed by or hurt, and for its recognition of those populations' signal intellectual and conceptual capacities in dealing with the hard realities of their natural and political environments. It inspires emulation, passion, and commitment. Achan Chayan has led the way; these essays movingly reflect the aura of his extraordinary mind, spirit, and conscience.

REFERENCES

Cowan, Jane K., Marie-Bénédicte Dembour, and Richard A. Wilson. 2001. *Culture and Rights: Anthropological Perspectives.* Cambridge: Cambridge University Press.

Denes, Alexandra. 2015. "Folklorizing Northern Khmer Identity in Thailand: Intangible Cultural Heritage and the Production of 'Good Culture.'" *Sojourn* 30:1–34.

Eriksen, Thomas Hylland. 2005. *Engaging Anthropology: The Case for a Public Presence.* Oxford: Berg.

————. 2015. *Fredrik Barth: An Intellectual Biography.* London: Pluto.

Escobar, Arturo. 2012. *Encountering Development: The Making and Unmaking of the Third World.* 2nd ed. Princeton: Princeton University Press.

Ferguson, James. 1990. *The Anti-Politics Machine: Development, Depoliticization, and Bureaucratic Power in Lesotho.* Cambridge: Cambridge University Press.

Gupta, Akhil. 1998. *Postcolonial Developments: Agriculture in the Making of Modern India.* Durham, NC: Duke University Press.

Herzfeld, Michael. 2002. "The Absent Presence: Discourses of Crypto-Colonialism." *South Atlantic Quarterly* 101:899–926.

————. 2009. *Evicted from Eternity: The Restructuring of Modern Rome.* Chicago: University of Chicago Press.

————. 2010. "Engagement, Gentrification, and the Neoliberal Hijacking of History." *Current Anthropology* 51, supplement 2: S259–67.

Low, Setha M., and Sally Engle Merry. 2010. "Engaged Anthropology: Diversity and Dilemmas: An Introduction to Supplement 2." *Current Anthropology* 51, supplement 2: S203–26.

Lowe, Celia. 2004. "The Potential of People: An Interview with Chayan Vaddhanaphuti." *positions* 12:71–91.

Thongchai Winichakul. 1994. *Siam Mapped: A History of the Geo-body of a Nation.* Honolulu: University of Hawai'i Press.

Contributors

KATHERINE A. BOWIE is Professor of Anthropology at the University of Wisconsin–Madison. She completed her undergraduate training at Stanford University (1972) and her PhD at the University of Chicago (1988). She joined the faculty at UW–Madison in 1988. She has served as director of the Center for Southeast Asian Studies, president of the Council of Thai Studies, president of the Midwest Conference of Asian Affairs, Eisenhower fellow, and Fulbright scholar. Her research combines political anthropology with history, gender, and religious studies. Focused on northern Thailand, most recently she has been conducting research on the Vessantara Jataka and the famous northern monk, Khruba Sriwichai.

OLIVIER EVRARD is a social anthropologist and researcher at the Institut de Recherche pour le Développement, where he has been since 2004. He received his doctoral degree from the Sorbonne University in Paris in 2001 based on research on the uplands of northern Laos. He has collaborated with the Faculty of Social Sciences at Chiang Mai University since 2005—mainly with the Center for Ethnic Studies and Development. His research concerns mobility patterns, interethnic relationships, and cultural heritage in northern Southeast Asia, with a focus on Mon-Khmer-speaking groups.

MICHAEL HERZFELD is Ernest E. Monrad Professor of the Social Sciences in the Department of Anthropology at Harvard University, professorial fellow at the University of Melbourne, IIAS visiting professor of critical heritage studies at Leiden University, and Chang Jiang Scholar at Shanghai International Studies University. Author of eleven books—including *The Poetics of Manhood* (1985), *Anthropology: Theoretical Practice in Culture and Society* (2001), *Cultural Intimacy* (2005, 2nd ed.), *Evicted from Eternity* (2009), and *Siege of the Spirits* (forthcoming)—two films (*Monti Moments* [2007] and *Roman Restaurant Rhythms* [2011]), and numerous articles, he served as editor of *American Ethnologist* in 1995–98. He has conducted extensive field research in Greece, Italy, and Thailand.

CHRISTOPHER M. JOLL is a New Zealand anthropologist affiliated with Chiang Mai University's Center for Ethnic Studies and Development. He has been based in Thailand for fifteen years, the first decade of which was in Pattani. He competed his PhD from the National University of Malaysia in 2009 and is the author of *Muslim Merit-Making in Thailand's Far-South* (2011). While his research interests are interdisciplinary, interreligious, and transnational, his primary ethnographic subjects have been from Thailand's diverse Muslim minority. He is completing research for a historical ethnography of Sufism in Thailand, based on fieldwork in Muslim communities between Ayutthaya and Narathiwat.

CHARLES KEYES, Professor Emeritus of Anthropology and International Studies at the University of Washington, has since the early 1960s carried out extensive research in Thailand, but also in and about Vietnam, Laos, Cambodia, Myanmar, and southern China. His research has focused on religious practice in Buddhist societies, ethnicity and national cultures, transformation of rural society, and political culture. He has published fifteen books, monographs, or special issues of journals and has published over eighty-five articles. His books include *The Golden Peninsula: Culture and Adaptation in Mainland Southeast Asia* (1977); *Thailand: Buddhist Kingdom as Modern Nation-State* (1987); and *Finding Their Voice: Northeastern Villagers and the Thai State* (2014).

RONALD DUANE RENARD, a native of California, lived in Chiang Mai for more than forty years. He held a PhD in Southeast Asian History from the University of Hawaiʻi (1980) and taught at Payap University and Chiang Mai University. His research included studies of the history of the North and the Tai areas outside Thailand, as well as of other indigenous peoples of the region. He used his considerable expertise to advise the United Nations Development Programme, the UN Office on Drugs and Crime, and several other international development agencies. He worked in many Southeast Asian countries, China, Nepal, and Afghanistan, and published six books and more than fifty academic papers, articles, and reviews. Ron Renard passed away prematurely on December 27, 2014, while working on his contribution for this volume.

MANDY SADAN is Reader in the History of Southeast Asia and Associate Dean (research) in the Faculty of Arts and Humanities at SOAS, University of London. She has been researching the social, political, and cultural history of the Kachin region since the mid-1990s and has written a number of articles on this and related subjects. She was a research fellow at RCSD during 2007–8. She published *Being and Becoming Kachin: Histories Beyond the State in the Borderworlds of Burma* (2013) and she is continuing her studies on the historical development of the border regions that connect East, South, and Southeast Asia.

OSCAR SALEMINK is Professor in the Anthropology of Asia at the University of Copenhagen and adjunct professor at the Institute of Religion, Politics and Society of the Australian Catholic University (Melbourne). He received his doctoral degree from the University of Amsterdam, based on research on Vietnam's Central Highlands. From 1996 through 2001 he was responsible for Ford Foundation grant portfolios in Thailand and Vietnam. From 2001 until 2011 he worked at VU University in Amsterdam, from 2005 as professor of social anthropology. His research concerns religious, ritual, and heritage practices in Vietnam and globally through the Global Europe project.

ROSALIA SCIORTINO SUMARYONO is Associate Professor at the Institute for Population and Social Research, Mahidol University, and Visiting Professor in the master's degree program in international development studies, Chulalongkorn University. Formerly, she was International Development Research Centre regional director for Southeast and East Asia (2010–14), senior adviser to the Australian Agency for International Development in Indonesia (2009–10), regional director for Southeast Asia of the Rockefeller Foundation (2000–2007) and program officer at the Ford Foundation Indonesia and Philippines offices (1993–2000). She received her doctoral degree in social science cum laude from the Vrije Universiteit in Amsterdam and has published widely on development and social health issues in Southeast Asia.

SHIGEHARU TANABE is Professor Emeritus at the National Museum of Ethnology in Japan and currently teaches social anthropology at the Center for Ethnic Studies and Development and the Japanese Studies Center, Chiang Mai University. His recent works include *Anthropology of Spirits: Politics of Communality in Northern Thailand* (Iwanami Shoten, 2013, in Japanese), an edited volume *Communities of Potential: Social Assemblages in Thailand and Beyond* (Silkworm, 2016), and "Spirit Mediumship and Affective Contact in Northern Thailand," in *Duai Rak: Essays on Thailand's Economy and Society for Professor Chatthip Nartsupha at 72*, edited by Pasuk Phongpaichit and Chris Baker (Sangsan, 2013).